STANDARD & POOR'S PRESS

THE **Standard
& Poor's
Guide to
Saving and
Investing
for College**

DAVID J. BRAVERMAN

McGRAW-HILL
New York | Chicago | San Francisco | Lisbon
London | Madrid | Mexico City | Milan | New Delhi
San Juan | Seoul | Singapore | Sydney | Toronto

The *McGraw·Hill* Companies

1 2 3 4 5 6 7 8 9 0   DOC/DOC   0 9 8 7 6 5 4 3

ISBN 0-07-141029-5

This publication is designed to provide accurate and authoritative information in regard to the subject matter covered. It is sold with the understanding that neither the author nor the publisher is engaged in rendering legal, accounting, or other professional service. If legal advice or other expert assistance is required, the services of a competent professional person should be sought.—*From a declaration of principles jointly adopted by a committee of the American Bar Association and a committee of publishers*

McGraw-Hill books are available at special discounts to use as premiums and sales promotions, or for use in corporate training programs. For more information, please write to the Director of Special Sales, Professional Publishing, McGraw-Hill, Two Penn Plaza, New York, NY 10121-2298. Or contact your local bookstore.

This book is printed on recycled, acid-free paper containing a minimum of 50% recycled de-inked paper.

Library of Congress Cataloging-in-Publication Data

Braverman, David J.
   The Standard & Poor's guide to saving and investing for College / by David J. Braverman.
      p. cm.
Includes appendix: state by state guide to 529 plans
   ISBN 0-07-141029-5 (pbk. : alk. paper)
   Student aid—College costs—Student loan funds—Parents—
   Students—United States—Finance, Personal
   LB2337.4B73 2003
   378.3 21
                              13146564

Contents

PREFACE

The odyssey that was to result in the creation of this book began in the summer of 1999 when I was visiting colleges with my daughter. In addition to the standard campus tours and information on how to go through the applications process, I had a great many questions about the financial end of going to college. We visited schools that cost upward of $35,000 per year, and quite frankly, I wasn't quite sure how it was going to be possible to just whip out my checkbook and pay not only for my daughter's college education but for the expenses quickly coming down the road for my three younger children. At each school we visited, the answer was the same: "We will meet 100 percent of your demonstrated financial need with an aid package."

I had no idea whether my family would actually have any "demonstrated need." So as an experienced securities analyst and portfolio manager, I did what came naturally: I asked questions. However, the answers started to surprise me. I went to one "financial aid seminar" sponsored by a local high school. The person leading the seminar was a financial aid officer at a university. The seminar consisted of an introduction to the Free Application for Federal Student Aid (FAFSA). After a detailed discussion of how the form was to be filled out, he asked for questions. "Great," I thought. "Now I'm going to learn something." I asked for some detail on how the financial aid formulas work and if he could give me some ideas on how my finances should be structured to make sure that if my children were entitled to financial aid that they would receive it.

The financial aid officer declined to answer my question. He said that whatever my finances were I should make no change. He said that anything that made sense to do without regard to financial aid, such as paying off credit cards or paying down my mortgage would probably also make sense from a financial aid perspective. He said that giving this group tips on how the aid formulas work would only enable this primarily upper-middle-class audience to look poorer and then drain aid from those students who are truly needy.

Those who know me will also know that this wasn't a satisfactory answer to me. I set out to learn as much as possible about college financing and paying for an education. I learned how the financial aid formulas worked and at the same time found out that I was not alone in wanting to learn more about saving for college. I discovered that almost every parent that I spoke to knew little or nothing about financial planning for college. Even those who had made an effort to save for college and were using some sort of savings vehicle, such as a Uniform Gift to Minors Act account or a state prepaid savings plan, didn't fully understand how their savings plan interacted with their taxes or with the financial aid process.

At the same time I was worrying about college savings, so too were our federal and state governments. The first 529 savings plans were starting to arrive on the scene, and the 1997 Taxpayer Relief Act had established the Education IRA. However, the debate over education funding was amplified during the 2000 Presidential election. The 2001 Economic Growth and Tax Relief Reconciliation Act (EGTRRA) made 529 savings plan earnings tax-free and created Coverdell Education Savings Accounts.

The establishment of these new savings vehicles created huge opportunities for families to save for college, but it created confusion as well. There has been debate and confusion on how these programs interact with new and existing tax initiatives which are designed to further aid college education. There has also been confusion, and at times misinformation, on how these programs work with financial aid programs.

It is my hope that this book provides families with the information they need to make sound decisions in planning for college educations. Obviously, I couldn't do this alone. In order to provide you with accurate information and an understanding of how college financing works, I have consulted some of the best experts around. I am especially indebted to Shauna Morrison, my former editor at Standard & Poor's who is currently the editor in chief of Collegeboard.com. She introduced me to Jack Joyce and Connie Betterton at the College Board, who are experts in the financial aid landscape in general and the CSS PROFILE in particular. I am also thankful to Linda Dagradi, EdD, the director of student financial services at Smith College in Northampton, Massachusetts. Linda is one of the foremost experts on financial aid in the United States and serves as a trustee of the College Board. Thanks also to Dan Madzelan, chief of forecasting and policy analysis in the Office of Post-Secondary Education for the U.S. Department of Education for keeping me informed of changes in treatment of 529 plans in the federal financial aid process.

My understanding of taxation and how it interacts with college savings was aided by Robert Friedman, CPA, my colleague at Standard & Poor's. When Rob can't answer a question (which is rare) he's almost always able to look it up or get an opinion from one of his many contacts in no time. Thanks also to Michael Director, another of Standard & Poor's analysts who helped me with some of the taxation research. I'm especially grateful to Michael's father, Howard Director, CPA, professor of accounting at Nassau County Community College, who agreed to read the taxation portion of the manuscript and offer his assistance.

Thanks also to Joshua Harari and John Krey, senior investment officers at Standard & Poor's, who were of invaluable assistance in building some of the asset allocation models in the book. They were a big help in adding discipline to the in-depth descriptions of some of the 529 plans described in Chapter 13. Analysts Michael Kaye and Numer DeGuia also assisted in this effort.

The assistance of Tim Milanich, Robert Hassimi, Gaurav Mehta, Houda Benali, and Dorota Czlapinska, graduate students at the Fordham University School of Business, was invaluable in helping me with the painstaking work of going through the documentation of nearly 90 different state-sponsored college savings plans. As a result, I believe we have detailed information on individual 529 plans that is more accurate than any other source.

This book would not have been possible without the support of George Gulla, who in conjunction with Jeffrey Krames and Kelli Christiansen of McGraw-Hill trade publishing, created the Standard & Poor's publishing imprint. Their confidence in me is most appreciated. The support of Standard & Poor's executives also made it possible for me to finish this book. Special thanks to James Branscome, who always inspires his employees to accomplish what only he thinks is possible. Thanks also to Portfolio Advisors executives Paul Aaronson, Tom Gizicki, and Steve Oyer for their support.

Those who have never written a book are blissfully unaware of the enormous time commitment needed to complete such a project. My family is now aware of that commitment, and they shared it with me in admirable fashion. Thanks to my daughter Stacy, who assisted me with some of the research, and my daughter Jennifer, who during the summer of 2002 accompanied me to eight different colleges where we investigated admissions for her and often investigated questions for the book. I'm also appreciative to my sons Jason and Aaron, who didn't see enough of me during 2002. I'm especially grateful to my wife Randi, who had enormous patience and understanding for this project (even when I was typing during the weekend of our twentieth anniversary). Randi's devotion to family is legendary to those who know her, and that trait made the completion of this book a reality.

About the Author

David Braverman is Senior Director of Standard & Poor's Portfolio Advisors. He has worked for Standard & Poor's and its parent, The McGraw-Hill Companies, for over 20 years. During this period he has also served as an economist, cash manager, and equity research analyst. He is a Chartered Financial Analyst and a member of the Standard & Poor's Investment Policy Committee. His comments on the financial markets are frequently carried by the media, including appearances on CNBC, CNBC Asia, Wall Street Journal Radio, and CNNfn. He lives on Long Island, New York, with his wife and four children.

CHAPTER 1

College and Savings

Although I am sure that you don't have to be convinced of the need to save for future educational expenses, you, like most well-meaning people, are probably not prepared for how hard it is to accumulate the sums needed to pay for a college education.

When you come right down to it, for every reason you can come up with to save for college, there's another reason, or excuse, that will keep you from following through.

Let's list some of the most common reasons that prevent people from saving for college.

➤ It doesn't pay to save because I have massive credit card debts.

➤ If I save for college, I'll reduce my eligibility for financial aid.

➤ If I put away money in my kids' names, the kids will just spend it on something else.

➤ I don't need to save; my kid is going to get a full academic merit scholarship to Harvard or Stanford.

➤ I'm waiting on an inheritance from my (name of relative). That will be my child's college fund.

➤ The child's grandparents said they would pay when the time comes.

➤ It's too early; my child is only three years old. I'll start when we're more established and can afford to save more.

All of these reasons make sense on some level, but in reality are just excuses for not accomplishing your goals. That's what it's all about—setting financial goals and then figuring out how these goals might be accomplished over some period of time. Quite frankly, by convincing yourself that some obstacle exists, you find yourself paralyzed by inaction. It's much better to recognize what the financial challenges are, what the misconceptions are, and then move to the next step. That next step is to figure out where you are now, figure out where you want to go, and then figure out how to get there.

Let's start with some of the reasons listed above and how to deal with them:

I can't save because I already have massive credit card debts.

It's true that paying off your high-interest debts ought to be a very high priority in your financial life. However, if you're just living hand-to-mouth and making the minimum payments on your credit cards, you will neither get out of debt nor accumulate any savings at all for college. What is needed here is a plan. You need to start by figuring out the date that you can realistically pay off the debt. You then need to figure out how large the monthly payment has to be to eliminate the debt. You need to cut your spending on "extras," and in some cases even things that appear to be necessities (but really are "extras") to accomplish this. Another route to consider is to borrow against your home equity to pay off the consumer debt. If you do this, however, I suggest you take out a five-year loan instead of a home equity line of credit. During the five-year payback period, get rid of your credit cards except for one card with a minimal ($1000 or less) line of credit. Your credit card issuer will usually approve your request to reduce your credit line. The whole idea is that once you've tapped your home equity to pay your credit cards, you want to make sure that you don't repeat the behavior that got you in this fix to begin with.

Be realistic though. If you can't figure out a way to get out of consumer debt in less than five years, you need to think about credit counseling or even bankruptcy to get back on track. Obviously, these are steps that are not to be taken lightly. However, it's far better to take a drastic step now and put yourself on a path toward achieving your financial goal instead of being paralyzed by your current situation and wondering 10 or 15 years later why things didn't quite work out.

What I suggest is developing a plan to get out of debt over a five-year period or less and then simultaneously saving a small amount (even $25 per month) for college. This gets you in the habit of setting a goal and achieving it as well as the habit of saving for college. Once you're out of debt, make sure you stay out so you'll be on track to execute your college savings plan.

If I save for college, I'll reduce my eligibility for financial aid.

This is actually not as valid a statement as most people think. While a high level of savings will reduce eligibility for financial aid, it shouldn't be an excuse not to get started with a savings program. In the federal financial aid formulas, a two-parent family, in which the older parent is 45, is allowed assets of $42,200 in the parents' name before any reduction in aid is calculated. That number excludes the value of retirement accounts and the equity in your home. The U.S. Department of Education calls this number the *education savings and asset protection allowance* used in calculating the *expected family contribution*. We'll have more about these terms later in the book. For now, it is best to worry about how you're going to accumulate $42,200 before you worry about any conditions that might limit financial aid.

If I put away money in my kids' names, the kids will just spend it on something else.

Recent changes in the tax laws expanding the use of 529 college savings plans has lessened or even eliminated most of the motivation for putting education funds in a minor's name. These 529 plans are usually set up whereby a parent or grandparent invests money for the future education of a child. Under this scenario, the parent or grandparent is the owner of the account up until the moment of withdrawal. No longer do you have to worry that the funds will be used for something other than the intended purpose.

I don't need to save; my kid is going to get a full academic merit scholarship to Harvard or Stanford.

No, that's not going to happen. At least not at these two schools. Harvard and Stanford are both very clear on their policy of providing need-based financial aid only. They don't give academic merit scholarships. They don't have to. They already get about 10 applicants for every available place, and the vast majority of their students are in the top 10 percent of their graduating class with scores higher than 1400 on the SATs. In fact, even stronger candidates than that are often rejected from some of the top schools. Even some candidates who are in the top 1 percent of their high school class and have perfect SAT scores don't always gain admission. However, many great schools that provide first-rate educational opportunities provide financial aid based on academic merit. Schools such as Duke University, Emory University, University of Chicago, and Washington University in St. Louis are among the top schools in the United States that award at least some merit aid to the most prepared applicants. In almost all cases though, this merit aid is given to only a small percentage of the student body. The trick is finding a school that will view the applicant as much better prepared than the average student applying to the same school. Merit aid can make college more affordable, but it's usually not a total substitute for developing and maintaining an education savings plan. The problem is that when you discover that you aren't getting merit aid, it's usually too late to start saving.

I'm waiting on an inheritance from my (name of relative). That will be my child's college fund.

Well, there's no sure thing in terms of waiting for an inheritance. If the relative is sure he or she wants to provide for your child's education, a college fund can be set up now instead of waiting for someone's demise. In fact, the new 529 college savings plans can be an effective estate planning tool because once funds are deposited into the account, they leave the donor's taxable estate. More importantly, though, the funds are already designated for the child so that effective financial planning can be accomplished. These accounts even have flexibility for the donor so that in case of an emergency, the donor can withdraw the funds for his or her own use. If this is a concern, the newly expanded Coverdell education accounts can be used as an irrevocable gift.

The child's grandparents said they would pay when the time comes.

Again, maybe yes, maybe no. The last thing someone wants to see is a misunderstanding when the bill for the first semester of school (possibly totaling as much as $20,000) arrives. A much better idea is that a college fund be set up in advance so that everyone knows what financial resources are available to the student. That way, the student and the family can make an intelligent decision as to what schools to apply to and what schools to attend. I've spoken to people who were shocked to find that their expected parental contribution to school is far in excess of what they thought they could afford. The whole premise of this book is to have some idea of what college is going to cost, how to realistically estimate what kind of financial aid is going to be available, and how to pay for the rest.

It's too early; my child is only three years old. I'll start when we're more established and can afford to save more.

This is the biggest misconception of all. Actually the reverse is true. If you save early, you might not have to bother saving later. Let's look at an example of this in Table 1-1. Let's say you, Parent A started saving $3000 when your child was born and put away another $3000 each year on the child's birthday. Let's also assume that you did this for the last time on the child's 10th birthday. Now compare that to Parent B, starting for the first time on the child's 10th birthday and putting away $5000 each year until the child was 18 years old.

In this example, Parent A put away $3000 at the child's birth and each of the next 10 birthdays for a total deposit of $33,000. Parent B put away $5000 on the child's 10th through 18th birthdays for a total deposit of $45,000. But look what happened. Assuming a 7 percent annual return, even though parent B saved $12,000 more, when the child is 18 years old, parent B has $21,467 less than parent A. This is

TABLE 1-1. **The Benefit of Saving Early**

| Year | PARENT A | | PARENT B | |
	Amount Deposited ($)	Balance ($)	Amount Deposited ($)	Balance ($)
0	3,000	3,000	0	0
1	3,000	6,210	0	0
2	3,000	9,645	0	0
3	3,000	13,320	0	0
4	3,000	17,252	0	0
5	3,000	21,460	0	0
6	3,000	25,962	0	0
7	3,000	30,779	0	0
8	3,000	35,934	0	0
9	3,000	41,449	0	0
10	3,000	47,351	5,000	5,000
11	0	50,665	5,000	10,350
12	0	54,212	5,000	16,075
13	0	58,007	5,000	22,200
14	0	62,067	5,000	28,754
15	0	66,412	5,000	35,766
16	0	71,061	5,000	43,270
17	0	76,035	5,000	51,299
18	0	81,357	5,000	59,890
Total	**33,000**		**45,000**	

all because Parent A's money had more years to accumulate. It is never too early to start to save. Later in the book, we'll even discuss the possibility of saving *before* your child is born.

On the other hand, while it's better to save early, *it's never too late.* Don't use this example to assume you can't make a dent in college savings expenses by starting now. It may seem obvious, but it's worth saying. It will always be later next year.

One thing that's important to state here is that while college saving is an important part of anyone's financial plans, it is just that—only a part. People should consider their college savings in relationship to their plans for retirement, their savings for other large purchases, such as a home, and whether their insurance coverage is adequate. The point is that saving for college is just another part of an integrated financial plan. It sounds complicated, but it really is no more than writing out your goals on a piece of paper and prioritizing what you realistically want to accomplish.

Even prioritizing these things is not easy. I heard one planner recently say, "Make sure you fund your retirement first. That's because if you don't save enough for college, your kids can get financial aid. But, there's no financial aid for retirement." I then heard another planner say "Make sure you save for college for your kids even if you have to cut back on your retirement savings. You can always work a year or two longer, but you don't want to tell your kids to delay college for a year or two." My own view is somewhere in the middle. Neither extreme is correct in all cases. When you plan for the future, only you can decide what is most important in your personal financial plan.

Now comes the time for some soul-searching: Are you going to do this prioritizing and planning yourself or are you going to hire an investment advisor to help you? There is, of course, no right or wrong answer to this question either. If you are the type of person who can stay informed about your savings (just reading this book is a good start) and stay disciplined about continuing to save, it is certainly possible to amass a significant amount of savings on your own. If instead, you find that you need someone to guide you through the various ways to save, and you value (and are willing to pay for) an advisor who can keep track of your various goals and report back to you on your periodic progress, then go ahead and use an advisor.

To me, the best analogy is when a room needs to be painted. Many people instinctively go to the paint store and buy the can of paint and all the supplies and do an adequate job. Others wouldn't consider doing anything other than hiring a professional painter. It's a matter of personal preference. Does the professional painter do a better job? Often yes, but not always. Is the professional more expensive? Usually, but if you're clumsy or inexperienced, you might spill a gallon of paint on your carpet, making the professional look like a bargain.

So, when it comes to college savings, I encourage you to try it yourself, but an advisor can also be invaluable when it comes to navigating these waters.

However, more important than the decision of whether or not to use an advisor is the decision to set goals and be focused on achieving them. Most people live day to day without thinking about what they want to achieve. If your goal is saving for college, then you need to think about that goal periodically. Ask yourself, "How much did I want to save for college this year?" Then translate that into, "How much did I want to save for college this month?" Once you start thinking about your goals on a periodic basis, you can start thinking about how you're going to achieve those goals. For example, each time you get paid you can ask yourself, "How much can I save toward my goal?" Better yet, ask yourself whether you can set up an automatic savings plan. Each time you make a major purchase ask yourself whether this purchase brings you closer to or farther from your goals. Not thinking about your savings goal is almost a guarantee that the goal will not be met. In saving for college, there are many decisions that need to be made. Most of this book will focus on what type of investment to make, who should be the owner of the account, and how to minimize taxes. However, none of that matters if you don't make the most basic decision first. That decision of course is, "Should I take this money and spend it on some immediate need or want, or should I use it to provide for college savings?"

A few years ago I was attending the Berkshire Hathaway annual meeting to hear Warren Buffett and Charlie Munger, two of the richest men in America, talk about their investing success. After being asked if they had any personal finance tips for the audience, Charlie answered, "Yes, make sure you underspend your income." It's so basic, yet so true. You have to spend less than you earn in order to meet your savings goal. Now that we understand that, let's go!

CHAPTER 2

The Cost
of College

N ow that you've decided that you should be saving for college, and that now is just as good a time as any to get started, the next step is figuring out what your financial goals should be. Remember that you are going to think of the college savings plan as just one of many goals in your financial life, such as saving for retirement, a car, or the down payment on a house. Just as there is a huge variation in what various people need to put away to achieve their particular retirement or purchase goals, college savings goals will vary with projected costs.

The first thing to do is to have some idea of what college costs today. These costs can vary considerably. A four-year college education can be had in certain situations for well under $15,000 or, at the other extreme, close to $200,000. Where you are in this continuum depends on the answers to a few questions:

➤ Will the college be public or private?

➤ What level of financial aid is likely to be available?

➤ Will the student commute from home or go away to school?

➤ What type of academic program is the student considering?

➤ Will the student need a car?

➤ What level of social activity will there be in school?

PUBLIC OR PRIVATE SCHOOL: I personally attended a public university for my undergraduate work and a private school for my graduate work. Clearly, public universities are substantially less expensive than most private schools. The argument is that your tax dollars are going to support these schools, so why not take advantage of the opportunity when the time comes to go to school. They are usually a bargain, but these schools are not for everyone. Some of these schools, including the University of Michigan, the University of Virginia, and the University of California at Berkeley are ranked by *U.S. News & World Report* as among the 50 best research universities in the United States. However, state schools tend to have larger classes and a reputation for somewhat less personal attention than might be found in a private institution. Even here, there are no absolutes. In visiting various colleges with my children, I found some very personalized attention at some state schools and some indifference at some private schools. My advice is to visit some private and public schools and decide for yourself when the time comes.

In terms of how much to save, I think it's best to keep an open mind. I've spoken to the parents of elementary school children who already believe they know which college their offspring will attend even though they don't truly know their child's interests and abilities and the parents haven't investigated the whole array of opportunities open to them. At that early stage, it seems that the best course of action is to keep as many options open as possible. It may make sense to assume for the time being that the student will be attending the more expensive private school. This enables the family to have as many options as possible later. Many families find that after need-based aid kicks in, the private school option is more affordable than previously thought.

LIKELY FINANCIAL AID: At this stage of the game, you need to forecast what your family would likely pay for school this year in today's dollars. One way of doing this is starting with one of the many financial aid calculators that are available on the Internet. Three of the best are the calculators at www.collegeboard.com, www.finaid.com, and www.usnews.com. All three tend to give similar results. The calculator at finaid.com can give you a detailed printout that shows some of the underlying formulas for computing aid. Basically, you enter your income and assets and then get an approximation of what the likely expected family contribution (EFC) would be. At this point, don't enter what you think your income will be when your child is in college, but do enter the likely number of children who will be in college each year. The reason is that you're trying to compute your savings goal for this year, not the likely aid you're going to get 10 or 15 years from now. You also need to calculate the EFC using both federal methodology and institutional methodology. Federal methodology is usually used for public schools, and institutional methodology is usually used for private institutions. The calculations are somewhat different. For most families, the biggest difference is that home equity is usually considered in the institutional methodology, while it is excluded from the federal methodology. There will be more detail on this subject in the financial aid section of the book.

TYPE OF ACADEMIC PROGRAM: When estimating future college costs, keep in mind that some academic programs cost more than others. Some scientific programs have extra lab fees and may entail more expensive textbooks. Study abroad programs invariably entail additional costs. Even if the school says that the normal tuition and room fees apply, there will almost always be additional funds needed for travel and spending money. Schools have been creative in the last few years in adding additional costs. While many schools have charged laboratory fees for years for science courses, these fees are now being imposed on language, math, and journalism courses at some institutions.

NEED FOR A CAR: At some schools and in some situations (such as commuting to school) a car may be a necessity. In most situations, however, a car is definitely a luxury. A large number of schools restrict resident freshmen from having cars on campus anyway. Some schools attribute the policy to a lack of parking; others want to avoid the distraction of the student having a car. In any event, when thinking about the total cost of going to college, your plans for a car should be factored in.

LEVEL OF SOCIAL ACTIVITY AT COLLEGE: I'm usually amazed when I see top private schools include a token amount for personal expenses or exclude the amount completely. According to Shauna Morrison, the chief editor of Collegeboard.com, students and their parents frequently don't consider the expense of joining a fraternity or sorority, attendance at sporting events, eating out with friends, or going to parties. I can now hear parents mumbling, "I didn't save up so that my kid could just fool around; I wanted my child to get an education." However to some extent, these social activities are part of the college experience. A student doesn't have to join every club and go to every single party, but social events should be at least part of the mix when figuring out the cost of going to a particular school.

How Much to Save— Your Annual Savings Goal

After you've gotten an early look at how your expected family contribution is calculated as described above, the next step is to find out how much a school that you may have some interest in will cost. Visit the Web sites of various schools and take a look at the costs. Once you've determined the costs of a few schools, here's how you would figure out your initial savings goals for an elite private school and for a state school:

Costs per Year at a Private School		Costs per Year at a State University	
Tuition	$25,800	Tuition	$3,400
Room and board	8,900	Room and board	6,800
Fees	300	Fees	200
Books	600	Transportation	400
Transportation	800	Books	500
Personal expenses	500	Personal expenses	500
Total	**$36,900**	**Total**	**$11,800**

Then let's say you calculated that the expected family contribution for the private school was $18,000 under the federal methodology and $20,000 under the institutional methodology. You need to calculate this for each year you have a different number of children in school. It may be that you have two children that will be in school together for two years. In the years that both children are in school, the institutional EFC might be $12,000 for each child.

Assuming you're saving for private school, the total savings needed for the six years of college, including the two children at school together for two years would be as follows:

> Four years at $20,000
> Two years at $24,000 ($12,000 × 2)
> Total = $128,000

We used the EFC instead of the cost of attendance because it's lower. We're assuming for the time being that we'll save the expected family contribution first, and then if we get ambitious, we'll save beyond that amount to help mitigate the likely cost of borrowing. When we talk about financial aid later in the book, we'll see that borrowing is usually a big part of the financial aid package awarded by schools. For now though, let's just concentrate on covering the lion's share of the financial burden.

You should initially set the goal to have the savings plan completed by the halfway point of the two childrens' college education. There are two reasons for this. The first reason is that you want to be done early so that if there are any additional expenses such as the purchase of a computer or the repayment of loans you can start early. The second reason is that if you fall short of your savings goal it gives you a bit more time to make a midcourse correction. In our example, the halfway point would be the end of third year of the older child's education, and the first year of the younger child's. Assuming the children are currently 7 and 9 years old, and are 11 and 9 years away, respectively, from starting college, you have 12 years to complete your plan. That means that this year's savings goal ought to be $128,000 divided by 12, or $10,667. Doing it this way assumes that the return on investments will cover the likely inflation that we'll see in college costs. Each year, you go through the exercise again to determine your savings goal for the next year.

A year later you might have $11,200 after return on your investments. However, you might find that with a higher income, your six-year EFC has risen to $130,000. So for the next year, you would take $130,000, subtract the $11,200 you already saved and divide the resulting $118,800 by 11 and get a savings goal of $10,800. Hopefully, the investment performance is strong enough to overcome the increasing cost of college. In addition, each time you reestimate the EFC you'll have more savings, which in turn could increase the EFC. Yes, there are quite a few moving parts to all of this. However, don't panic about all of this. Keep in mind that having substantial savings is the name of the game. If you can't meet your goal for this year, save what you can. By the way, a family with an EFC of $25,000 usually has income of over $100,000. So if your earnings are less, your savings goal will also be less. On the other hand, this calculation doesn't really consider some of the additional things we mentioned above such as a car or a more expensive academic program or some additional social activities.

One of the reasons it's necessary to be so aggressive in saving for college is that costs are continuing to rise more rapidly than household incomes. That's why it's important to start saving early, and to keep up with reestimating your annual savings goal. This is particularly important for those upper-middle-income and upper-income families that won't be qualifying for much of any need-based grant aid.

Over the five years ended in 2002–2003, private four-year college tuition costs rose 5.8 percent per year and public four-year tuition costs rose 5.6 percent compared with 2.2 percent for the Consumer Price Index. It's important to find investment vehicles that will let you keep up with inflation. It's also important to make sure that the level of investment risk is not so high as to raise the possibility that your savings goals can't be met late in the savings game. This will be covered in more depth in the investment strategy section.

Hopefully, this discussion hasn't scared you off, but instead has encouraged you to start your savings plan. In Chapter 3, we discuss some of the ways to save for college and save money on taxes at the same time.

529 Plans

F or many families, a new and attractive way to save for college has arrived. These accounts, commonly known as 529 plans, are rapidly gaining assets. The reason for the quick rise in popularity is clear.

➤ Income and returns from investments accumulate tax free when used for qualified college expenditures.

➤ Contributions in many states can be deducted from income on state tax returns.

➤ The owner (usually also the contributor) of the account (such as a parent or grandparent) retains control of the account until the moment the funds are withdrawn.

➤ The account is treated as a completed gift for estate tax purposes.

➤ These accounts can be advantageous in maintaining eligibility for financial aid when compared to custodial accounts for minors.

What Are 529 Plans?

Officially named Qualified Tuition Plans, 529 plans are state-sponsored savings plans that can be used to pay for college expenses. There are basically two types of 529 plans: prepaid tuition plans and college savings programs. Most of the explosive growth has been in the college savings programs, but the prepaid plans deserve some mention here.

Most of the prepaid plans are analogous to a defined benefit pension plan, where you contribute an agreed amount in exchange for future benefits. What's nice about these plans is that there is sometimes a full faith and credit backing by the state that once the contract is purchased, there will be sufficient funds to pay tuition (usually at the state university level). College savings plans, on the other hand, are more like defined contribution plans, such as IRAs or 401(k) plans. These plans usually don't have any state guarantee (although some do), but they have more flexibility to accept various levels of contributions and offer at least the possibility of higher returns on investments.

Although some form of prepaid tuition plans have been around since the late 1980s, section 529 of the tax code wasn't established until 1996. States then had the ability to offer savings plans as well as prepaid tuition plans. These savings plans were further improved as part of the 1997 Taxpayer Relief Act when room and board and books were added to the list of qualified expenses. However, the biggest revision to 529s was a result of the Economic Growth and Tax Relief Reconciliation Act of 2001 (EGTRRA). These changes, which took effect in January 2002, permitted tax-free distributions for qualified educational expenses. In addition, the law expanded the transferability of 529 funds, adding a first cousin of the present beneficiary to the list of those eligible to become a revised beneficiary of the account. EGTRRA also permits schools to establish 529 plans (prepaid plans only) with tax-free withdrawal status beginning in 2004. Interestingly, the EGTRRA provisions expire on December 31, 2010, so at that time (unless Congress renews the provisions) withdrawals once again will become taxable.

The question of whether tax-free treatment of 529 plans will be extended beyond 2010 has been the subject of a great deal of debate. Many advisors say they can't imagine a scenario where the current treatment is allowed to expire, given how many families are depending on 529 plans to save for college. In fact, early versions of the tax bill debated in 2003 included a provision to make the tax-free treatment of 529 plans permanent. The final version of the bill failed to make the change. On the other hand, some economists and political analysts point to growing federal deficits and say that letting the provisions of EGTRRA expire in 2010 will be a back door way of raising revenue at the point where Social Security expenditures will be growing rapidly. Stay tuned.

While 529 savings plans are state sponsored, they are mostly managed by well-known financial services companies. Most plans offer a variety of investment choices. However, not every plan offers every type of investment, and the fees charged by the various plans can vary widely. You don't have to necessarily invest in the plan offered by your home state. The same federal tax benefits apply regardless of which state plan you invest in. However, many states offer tax benefits to those who contribute to the plan in their home state.

Tax-Free Withdrawals

The ability to have funds distributed on a tax-free basis is an enormous advantage for families who want to maximize their savings. Here's an example. Let's say a married couple earns $95,000 per year, and in 2003 had a federal marginal tax rate of 27 percent. They want to save $5000 per year for the next five years for their son's college education. Let's say they have three choices:

1. An investment that is taxable (at 27 percent) and pays 7 percent a year.

2. An investment that is tax-deferred (with taxes paid at withdrawal at the 15 percent capital gains rate) and pays 7 percent a year.

3. An investment that is tax-free and pays 7 percent a year.

Table 3-1 shows the results of these three scenarios.

Tax-free scenario 3 provides $1663 more at the end of the five years than does taxable scenario 1. The ending balance is 5.7 percent higher without any additional deposit or any higher return.

State Tax Deduction

Now let's assume the same married couple lives in a state in which they can deduct their contributions and the state tax rate is 6 percent. We'll also assume that this couple also itemizes their federal deductions, so by getting a reduction in their state taxes, they get a slight increase in their federal tax. This nets out to getting a tax savings of 4.38 percent. The formula is $(1 - 27\%$ federal tax rate$) \times (6\%$ state tax rate$) = (73\% \times 6\%) = 4.38\%$.

TABLE 3-1. Benefit of Tax-Free Savings

Year	Deposit (at (beginning of year) ($)	Earnings ($)	Taxes Paid ($)	End of Year Balance ($)
Scenario 1: Taxable				
1	5000	350	95	5,255
2	5000	718	194	10,779
3	5000	1105	298	16,586
4	5000	1511	408	22,689
5	5000	1938	523	29,904
Scenario 2: Tax-Deferred				
1	5000	350	0	5,350
2	5000	725	0	11,075
3	5000	1125	0	17,200
4	5000	1554	0	23,754
5	5000	2013	865	29,902
Scenario 3: Tax-Free				
1	5000	350	0	5,350
2	5000	725	0	11,075
3	5000	1125	0	17,200
4	5000	1554	0	23,754
5	5000	2013	0	30,767

TABLE 3-2. Additional Benefits of State Tax Deduction

Year	Deposit (at (beginning of year) ($)	Earnings ($)	Taxes Paid ($)	End of Year Balance ($)
1	5219	365	0	5,584
2	5229	757	0	11,570
3	5229	1176	0	17,975
4	5229	1624	0	24,828
5	5229	2104	0	32,161

3342076

Table 3-2 shows what happens when this couple adds their tax savings to the account each year.

We now have $1394 more than the tax-free scenario 3 and $3057 more than the taxable scenario 1. Note that the amount deposited in years two through five are higher. That's because you are now getting tax savings on your tax savings for the prior year. Obviously, if you save more or save for longer than five years, your savings with the 529 plan will be even greater (depending on limits for deductions in each individual state).

How 529 Plans Work with Your Taxes

When you make a deposit to a 529 plan, there is no tax impact at the federal level. You can't deduct the contribution. However, in many states, the contributions are deductible from state income tax. The following states allow deductions from taxable income for contributions to 529 plan accounts:

Colorado	Nebraska
District of Columbia	New Mexico
Georgia	New York
Idaho	Ohio
Illinois	Oklahoma
Iowa	Oregon
Kansas	Rhode Island
Louisiana	South Carolina
Maryland	Utah
Michigan	Virginia
Mississippi	West Virginia
Missouri	Wisconsin
Montana	

The tax benefits accrue at the time of withdrawal. Each withdrawal (or distribution) from a 529 plan account is totaled on form 1099Q at the end of the year. If the distribution was used for a qualified higher educational expense (QHEE), then the entire distribution is excluded from taxable income at the federal level. Most (but not all) states also exclude the qualified distribution from taxable income. QHEE is defined as tuition, fees, books, supplies and equipment. Room and board is also a qualified expense. Generally, the school's posted room and board rate qualifies for students living on campus and an allowance for off-campus living also qualifies. Usually, transportation, personal expenses (televisions or stereos) don't qualify.

If all or part of the distribution is not qualified, in other words, the QHEE was less than the distribution, then all or part of the earnings will be taxable and subject to penalty. Only the earnings are subject to taxes and penalties. The initial contribution is not subject to penalty, although some states will "recapture" the state tax deduction on nonqualified distributions.

EXAMPLE: George has saved $3000 per year for seven years in a 529 savings plan with his son Bill as beneficiary. The balance is $30,000 of which $9000 represents earnings and $21,000 represents principal. George lives in a state without an income tax. In August, George asks for a distribution of $10,000 to be sent to pay for Bill's freshman year of college. However, Bill only had $8000 of qualified expenses in his first semester and George didn't pay for the second semester until January of the following year. As a result, $2000 of the distribution is nonqualified and subject to tax and penalties. However, only the earnings portion is taxable. Here's how the tax and penalty is figured:

1. Balance (including all distributions) $30,000
2. Earnings $9,000
3. Line 2 divided by line   30%
4. Distributions for the year $10,000
5. Earnings portion of distribution $3,000
   (multiply line 4 and line 3)
6. Qualified higher education expense $8,000

7. Nonqualified distribution (line 6 minus line 4) $2,000
8. Line 7 divided by line 4   20%
9. Taxable earnings (line 8 multiplied by line 5) $600

What's interesting in this example is that the $600 is taxable to George, not Bill. Assuming George is in the 27 percent marginal tax bracket, the tax would be $162 and the 10 percent penalty would amount to $60. There are two lessons in this example: The first is that even when some of a 529 plan withdrawal is taxable, the tax burden is not overly severe because only the earnings, not the principal are taxed. The second lesson is that with a bit of planning, taxes and penalties could often be avoided. The best bet is to try to match the qualified educational expenses in the same calendar year with the 529 plan distribution. George and Bill could have prepaid the second semester of tuition in December and increased the amount of qualified expenses, thus eliminating the penalty. Also, George, as owner of the account, could have directed the funds sent directly to the school. As long as the school is not making a refund, there would be no question that the expenses were qualified. The school would have just applied the excess to the next semester. Even if a refund were made, the school would have paid it to Bill. That way, the taxes would be payable at Bill's lower tax rate.

Note: The IRS has not explicitly required a strict matching of qualified expenses to withdrawals. However, it is reasonable to expect that they could at a later date. Thus, it's a smart idea to keep your 529 withdrawals and your payments to the college in the same calendar year.

In some 529 plans, the distribution can be paid directly to the beneficiary. In others, the choice is between having a distribution paid either to the account owner or directly to the school. When a distribution is paid to the school, it is construed as having been paid to the beneficiary. It's not a bad idea to have a look at the account withdrawal forms from your 529 plan long before a distribution is going to be made. It's not even a bad idea to look at the withdrawal forms when initially choosing a 529 plan.

Sometimes it's *advantageous* to pay the taxes and penalties on a 529 plan distribution. Assume for a moment that Bill actually had

$10,000 of qualifying higher educational expense, but chose to only claim $8000 of those expenses. The reason for doing that is to claim the Hope Credit, one of two major tax credits available for college tuition, which will be discussed further in Chapter 6. (You cannot use tax-free 529 plan proceeds to pay expenses to qualify for the Hope Credit, but you can choose to make part of the 529 distribution non-qualified in order to get the credit. The credit ends up being more than the taxes and penalties paid on the 529 plan distribution.) George can claim 100 percent of the first $1000 of tuition paid and 50 percent of the second $1000 of tuition paid as a Hope Credit. This $1500 credit far exceeds the $222 of taxes and penalties paid by George. George is allowed to get the credit even if the tuition payment was actually paid by Bill. George also qualifies to take the Hope Credit because he and his wife file jointly and have modified adjusted gross income (MAGI) of less than $80,000. The credit phases out for MAGI between $80,000 and $100,000. Single taxpayers are eligible for the Hope Credit with MAGI of less than $40,000 and the credit phases out between $40,000 and $50,000. In general, 529 distributions can't be used for expenses that are deductible or eligible for a credit at the federal level. You have to either (a) forgo the federal credit or deduction or (b) take the distribution on a nonqualified basis. We'll have more details on the Hope Credit, the Lifetime Learning Credit, as well as other tax credits and deductions for educational expenses in Chapter 6.

Who Controls a 529 Account?

When a 529 account is set up, the state (or account administrator) will ask for an account owner and an account beneficiary. The guiding principle here is that usually the contributor of the money should be the owner of the account. Typically, the owner is a parent or grandparent, and a minor child is the beneficiary.

One of the big advantages of 529 plans is that control of the money stays with the owner until the request for a distribution is made. This usually makes 529 plans a preferred choice for college savings over making an irrevocable gift to a child and putting it into a custodial account. There are two reasons for this. First, an irrevocable gift is just that. It has to be spent on the beneficiary or turned over to the child when he or she becomes an adult. There's no control over the funds eventually being spent on new cars, clothing, entertainment, and vacations by a young adult, when the funds were actually intended for education. The second reason is that because the funds in a 529 savings plan remain under the control of the owner, they are generally not counted as the child's assets when computing financial aid. In most financial aid formulas, funds owned by the student are assessed much more heavily than funds owned by the parents. Accounts owned by grandparents are usually not considered at all. Later in this chapter, I'll describe a significant difference between how 529 prepaid plans are treated in financial aid formulas and the treatment of 529 savings plans.

Estate Planning

529 plans have a unique feature that can make them an interesting part of one's estate planning arsenal. Although the owner retains control of the funds, the establishment of a 529 plan account is treated as a completed gift to the beneficiary. As such, it is no longer a part of the account owner's taxable estate. What does this mean? It means that if you're a person of significant means, you can reduce the size of your taxable estate and ultimately the estate taxes due while helping your heirs pay for college and while maintaining control of the principal.

It's a triple play! Just keep in mind that fewer and fewer individuals are subject to estate taxes as a result of the Economic Growth and Tax Relief Reconciliation Act of 2001 (EGTRRA). Yes, the same law that expanded 529 plans also sharply reduced the bite of estate taxes. For 2002 and 2003, estates of less than $1 million are exempt from federal taxes. For 2004 and 2005, that amount is increased to $1.5 million. For 2006 through 2008 the limit is $2 million and for 2009 the exempt amount is $3.5 million. Interestingly for 2010, there is no estate tax at all, although gift taxes continue at a reduced rate. However, like the rest of EGTRRA, the rules expire at the end of 2010, so unless extended, estate taxes make a reappearance in 2011.

Each time you make a contribution to a 529 plan account, it is treated as a gift to the beneficiary of the account. You can make small or large contributions to the account at any time. If you make a gift in excess of the annual gift tax exclusion, you need to either pay gift tax or use part of the lifetime gift/estate tax exemption. In 2003, the annual gift tax exclusion is $11,000, with that amount indexed for cost of living increases in future years. That means that a married couple can currently contribute $22,000 per year with no tax consequence to each child's 529 account. In addition, if by chance that's not enough, it's also possible to "front load" five years' worth of gifts in a single year. That way, an individual can put up to $55,000 into a 529 plan account at one time. (A married couple can contribute $110,000, but each should open their own 529 plan account for a single beneficiary.) The election to average five years of gifts has to be reported to the IRS on form 709 (probably with the assistance of a tax professional). Two other things to keep in mind are that you can then not make any additional contributions to that beneficiary during that five-year period. Also, if the donor were to die before the beginning of the fifth calendar year of the gift, the portion of the contribution allocated to years following the donor's death would be included in the donor's estate.

Another thing to keep in mind is that just because the 529 plan represents a completed gift for estate purposes doesn't mean that the funds still aren't under the donor's control. The implication is that an elderly person may find that funds contributed into a 529 plan account are still considered available for the contributor's long-term care. Medicaid, for example, considers all transfers within 36 months to be available for a patient's care. A grandparent may want to consider making a gift to the child's parents so that the parent can be the owner of the 529 account. The gift should be made well in advance of the need for long-term care if this is a concern.

Financial Aid Benefits and 529 Plans

We'll get into more detail in Chapter 7 about financial aid. At that point we'll talk about the various methodologies for computing need-based aid. For now, keep in mind the following tenets that are common to almost every financial aid formula:

➤ The student's assets are assessed at a higher rate than the parents' assets.

➤ The student's income is assessed at a higher rate than the parents' income.

Assets and income owned by relatives other than the parents are not usually assessed.

529 plans are unique in that while they are dedicated to a particular student as beneficiary, they need not be owned by the beneficiary. A parent or grandparent can open the account for a child and maintain ownership of the account until the moment the funds are withdrawn. Thus, unlike custodial accounts for minors, such as those made under the Uniform Transfers to Minors Act or Uniform Gift to Minors Act (UTMA/UGMA), which count as a student asset, 529 plans, owned by a parent, count as a parental asset and are much less heavily assessed.

The question of how the 529 plan is treated upon withdrawal is less clear. Interestingly, a distinction is made between 529 prepaid plans and 529 savings plans. Currently, distributions from 529 prepaid plans are treated as a resource, much like a scholarship and added to the expected family contribution. So, in effect, the assessment (or tax) on a 529 prepaid plan is 100 percent. Currently, distributions from 529 savings plans are not treated as a resource. In years prior to 2002, they were only counted in the financial aid formulas to the extent that the earnings portion of the distribution was included in the student's income. Clearly, this makes the 529 savings plan far superior to the prepaid plan in that at least the principal portion of the distribution escapes consideration.

For the financial aid forms that came out in late 2002, it appears that since 529 earnings are not subject to income tax, that the entire distribution from a 529 savings plan escapes consideration from the financial aid formulas as a resource or as income. Will this continue? It's hard to say. The current treatment of a 529 savings plan is now not particularly different from that of a parent who saves under his or her own name and then withdraws the funds to pay for college. However, it's entirely possible that in the future the rules will change to some sort of unified treatment for 529 savings plans and prepaid plans. I'll discuss the reasoning further in Chapter 7, but for now, despite some advisors and columnists claims to the contrary, we believe that the income component of a distribution from a 529 savings plan owned by a parent with a child as a beneficiary *is not* treated as the child's income when it's time to compute need-based financial aid.

Make sure you stay alert for changes in the financial aid landscape. This brings us back to the advice I had in Chapter 2. On a periodic basis, take a look at the online financial aid calculators. See how various types of savings affect financial aid for your family's situation. For most families, 529 savings plans will be superior to UTMA/UGMA accounts from a financial aid perspective.

Transferring Funds from a UTMA/UGMA Account to a 529 Plan

This is technically possible, but there are a few pitfalls. First and foremost is the fact that legally this is the child's money. Thus, if custodial money is transferred to a 529 plan, that ownership is supposed to be maintained. Different plans handle the transfer of UTMA/UGMA funds in a couple of ways. Either the minor child becomes the owner of the account as well as the beneficiary, or the parent remains the owner, but often with restrictions on future changes to beneficiary. A better idea may be to "spend down" the custodial account on items that would have been purchased for the child anyway. The test is whether the expenditure was for the "benefit of the minor." In addition, the expenditure can't be for an item that is a normal parental obligation, such as food and shelter. Some advisors though, say you can go back in time and make an itemized list of "nonessential" expenditures such as music lessons, summer camp, etc., and reimburse yourself out of the UTMA/UGMA account. You would then make a contribution equal to the expenditure into the 529 savings plan.

If, however, you do make a direct transfer into a 529 savings plan, it would be wise to keep those transferred funds segregated in a separate account and not comingled with other 529 funds.

Dealing with Some of the 529 Plan Pitfalls

All this sounds great. I'd like to take some of the stock I own and put it into one of these 529 savings plans.

That can't be done. Only cash can be contributed to a 529 savings plan. If you want to move some of your current investments to a 529 savings plan, they need to be liquidated first. This will usually be a taxable event.

What if I set up a 529 plan for my child and he or she decides not to attend college?

You have a few choices: You can do nothing, leaving open the possibility that your child may change his or her mind and attend college later in life. If you decide to do nothing, you can make your child the contingent owner of the account, and when you die, your child will become the owner and can change the beneficiary from himself to one of his or her children. This way, the funds pass from you to your grandchildren without passing through your estate.

Another choice is to change the beneficiary yourself. The new beneficiary has to have an approved relationship to the previous beneficiary, as follows:

Allowed relationships for 529 plan account beneficiary changes (relationship to prior beneficiary)

Son or daughter or descendent of either

Stepson or stepdaughter

Brother or sister or stepbrother or stepsister

Father or mother or ancestor of either

Stepfather or stepmother

Son or daughter of a brother or sister (nephews and nieces)

The brother or sister of father or mother (uncles and aunts)

The spouse of any individual listed above

The original beneficiary's spouse (provided they are a member of the same household)

A first cousin

A third choice is to withdraw the money for your own use. In most cases, there will be a 10 percent penalty on the earnings portion of this nonqualified distribution. The earnings will also be taxable at ordinary income rates. Remember, the funds originally contributed can be withdrawn without tax or penalty.

What if I set up a 529 plan for my child and I die before he or she starts college? Can my spouse withdraw the money if it's needed for living expenses?

Provided the spouse is named as the contingent owner, he or she becomes the owner of the account. If he or she decides that the funds are needed for living expenses, the funds can be withdrawn but, because this is a nonqualified distribution, the earnings will be subject to tax and penalty. In many states, if no contingent owner is named, the beneficiary becomes the owner.

What if my child gets a scholarship, and we don't need all of the money in the account?

Two choices: You can either (a) use the money for other qualified expenses and change the beneficiary on the remainder or (b) withdraw the remainder. In this case, the earnings are still taxable, but the 10 percent penalty is waived on the amount of the scholarship. One caveat: the scholarship has to be tax-free. That means that the scholarship has to cover tuition. The portion of a scholarship that covers room and board is technically taxable income and is not eligible for exemption from the 10 percent penalty.

What if the beneficiary dies before the funds in the 529 plan are distributed?

The rules on this are not completely clear, but it appears that the account owner can either have the funds distributed to the beneficiary's estate, in which case the earnings are taxable and the 10 percent penalty is waived; or the beneficiary can be changed, which would have no immediate tax consequence.

What if I have a loss on my investments on my 529 plan account? Can I deduct the loss on my income tax return?

Yes, you can, but with some limitations. A miscellaneous deduction (which is reduced by 2 percent of adjusted gross income) can be taken for the loss. The basis for this is the allowance of IRA loss deductions. As is the case with an IRA, the entire 529 plan account has to be liquidated. So, this would only apply in the case of a 529 plan that was also totally liquidated. With many people suffering losses on equity investments in 2001 and 2002, it's clear that many will be in this situation. Keep in mind that in this situation you can usually take out the funds from your 529 account without federal taxes or penalty, even if there are no qualified educational expenses that year, since the computation of tax is based on the accumulated earnings (which in this case are nonexistent). However, be careful about taxes on the state level. Many states that allowed a tax deduction for contributions, will recapture that deduction when you take a nonqualified distribution.

I don't like how my investments are performing within the 529 plan that I'm currently in. Can I direct the investments myself? Can I change to another option within my plan? Can I switch to another state's plan?

You can't direct the investments yourself. You can't decide which individual stocks and bonds you can buy and sell. So if you have a hot stock tip, your 529 money is not going to be available to you. As we'll see in Chapter 4, Coverdell Education Savings Accounts have the flexibility to permit self-directed investments. Some 529 plans however, have over a dozen investment options, so you can get fairly close to directing the investments. In most 529 savings plans, you can move funds from one investment option to another once a year. In addition, most states are now allowing rollover investments from other states' plans. However, be careful. Some states are assessing taxes on money withdrawn for rollovers. In addition, federal law limits these rollover investments to one per year.

I really want to minimize paperwork. I have four children. I'd like to just open one 529 account and name each of my four children as equal beneficiaries. Can I do that?

No, the rules are clear that there can only be one beneficiary per account.

CHAPTER 4

Other Ways
to Save
for College

O f course, 529 plans are not the only way to save for college. This chapter will deal with a variety of additional savings vehicles that families can use to create a college savings plan.

Coverdell Education Savings Accounts (Formerly Education IRA)

The Taxpayer Relief Act of 1997 created the Education IRA. Although this college savings vehicle was the first to allow for tax-free withdrawals for qualified college expenses, the Education IRA was not frequently used because of its rather puny $500 contribution maximum. During 1998 and 1999, Congress considered expansion of 529 plans to make distributions tax free like the Education IRA. This ended up becoming a partisan battle, and one of the thorniest disputes centered on whether to expand 529s to K–12 expenses. Republicans, led by Senator Paul Coverdell of Georgia wanted to expand the use of 529 plans to private elementary and secondary education. Democrats were concerned that this represented an attack on public schools. In the end, a compromise provision was placed inside the Economic Growth and Tax Relief Reconciliation Act (EGTRRA). The 529 plans remained for college expenses only, but the Education

IRA was expanded to allow for payment of elementary and secondary education. The contribution limit was raised to $2000 and the vehicle was renamed the Coverdell Education Saving Account (ESA) as a memorial to Senator Coverdell, who died in 2000.

Comparison of 529 and Coverdell Education Savings Accounts

ADVANTAGES

➤ The Coverdell Education Savings Account can be self-directed, with a wider array of investment products available.

➤ The Coverdell funds can be used for private elementary and secondary education, not just college.

➤ The tax-free status of these Coverdell plans will continue after 2010, while the tax-free status of 529 savings plans is currently scheduled to end at that time.

DISADVANTAGES

➤ Contributions to Coverdell Education Savings Accounts are limited to $2000 per beneficiary per year.

➤ The age of the beneficiary is limited in a Coverdell account.

➤ The contributor relinquishes ownership of Coverdell funds.

➤ The effect on need-based financial aid eligibility is probably less favorable for a Coverdell than for 529 savings plans.

➤ There is less flexibility in changing beneficiaries in a Coverdell ESA.

➤ There is a 6 percent excise tax on excess contributions in a Coverdell ESA.

➤ The Coverdell ESA is not eligible for the state tax deductions available to some 529 plans.

Some Attributes of the Coverdell Education Savings Account

The beneficiary must be under 18 when the contribution is made. There is an exception to this rule for "special needs beneficiaries."

A maximum contribution of $2000 can be made per year to an account. The contribution limit is figured in two ways:

➤ An individual can contribute no more than $2000 per year for any one beneficiary.

➤ No beneficiary can have more than $2000 per year contributed on his or her behalf.

Example: A couple wants to open a Coverdell account for their son and daughter. They contribute $2000 to their son's account and $1800 to their daughter's account. The children's grandfather would also like to open a Coverdell account for his grandchildren. He may not make a contribution for his grandson, but he may open an account with $200 for his granddaughter.

The contributor has to have modified adjusted gross income of $95,000 or less ($190,000 if filing a joint return). The ability to make the contribution is phased out between $95,000 and $110,000 (between $190,000 and $220,000 for a joint return).

How Coverdell Accounts Work

Coverdell Education Savings Accounts are actually trust or custodial accounts. They can be opened at most banks, mutual fund companies, or brokerage firms. A maximum of $2000 can be contributed before April 15 of each year (for the previous calendar year). In the account opening forms two individuals need to be named: a beneficiary and a responsible party to direct the investments. The form usually designates the beneficiary's parent or guardian as the responsible party. The "responsible party" does not necessarily have to be the contributor to the account. Each contribution must be made before the beneficiary's 18th birthday (except for "special needs beneficiaries"). The funds in the account grow tax free and can be withdrawn by the designated beneficiary at any time. If the withdrawal is for a use other than as a qualified education expense, then the income portion of the withdrawal is subject to income tax (at the beneficiary's tax rate) with an additional 10 percent tax penalty.

INVESTMENTS

The account can be invested in almost any type of investment, such as bank CDs, individual stocks and bonds, mutual funds, unit investment trusts, and exchange-traded funds. The account cannot be invested in life insurance contracts. This gives a great deal more flexibility to those who feel limited by the array of choices available in 529 plans. This can be an opportunity to implement a specific investment strategy you might have, or it might be a way to find a mutual fund or exchange-traded fund that has lower expenses than a typical 529 plan.

LIFE OF THE COVERDELL

The Coverdell account has a limited life. No contributions can be made after the beneficiary reaches his or her 18th birthday, and the account must be liquidated by the time the beneficiary reaches 30. It is possible though to roll over the balance into a 529 savings plan to extend the tax-free accumulation of account balances.

FUNDING FOR ELEMENTARY AND SECONDARY EDUCATION

Certainly, if you're sending your children to private elementary or secondary school, the Coverdell ESA is a great way to save. There may be a use for these accounts even for children who are in public school. The definition of qualified elementary and secondary school expenses is rather broad, including such things as expenses for tuition, fees, books, and supplies. Interestingly, a home computer purchased for educational use and fees for Internet access are also considered qualified expenses.

TAX CONSIDERATIONS

An advantage of the Coverdell is the certainty it provides on the tax side. As explained above, the Coverdell Education Savings Account resulted as an expansion of the Education IRA in the EGTRRA (which expanded the 529 savings plans and which is going to sunset on December 31, 2010). Hence, because withdrawals for the Education IRA already were tax-free before EGTRRA, contributors can be assured of the ability to continue to make tax-free withdrawals from the Coverdell for qualified expenses in 2011 and beyond.

On the other hand, if you decide to invest in a Coverdell ESA, you may be forgoing state tax benefits that would have been available had you instead put the money in your home state's 529 savings plan. Of course, a state tax deduction is not the only reason to choose an investment. Make sure that you believe that you have chosen an alternative that provides a higher expected return for a similar level of risk. You may find that you are able to more than offset the value of the tax deduction in your Coverdell ESA, or for that matter, in another state's 529 plan. Then again, particularly if you live in a high-tax state, you may find that your home state represents the highest expected return.

There is another tax implication to Coverdell ESAs. Funds withdrawn from the accounts to pay college expenses can disqualify those expenses from eligibility for the Hope Credit, Lifetime Learning Credit, and college tuition tax deduction. You can always elect to make the withdrawals taxable in order to qualify. Perhaps a better idea is to save some money outside the Coverdell accounts to qualify for these tax breaks. There will be more discussion of these tax breaks and the income limitations needed to qualify for these credits and deductions in Chapter 6.

CONTRIBUTION LIMITATIONS

There are some disadvantages as well to Coverdell ESAs. First and foremost, are the contribution limitations. At $2000 per year, it would be tough to make that the entire college savings plan. However, with the combination of starting early and getting good investment returns it's possible to make a significant dent in college savings. For example, if you put away $166.66 per month ($2000 per year) for 216 months (18 years) and got an annual return of 9 percent compounded monthly, you would end up with $89,391. If you received perhaps a more realistic 6 percent, you would have a still-respectable $64,559. Both figures are much less than what you're going to need to pay for a private college 18 years from now. However, just doing this could be a tremendous head start.

The next disadvantage is that you can't make contributions after the beneficiary turns 18. Since not everyone starts saving for college on the day their child is born (some start thinking about it around the senior year of high school), the Coverdell ESA is a less effective way to accumulate a large sum of money for college.

ACCOUNT OWNERSHIP

In contrast to a 529 savings plan where ownership of the account remains with the contributor until the funds are withdrawn, Coverdell accounts are technically an irrevocable gift. A parent can't open a Coverdell account and then take the money back for his or her own use. In most cases the parent is the responsible party prior to the beneficiary reaching age 18; after that, control of the funds usually passes to the beneficiary. In many cases, the parent can opt to retain control until the last possible distribution date, which is age 30. The eventual transfer of control to the beneficiary can be either a disadvantage or an advantage. It becomes a disadvantage if the beneficiary decides to divert the funds to a use other than its original intent. It becomes an advantage if the goal is to protect parental assets from judgments or creditors.

There is some ability to change the beneficiary, just as in a 529 account. Prior to the beneficiary gaining control (usually at age 18), the responsible party (designated at the time the account is opened) can change the beneficiary to another family member provided the family member is under 30. However, after the beneficiary obtains control of the account, it may very well be that only the original beneficiary can decide to switch to a new beneficiary.

The law places the burden of determining whether contributions from one or more Coverdell ESAs are under the $2000 annual limit on the beneficiary. If contributions are over $2000 or if a contribution is made subsequent to the beneficiary's 18th birthday, then a 6 percent excise tax must be paid by the beneficiary for each year that the account is out of compliance.

Other Ways to Save for College

Uniform Gift to Minors Act/Uniform Transfer to Minors Act

The best part of a UGMA/UTMA account is that it's simple. All you have to do is open an account with a financial intermediary such as a bank, mutual fund company, or brokerage house and deposit the funds. One advantage that this account has over Coverdell and 529 accounts is that you can deposit securities into the account. You may want to do this in order to move appreciated securities into a child's account as a gift, so that when the securities are sold, the capital gains are taxed at the child's rate instead of the donor's rate. Currently, you can provide a gift to your child of up to $11,000 per year without having to consider gift taxes. Two parents can provide up to $22,000 per year.

UGMA/UTMA accounts are custodial accounts opened on behalf of a minor. Once funded, the gift is considered irrevocable; any withdrawals by the custodian are required to be for the benefit of the minor. Interest income and capital gains are taxed at the minor's rate. Ultimately, the balance of the account is turned over to the minor at age 18 or 21, depending on the individual state in which the account is opened. This may be a definite disadvantage to parents and grandparents who may watch in dismay as funds set aside for education get spent by the child elsewhere as soon as the age of majority is reached. UGMA/UTMA accounts have the additional disadvantage when computing financial aid of being considered the child's asset instead of the parent's asset.

However, unlike 529 savings plan accounts and Coverdell ESAs, you can use these funds for college and still qualify for the Hope and Lifetime Learning tax credits as well as the new deduction for college tuition. In addition, you have the advantage of being able to self-direct the investments in the account. On balance, though, given the array of other investment structures available, UGMA/UTMA accounts ought to play only a small role in college savings plans. Upper-income families should probably first consider 529 savings plans to obtain tax-free buildup of assets, while lower-income families should probably save under the parent's name to maximize need-based financial aid awards and preserve the ability to qualify for college tax credits and tax deductions.

Savings Bonds

Families who are concerned about preserving their principal and who are also concerned about maintaining eligibility for financial aid might want to consider U.S. Savings Bonds. Many middle-income and lower-income families will find that the interest on these bonds will be tax-free when used for qualified education expenses.

There are two kinds of Savings Bonds that are eligible for the interest tax exclusion: Series EE (now also known as Patriot Bonds) and Series I. Both series of bonds have their interest rates adjusted twice a year using somewhat different formulas. Series EE bonds will pay 85 percent of the yield on 5-year Treasury notes, while I bonds will pay a fixed minimum rate (currently 1.1 percent) plus the previous six months' annualized increase in the U.S. Consumer Price Index. Over the past several years, I bonds have frequently paid more than Series EE bonds; however there have been times, such as the May to October period of 2002, that Series EE bonds paid a slightly higher rate of return.

There is a $30,000 face value limit to the amount of EE bonds that an individual can purchase per year. This amounts to a $15,000 maximum expenditure. In addition there is a $30,000 annual limit per individual for the purchase of I bonds. Thus any individual can buy no more than $45,000 worth of U.S. Savings Bonds per year. Forms to purchase bonds can be obtained at virtually any bank. Years ago, the banks sold you the bonds directly. Today, you fill out the forms and pay and the bonds are mailed to you. The best way, however, to buy

Savings Bonds may be on-line. You can buy directly from the U.S. Treasury at www.savingsbonds.gov. You can pay with a credit card, and if you have a card that provides you with some sort of rebate, all the better. In effect, let the government pay for a cash rebate or for some frequent flyer miles. However, make sure that the credit card that you use to buy the bonds doesn't have a balance that you are currently paying off. If you haven't been paying the balance in full each month, then you'll have to pay interest on your savings bond purchase. That's probably not a great idea because the interest on the credit card debt is likely to exceed both the interest earned by the bonds and the value of the credit card rebate. The Treasury has said that it is considering phasing out the use of credit cards for the purchase of Savings Bonds during 2004,

Series EE bonds are sold at half of face value and gradually grow toward their face value and beyond. I bonds are sold at full face value and accumulate interest, which is added to the bond's value. Both bonds have a set value for an entire month. You end up with the same amount of money regardless of which day of the month the bonds were bought or sold. Thus, it's most advantageous to buy bonds late in the month and redeem them early in the month. Both series of bonds can't be cashed in for the first 12 months after issue. In addition, during the first five years after issue, there is a three-month interest penalty if the bonds are redeemed.

Like other U.S. Treasury securities, Savings Bonds are always exempt from state and local taxes. That includes both state income taxes and personal property or intangible taxes. Usually, the interest on savings bonds is taxable at the federal level, but there is a tax break for bonds used to pay educational expenses. If all requirements are met, the interest is then excluded from federal tax. First, the proceeds from the bonds must be used for a qualified higher educational expense. This includes tuition and fees, but does not include room and board or books. What's really interesting is that a qualified expense happens to include a contribution to a 529 plan or a Coverdell ESA. There are some deductions from qualified higher education expenses as well. The total of qualified expenses has to be reduced by any tax-free scholarship, a tax-free withdrawal from either a 529 plan account or Coverdell ESA, and finally, any expenses used to figure the Hope and Lifetime Learning tax credits.

Next, the qualified higher educational expense has to be for yourself, your spouse, or a dependent who is claimed as a dependent on your tax return. Finally, the bond has to be qualified. A qualified bond is a Series EE or Series I bond issued after 1989 and issued to the person taking the tax deduction or jointly with the bond owner's spouse. In addition, the bond is qualified only if the owner of the bond was at least 24 years old on the day the bond was issued.

If you meet all of these criteria, there's only one more hurdle. Your modified adjusted gross income has to be below $70,750 or $113,650 for a joint return. The interest exclusion is then claimed with your tax return on form 8815. You have to give the IRS the name of the student on the form as well as the name of the school. If the funds are not going to a school, but instead are being contributed to a 529 account or a Coverdell ESA, you should list the name of the 529 plan or the financial intermediary where the Coverdell account resides.

What does all this mean? It means that bonds bought in your child's name don't qualify for the tax-free program. It also means that Savings Bonds probably shouldn't be the only way you save for college. That's because those families who would qualify for the Hope and Lifetime Learning tax credits still need to save outside tax-exempt plans to get the tax credits. Of course, if there are excess funds, the Savings Bonds can always be cashed in on a taxable basis to qualify for the tax credits.

The other interesting aspect is the ability to move funds on a tax-free basis from Savings Bonds to 529 or Coverdell accounts. This provides parents who are concerned that they may have incomes above the limits by time their child goes to school the ability to move the funds out of Savings Bonds while their incomes are lower and preserve the tax-free status of the funds. By moving the funds into a 529 or Coverdell account, you also have the advantage of broadening the type of educational expenses that can qualify for tax-free treatment. Once transferred into a Coverdell account, the funds can then be used for elementary and secondary school expenses. If transferred into a 529 account, expenses for room and board or books now become qualified expenses.

Some advisors have indicated that these rules also give other relatives besides parents the ability to get tax-free treatment of their Savings Bonds. Let's say an uncle wants to provide for his niece. He can take his Savings Bonds and open a 529 savings plan account and name himself as both owner and beneficiary. This would allow him tax-free treatment of the interest. A year later he changes the beneficiary of the 529 plan to his niece. This is a fairly aggressive position and there is always the risk that the IRS would consider such a transaction "abusive." Once that happens, the IRS can retroactively deny the original interest exclusion. Interest and penalties could also be tacked on. Get the advice of a tax professional if such a transaction is contemplated.

Saving in Your IRA

Usually, IRA distributions taken before the age of 59 1/2 are subject to a 10 percent penalty tax. However, if you make a withdrawal for qualified higher educational expenses for yourself, your spouse, your children, or your grandchildren (including your spouse's children or grandchildren), the 10 percent penalty tax is waived.

Qualified expenses include tuition, fees, books, supplies, and equipment. If the student is at least a half-time student, room and board is also qualified. However, the total must be reduced by any tax-free withdrawals from a Coverdell ESA, a tax-free scholarship, tax-free employer educational assistance, or any other tax-free payment (including the tax-free redemption of qualified Savings Bonds). There is an exception to this list of reductions: you do not have to reduce your qualified expenses by the amount of distributions from a 529 account.

If you withdraw funds from a traditional IRA, the earnings will still be taxable. In addition, if the contributions were originally deducted (a deductible IRA), then the principal will also be taxable as ordinary income. However, contributions to a Roth IRA make for an interesting educational savings strategy. Withdrawals from a Roth IRA are tax-free for account owners who are older than 59 1/2 and have had contributed to the account more than five years ago. Let's say, however, you're younger than 59 1/2 and you want to use some of your Roth IRA balance to fund your child's education. Any withdrawal from the Roth IRA is first assumed to be your contributed principal. Thus, you can take out your contributions to fund the college expenses and leave in any accumulated earnings to grow until after you're 59 1/2. The withdrawal of principal will be tax-free now, and the future withdrawal of the earnings will also be tax-free after retirement age is reached. The other added advantage is that withdrawals from Roth IRAs will continue to be tax-free under these rules after 2010, while the tax exclusion for 529 plans is scheduled to end in 2010. The other advantage of using IRAs as a savings vehicle is the ability to self-direct the investments among a wider array of choices. However, the annual contribution limits for IRAs may make them somewhat inadequate as the primary savings vehicle.

Using IRAs as a savings vehicle also requires a slightly different strategy when coordinating with need-based financial aid programs. The federal financial aid methodology, and most versions of the institutional methodology, excludes retirement accounts from the calculation of total parental financial assets. However, the formula does include distributions from IRAs even when nontaxable as parental income. As a result, the best strategy for those families that will qualify for financial aid is to keep the funds in the IRA as long as possible to preserve the exclusion from financial aid asset status. The funds should ultimately be used to finance the child's senior year so that the income from the IRA distribution is not included in the financial aid formulas for a subsequent year of college. Another way of doing the same thing is to use the IRA proceeds for the youngest child instead of the oldest child. Again, if possible, wait until the last possible opportunity to use the funds.

Savings in the Parent's Name on a Taxable Basis

You don't necessarily have to save in a tax-advantaged plan to accumulate funds for college. There are times when it may actually be the best alternative for a family to invest on a taxable basis. Some people consider it a huge advantage to be able to have full discretion over their investments. Others who made ill-advised choices wish they had used professional management. Another advantage is that saving on a taxable basis preserves the ability to take full advantage of the tax credits and tax deductions available for education. Keeping the funds in the parent's name will probably lead to higher taxation of the income and capital gains. This is a decided negative. On the other hand, there is the offsetting benefit of maintaining higher eligibility for need-based financial aid and it helps ensure that the children don't spend the money on noneducational expenses. What it doesn't always do, however, is get to the children. Things have a way of going wrong sometimes, and despite the best of intentions, funds not specifically designated as a college fund can end up getting divided in divorce proceedings or being diverted to pay other bills. You have to ask yourself: After saving this money, will you have the discipline to resist withdrawing the money when faced with some discretionary expense?

Borrowing or Withdrawing from Your 401(k) Account

Many employers will permit you to take a loan or a hardship withdrawal from your 401(k) account to pay college expenses for your children. It can be tempting to do this. In the case of a loan, instead of paying interest to a bank or finance company, the interest is credited back into your account. It seems pretty painless. There can be a big risk, however. If you quit your job or are laid off, the loan can be immediately due and payable. If you decide that you don't want to pay the loan back or can't afford it, then the balance of the loan would be considered an early distribution and would be subject to ordinary income tax and a 10 percent tax penalty. If you borrow $20,000 for your child's educational expenses and then get laid off, assuming you're in the 27 percent marginal tax bracket, you will be faced with the unfortunate choice of having to come up with either the full $20,000 or a $7400 additional tax bill. It might be difficult at that point to get an educational loan given the school has already been paid and you are newly unemployed.

A withdrawal from a 401(k) plan makes the ordinary income tax and the penalty tax due for the tax year the withdrawal is made. In addition, you may find that following a hardship withdrawal, you are limited in the amount of contributions you can make to your 401(k) plan in the following year. As a result, you may be missing out on some of your employer's matching benefits to fund the child's education. This can result in a significantly lower balance in your 401(k) account when it is time to retire. The bottom line is that tapping your 401(k) account is possible but could end up being a very expensive alternative. Certainly consider the option of borrowing from the 401(k) before taking the hardship withdrawal and realistically measure the risk your employment ends before the loan can be repaid.

Conclusion

It's important to know yourself and think through your own situation when deciding how to allocate your investment dollars among different college savings vehicles. The conventional wisdom is that individuals with incomes below $50,000, or married couples with incomes below $100,000 when filing a joint return, should steer clear of 529 plans and just save on their own in mutual funds, bank accounts, and Savings Bonds. There is some merit to this, since the tax benefits of 529 plans are less valuable to taxpayers in lower tax brackets and saving outside a tax-advantaged plan preserves eligibility for tax credits and deductions. On the other hand, 529 plans with their penalties for nonqualified distributions provide a psychological barrier to withdrawing the funds for a nonessential expense. In addition, 529 savings plans don't generate capital gains, which may allow you to file your taxes on Form 1040-A or 1040-EZ. This could provide more favorable financial aid treatment (more about this in Chapter 7). My advice is to consider saving only those funds needed to qualify for educational tax credits and deductions in taxable accounts, and save the rest in 529 savings plans or other tax-advantaged instruments. Chapter 6 will have a discussion on the tax credits and deductions and how much to save in taxable accounts when you qualify.

CHAPTER 5

The College Investment Process

Within the various college savings plans dis-cussed in Chapters 3 and 4, there is a huge array of choices that you can employ to meet financial goals. For example, depending on which 529 plan you select, you might find age-based portfolios, aggressive growth portfolios, small and mid-cap equity portfolios, guaranteed investment certificates, index funds, passive investments, active investments, long-term bond port-folios, money market accounts, and certificates of deposit. Moreover, this is not even a complete list. When you examine Coverdell ESAs or saving on a taxable basis, you will find that the array of invest-ment possibilities grows even further.

So how do you decide what the best mix of investments might be to meet your financial goals and have funds available for your child's education?

The first step is understanding that different investments have dif-ferent risk profiles. It's important to also understand that investment risk is not the probability that you lose your money (although that's obviously part of risk). It's actually the likelihood that you receive a different return than you expect. Let's compare some types of invest-ments and see what I'm talking about.

[45]

5-Year Versus 10-Year Treasury Notes

In both cases, the risk of loss when the instrument is held to maturity is nil. These government instruments are full faith and credit obligations of the U.S. Treasury. However, they have different risk profiles. If you want to sell your investment before maturity, you will have a gain if interest rates go down and you will have a loss if interest rates rise. In general, the instrument with the longer maturity will gain more when interest rates go down and fall more when interest rates rise. Because each year, your return (if you were to sell) is more variable with the longer maturity instrument, the 10-year note is more risky than the 5-year note. Normally, because of that higher risk, the return is usually higher on the 10-year than on the 5-year note. Another way of looking at this is that your *expected return* is higher.

Treasuries Versus Corporate Bonds

Let's say you were presented with the choice of a 10-year Treasury Note with a 5 percent coupon (the stated interest rate) and a 10-year bond issued by a well-known corporation that also had a 5 percent coupon. If both were selling at the same exact price, which one would you buy? The answer is the Treasury Note every time. The reason is that no matter how well known, the corporation has a lower probably of repaying the principal at maturity than the U.S. Treasury. There is also a higher probability that the corporation will stop paying interest (known as a default). As a result, you will always find that the corporate bond has either a higher coupon or a lower price to compensate for the possibility that these problems will occur. Again, because of the higher probability that your return will be very different if the company defaults on its interest payments or doesn't repay at maturity, the corporate bond has a higher risk and again, a higher expected return.

Corporate Bonds Versus Common Stocks

With corporate bonds you're getting a fixed return. The company makes the same interest payment when profits are strong as when profits are weak. As the company's profits improve, the bonds may rise in value because the probability of repayment has improved; the company's stock will rise even more as profits improve because the company is that much more valuable. The reverse is also true. As profits deteriorate, the stock will almost always fall faster than the bonds. If a company were to fail, bondholders become the creditors of the company and share in the liquidation of the assets. When this happens, stockholders usually lose all or most of their investment. Again, the return is more variable with stocks than with bonds, and the expected return for stocks is higher. Over the long run, despite their ups and downs, stocks have done quite well. Figure 5-1 depicts the S&P 500, a well-known benchmark primarily consisting of large-capitalization domestic stocks. In June of 1979, the S&P 500 fell below 100 for the last time. By February of 1998, less then 19 years later, the index reached 1000, a 10-fold gain and an average annual increase of over 13 percent.

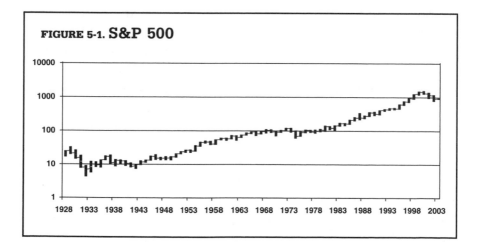

FIGURE 5-1. **S&P 500**

Small-Capitalization Stocks Versus Large-Capitalization Stocks

It's certainly true that large companies can get into difficulty and go bankrupt; just look at K-Mart, Enron, and Worldcom over the last couple of years. However, difficulty occurs with small companies even more frequently. More importantly, there is a greater degree of earnings variation with smaller companies, and as a result, more volatility in stock prices. That volatility moves both ways. There are more earnings surprises on both the upside and downside with smaller companies. Again, you wouldn't take on this volatility unless you thought you were being paid for it. So once again, the expected return is higher with smaller companies.

In general, you move up the ladder in risk and expected return as you move toward emerging market companies, leveraged investments (purchased with borrowed money), and undiversified investments (one company or a single sector).

So does this discussion about the relationship between risk and expected return mean that you should just maximize your risk to get the highest return? Well, in a word, no. Let's go back to our original definition of risk: It's the probability that you get a different actual return than your expected return. The problem with risky assets is that although you *expect* a higher return you often don't *receive* that return. What is generally needed is to balance risky and less risky assets together to get a total level of risk, so that over the long run, you have some likelihood that actual returns will bear some resemblance to expected returns.

One way of quantifying this risk is to measure actual historical returns of particular assets and measure how far they fluctuated from average. Looking at the mean (the average) and standard deviation of the returns can do this. For those who are aren't (and don't want to be) statisticians, *the standard deviation* is merely a measurement of how far away from the average return you are likely to be. The average of the historical returns can be a good indication as to what the expected returns should be. In general, the higher the historical mean, the higher the expected return. The higher the standard deviation, the higher the likelihood your actual return for a given period time is different from the average or expected return. This past history is never going to be an exact predictor of the future, but in most cases, it's the best indication you have.

Your Risk Comfort

Only you can judge your risk comfort level, but the following exercise puts into place some of the thoughts we went through in the preceding paragraphs: Let's say your goal is to save $50,000 for your child's education over the next five years. If your expected return were 4 percent, you would have to invest $754.16 each month to reach your goal. If you did this with Treasury securities or with the one of the more conservative options in a 529 plan, you might find that the standard deviation of the historical returns is 1 percent. That's another way of saying that two-thirds of the time when the expected return is 4 percent, the actual return is between 3 and 5 percent. Now if things go wrong and it turns out after four years your return was only 3 percent, you would have to catch up and start investing $856.58 per month in order to reach your $50,000 goal. Or conversely, you could keep investing the $754.16 and miss your goal. You would end up with $48,754 instead of the $50,000.

Now let's suppose you weren't quite that conservative. You want to receive the higher returns that have been traditionally found in the stock market. So you assume that the returns will be higher. When you look back, you find that the average return is 10 percent and the standard deviation is 20 percent. Another way of looking at this is that about two-thirds of the time, you will receive a return of between negative 10 percent and positive 30 percent. Now, if you want to save the same $50,000, and your expected return is 10 percent, you need to put away $645.59 per month, quite a bit less than when you invested in Treasuries. The problem is what if you had four years in a row when the return on the stock market was a negative 10 percent instead of a positive 10 percent. You would find that after four years of saving, you were only halfway toward your five-year goal. You would have to increase your saving to $2251 per month to reach your goal (provided that you finally got a positive 10 percent return in the fifth year).

Of course, that's assuming that you get below-average returns. It's also possible with the riskier portfolio to get above-average returns. Let's say that instead of getting a negative 10 percent return, you got a 25 percent return for each of the first four years. You would find that you already had $52,386. You could stop saving a year early, since your goal had already been met.

There's nothing wrong with either a conservative or aggressive approach as long as you know the implications of each. If you're too conservative you might have to save more and for a longer period of time to compensate for the lower returns. If you're too aggressive, you might have to save more for a longer period of time to compensate for your losses! There is no free lunch. Most people try to find a happy medium between risky and less risky investments. In general, the conventional wisdom is to figure out how much time you have before you need the funds, that is, when will the bill be due at the college? When you are many years away from the expenditure, you can afford to take on more risk. The idea is that if you have losses (or below-average returns), you can slightly step up your periodic investments and make up the difference. As you get closer and closer to the time you need the money, you get more conservative. That's because it can be impossible to make up the losses through increased contributions if they occur close to the time the college tuition bill arrives at your home.

Bang for the Buck

The Holy Grail in investing is getting the maximum amount of return for a given level of risk. If you had a choice of two investments, one with a guaranteed a return of 10 percent a year and the other investment with an averaged 10 percent return a year that was sometimes up 40 percent and sometimes down 20 percent, a rational person should take the guaranteed return. That's because the second investment provides risk that you're not being paid for. Let's take a look at Figure 5-2. Each point on the chart represents a randomly selected mutual fund. The funds in the lower-right quadrant represent the worst of all worlds; they have the highest risk and the lowest return. In general, you would strive for the reverse; the upper-left quadrant

which has the highest return and lowest risk. What you really want
to do is to develop a blend of assets that gives the most return for a
given level of risk.

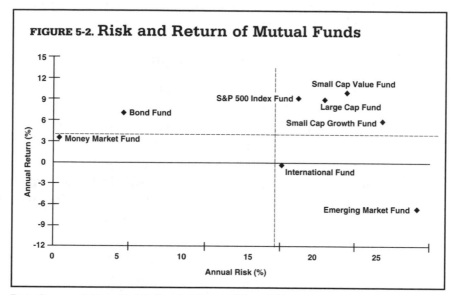

Data Source © Standard & Poor's Micropal Inc. (2001)—http://www.micropal.com

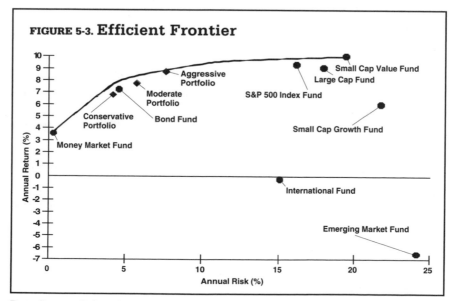

Data Source © Standard & Poor's Micropal Inc. (2001)—http://www.micropal.com

Figure 5-3 shows various asset allocations; the curved line, known as the *efficient frontier*, has the theoretically best portfolios. The portfolios that fall on the efficient frontier have the best combination of risk and return. As you move below the efficient frontier it means that you have a portfolio that contains risk that you're not being paid for.

Diversification Versus a Focused Approach

As you diversify, or blend more assets together, you generally reduce the standard deviation and cut risk dramatically. I did an experiment a few years ago and measured the average monthly return and standard deviation of each stock in the Standard & Poor's 500 and calculated the ratio of return to risk (on an annualized basis). I then compared that to the return/risk ratio of the S&P 500 itself. Interestingly, the S&P 500 had the 11th best ratio calculated. Another way of looking at this is that you have only a 10 out of 500 chance of beating the index on a risk-adjusted basis with a single-stock portfolio.

On the other hand, many people (including fund managers) over-diversify. So many fund managers who are supposed to be active investors buy 150 or more stocks. When they do this, they increase the odds that they will get index-like returns. Since most active funds have higher fees and expenses than index funds, the majority of active funds end up underperforming, in large measure because of this overdiversification.

The trick is to find an active fund that outperforms. This outperformance should be for a long period of time. You want to see that there is some investment skill and not just luck. Many people can outperform the market for brief periods of time; to do so over a longer period may indicate some special skill. The performance record should also be fairly consistent. Obviously, you don't want a fund that has outperformed over a 20-year period, but you find that it was up 400 percent 11 years ago and underperformed in 15 of the last 20 years.

Selecting an Equity Fund

My view is that in choosing an equity fund, one should take either of two approaches:

1. An active fund that takes a focused approach, and as a result of superior stock selection, has a long record of outperformance. It's not sufficient to have done well for the last 18 months or so.

2. An index fund that provides the most diversification for the lowest possible expense.

Comparing 529 Plans

Here are a few things to keep in mind when comparing plans:

➤ A long history is better than a short history. Many of the 529 plan distributors use new investment products in their plans. That provides relatively little information on how these investments perform in both up and down markets and how stable the performance might be.

➤ The history of outperformance. Take a look at how the investment did compared to an established benchmark. If you're looking at a large-capitalization equity fund and it has done worse than the S&P 500 or Russell 3000, why would you be interested in the fund when you could have instead bought a fund that invests in the index itself?

➤ Level of fees and expenses. All things being equal, low expenses are better than high expenses. However, the level of expenses always has to be judged in the context of performance and service. You ought to gladly pay additional expenses if you're getting better performance. Keep in mind though that paying higher expenses doesn't guarantee better performance.

In Chapter 13 we will take an in-depth look at six 529 plans. Some are available for direct purchase by mail, phone, or through a Web site; others are advisor-sold.

Typical Asset Allocations

Two factors will determine your asset allocations:

➤ How much risk you are comfortable with

➤ How much time you have until the money has to be spent on college

Let's take a look at a typical asset allocation in a 529 savings plan account: If you were saving for a 10-year-old child who would be going to college in eight years, the account might be invested in a moderate portfolio as follows:

    60% equity (stock) fund

    25% fixed-income fund

    15% in a money market fund

If you were more aggressive, you might decide that you wanted to be invested as follows:

    80% in an equity fund

    20% in a fixed-income fund

If you were much more conservative, you could be invested as follows:

    40% in an equity fund

    30% in a fixed-income fund

    30% in a money market fund

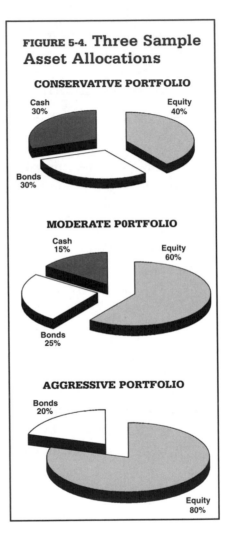

FIGURE 5-4. Three Sample Asset Allocations

CONSERVATIVE PORTFOLIO
Cash 30%
Equity 40%
Bonds 30%

MODERATE PORTFOLIO
Cash 15%
Equity 60%
Bonds 25%

AGGRESSIVE PORTFOLIO
Bonds 20%
Equity 80%

Figure 5-4 displays those choices.

Now, let's see what a typical allocation might look like when the child is 16: Since the child is only two years away from college, the average account that was 60 percent in equities back when the child was 10 might now be invested 40 percent in equities (with 30 percent in fixed income and 30 percent in the money fund). The aggressive investor might have moved from 80 to 60 percent in equities, and the conservative investor might have moved from 40 to 20 percent in equities. The point is that as you get closer to the time that the money will be spent, the more conservative you should get in your allocation.

Investment Vehicles

Guaranteed Investment Certificates

Often an investment option in 401(k) plans, guaranteed investment certificates (GICs) are also available in some 529 plans. This investment pays a fixed rate of return. The issuer (usually a large life insurance company) guarantees both the principal and the fixed rate of return. This type of investment is attractive in a 529 plan because it usually has a similar rate of return to fixed-income funds and generally a higher rate of return than money market funds. On a short-term basis, the GIC fund will usually fluctuate much less than a typical fixed-income fund. In 529 plans that offer this type of investment, one could substitute the so-called guaranteed option for the fixed-income–money market allocation. Most of the plans issued by TIAA-CREF, for example, offer this type of investment.

Age-Based Portfolios

Earlier, I mentioned that as you get closer to the point in which you need to spend the money you've invested, you need to get more conservative. This isn't rocket science and most of the sponsors of 529 plans realize this. As a result, most of the plans offer an age-based portfolio system. With age-based portfolios, the sponsor sets up an allocation appropriate for the age of the beneficiary and then gradually shifts the funds into more stable investment vehicles as the child gets closer to college age. This can be a convenience, but first take a look at what the underlying investments are in the age-based portfolios. I've found them at times to be less satisfactory than building your own allocation with available options. Some plans for example, don't use a well-diversified equity component in the age-based plan. You may find that the age-based portfolios are either too conservative or too aggressive to meet your needs. Nevertheless, when starting an investment program in a 529 plan, take a look at the age-based portfolios, if only as a guide to a "base case" average allocation. Then, if you decide not to use the age-based portfolios, you can still continue to refer to them in order to help you direct your future investments into the account and as a guide to perhaps moving some of the existing funds into more conservative investments as your beneficiary gets closer to college age.

Types of Equity Funds

In some 529 savings plans, there may be various options among the equity funds. Outside the 529 plan universe, you will generally find the same kinds of options among mutual funds. Whether you are using a 529 savings plan, a Coverdell account, or just investing in mutual funds on a taxable basis, here is a brief primer on some of the choices that may be found:

GROWTH FUNDS: Tend to buy companies that are concentrated in technology, health care, and consumer staples. Often, these companies sell at higher price to book value ratios. During the early and middle 1990s these companies significantly outperformed the market, while they significantly underperformed in 2000 and 2001.

VALUE FUNDS: Tend to buy companies in the consumer discretionary, financial, industrial, and energy sectors. These companies sell for lower price to book value ratios than their growth counterparts. Over very long periods of time, value stocks tend to outperform growth stocks. But there are times (such as the 1990s) where value stocks can be out of favor for long (5–7 year) periods of time. Figure 5-5 shows the difference in performance between growth and value stocks over the last 10 years.

SMALL-CAP FUNDS: Mostly own companies with market capitalizations (the value of all the company's common stock outstanding)

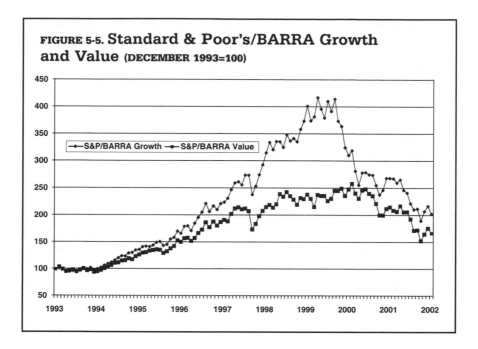

FIGURE 5-5. Standard & Poor's/BARRA Growth and Value (DECEMBER 1993=100)

of less than $1 billion. Some funds may go somewhat beyond the $1 billion in order to maintain fund liquidity. In general, these funds are more speculative than average because the companies purchased are often earlier in their product life cycle, are less known, not as widely followed by the analyst community, and often less financially secure. For many of the same reasons, however, the returns on these investments are often higher.

MID-CAP FUNDS: These funds own companies with market capitalization generally between $1 billion and $5 billion. These stocks have outperformed their larger brethren over the last several years. These companies often have better growth prospects than larger companies, but better access to capital than small-cap companies. The idea is to buy these companies as they are on their way to becoming large-cap companies. It usually works out this way, but unfortunately, more than a few mid-cap companies are on the road to becoming small-cap companies, losing their investors' money along the way.

LARGE-CAP FUNDS: Buy large, mostly well-known companies with capitalization usually above $5 billion. These companies are usually stronger financially and tend to benefit from good access to capital. There should be some emphasis on the word "usually." Enron, Worldcom and Global Crossing were large-cap companies that had (at one time) good access to capital. All three companies managed to go bankrupt, leaving investors with billions of dollars in losses. Large size doesn't prevent mismanagement. In most cases, though, larger companies are somewhat more stable than smaller companies.

GLOBAL FUNDS: A diversified portfolio of U.S. stocks such as the S&P 500 provides about 25 percent of income and sales from overseas. However, it doesn't provide any exposure to stocks that primarily trade outside the United States. These stocks often move up and down at different times than U.S. stocks. As a result, a global portfolio that contains both U.S. and overseas stocks may have a lower standard deviation of returns and represent a bit less risk than a purely domestic portfolio.

INTERNATIONAL FUNDS: Usually a portfolio that doesn't contain stocks traded in the United States. It's not a bad idea to diversify outside the United States. There are times when the economy is strengthening in other parts of the world faster than our own economy. There are also times when the U.S. dollar is weakening and investments that are not dollar-denominated will outperform a domestic portfolio. Don't overdo it, though. Keep in mind that eventually you want to spend the proceeds of your investments at a school that sends its bill in U.S. dollars. Even the most aggressive investors should probably limit their overseas equity investments to 25 percent of the total.

EMERGING MARKET FUNDS: Developing nations have the advantage of lower labor wage rates, growing productivity, and large pent-up demand for consumer goods and services. This provides long-term opportunity for outsized gains. It also provides substantial risk in that there is more likely to be political upheaval in developing countries. There is a greater likelihood of both economic and currency risk in this type of investment.

Indexing Versus Active Management

There are thousands of actively managed mutual funds. For the three years ended September 2002, on average, active management has managed to beat the S&P 500. According to Standard & Poor's Fund Services, 65 percent of actively managed domestic equity funds beat the S&P 500 for the three years ended September 2002. Before you get too excited, keep in mind this only means that for that particular period, active management has lost less than the index funds have lost. Over longer periods of time, indexing has done very well. Standard & Poor's research indicates that for a 10-year period (ended September 2002) the S&P 500 beat 64 percent of all actively managed domestic equity funds. For 20 years, the index was ahead of 85 percent of the domestic equity funds. Vanguard has published research with similar conclusions. Indexers believe that over time, the lower fees of index funds wipe out the advantage of most active managers. I believe that some active managers have the ability to provide long-term returns with the same or less risk than the market. However, you have to search for those managers, and you have to consider that some outperforming managers will underperform in the future while some underperforming managers will be the stars of the future. Another way of looking at this is that many fund investors will not successfully find an outperforming manager ahead of time.

Investing in Individual Stocks

First of all, as a reminder, you can't invest in individual stocks in a 529 plan. However, you can do this in either a Coverdell ESA or in a Uniform Gift to Minors/Uniform Transfer to Minors Account. Of course, a parent or grandparent can also do this on a taxable basis. There are advantages and disadvantages to investing in individual stocks:

ADVANTAGES

➤ It's possible to "beat the pros." In fact it happens every day. I've actually tried this experiment using the Standard & Poor's data-bases. Time and time again, a randomly selected portfolio of stocks held for a year beats a randomly selected mutual fund.

➤ With some research, you can improve your odds even more. By walking around town, talking to friends and relatives, sampling new products, being satisfied with service you get from national companies, you may actually find out about new investment opportunities before the pros. For example, I've heard about inter-esting retail businesses that turned out to be good investments from my children.

➤ You can buy and sell stocks that are thinly traded when the pro-fessionals can't. There may be a stock that trades only 50,000 shares per day. If you have a $50,000 portfolio, you might decide that you want to buy 100 shares of a $20 stock. It would represent 4 percent of your portfolio, and you could do this easily. If instead, you were managing a $1 billion mutual fund and wanted to gain only a 1 percent position, you would have to buy 500,000 shares, representing 10 times the average daily volume of the stock. The professional would quickly find that the stock couldn't be pur-chased without pushing the stock substantially higher. More importantly, the stock would be pushed much lower when the professional decided to sell. The individual can quickly maneuver around these giants and profit in companies that won't always be found in a typical mutual fund.

➤ You can benefit from lower turnover. A typical mutual fund ends up with a completely different portfolio at the end of the year than it had at the beginning, a 100 percent turnover rate. All of this repositioning at the mutual fund may help returns, but then again it may not. In any event, mutual fund turnover is going to happen. Look at it this way: Almost every mutual fund has the internal infra-structure to research new investments and trade securities. What if the fund decided not to use those resources? Can you imagine the conversation that the portfolio manager would have with his or her boss? The boss says "let's go over your performance this year." The portfolio manager says "I made no changes this year, but I watched the portfolio very carefully." It would be difficult to justify the manager's employment if absolutely nothing were done for the whole year. The individual though, can buy good stocks and hold on to them for long periods of time. The individual gets the reward of lower transaction costs and a more tax-efficient portfolio.

DISADVANTAGES

➤ The professionals are doing this full-time. You're not. By being in the market, the mutual fund managers are talking to companies, talking to analysts, maybe finding opportunities that you didn't immediately see, or perhaps will never see.

➤ Professionals are "watching the tape." There may be opportunities that last a day or two, or perhaps sometimes last only momentarily, that professionals can exploit.

➤ Individuals can sometimes be "more emotional" in their investing, getting euphoric as prices are rising and depressed as prices fall. Actually, investors should do the reverse in order to avoid the "buy high–sell low" syndrome.

Individuals can mitigate some of those disadvantages by being plugged in to information. There is a wealth of information on individual companies in the financial press. Also, many investors rely on the opinions of financial analysts who work for a number of firms.

Standard & Poor's is one such firm. Since 1987, Standard & Poor's has been making buy and sell recommendations on hundreds of stocks though its Stock Appreciation Ranking System (STARS). On average, those stocks ranked Five Star (strong buy) have outperformed the S&P 500 by a wide margin. Figure 5-6 depicts the performance of STARS for the 16 years ended December 31, 2002. Individuals can obtain the buys and sells in STARS through Standard & Poor's weekly newsletter *The Outlook*, which is available through subscription or through many public libraries. In addition, a selection of Standard & Poor's investment advice can be found on the Web site of our sister publication *Business Week*. Just go to the investing section of www.businessweek.com.

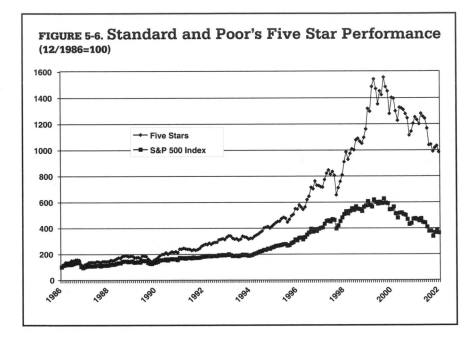

FIGURE 5-6. **Standard and Poor's Five Star Performance** (12/1986=100)

Whether you invest in mutual funds, in individual stocks, in fixed income, in money market funds, in guaranteed investment certificates, or in any of the various investment options available to you, observing the following caveats may save you a great deal of worry and perhaps money:

1. Try to understand what you are investing in and what the risks are.

2. If you don't understand what you are investing in and what the risks are, ask questions and do research.

3. If you have asked questions and still don't understand, don't invest!

The key to allocating your assets is to take a level of risk that you are comfortable with and *then* try to get the best return for that level of risk.

CHAPTER 6

The Tax
Challenge

T ax planning should play an important role in your college savings program. You should understand how the savings vehicles you've chosen interact with the various tax credits and deductions that are available for education. This understanding can help you figure out where to save, and more importantly, when and how to make withdrawals from your savings.

Tax Credits

There are two major federal tax-credit programs for undergraduate education—The Hope Credit and the Lifetime Learning Credit.

You can have a 529 savings or prepaid account or a Coverdell ESA and still be eligible for the Hope or Lifetime Learning Credit. You can even receive a tax-free distribution from one of these plans in the same year in which you claim the tax credit. However, you cannot use the tax-free distribution for the same expenses for which the tax credit is claimed. That gives you four choices:

1. Save enough money outside tax-advantaged plans to cover expenses that will be eligible for the tax credits. That usually amounts to up to $2000 for each of the first two years of college (for the Hope Credit) and up to $10,000 (starting in 2003) for each of the last two years of college (for the Lifetime Learning Credit). Because most students are in college for at least a portion of five calendar years, you may want to assume that the Lifetime Learning Credit could be taken three times.

2. Use proceeds from student loans for expenses that qualify for tax credits while using tax-deferred savings for other expenses. For example, use loan proceeds for the first $2000 of tuition, but use 529 savings for room and board.

3. Take nonqualified distributions from 529 or Coverdell accounts to cover the expenses that qualify for tax credits and take qualified distributions to cover the rest.

4. Forgo the tax credits. This is almost never a wise move when you qualify for the Hope Credit, but it may occasionally makes sense to forgo the Lifetime Learning Credit when you are faced with taxes and additional penalties from a nonqualified distribution from a 529 plan or Coverdell ESA.

The key to all of this is to understand the credits and determine whether you're eligible.

The Hope Credit

The Hope Credit can provide up to $1500 in tax reduction. This is not a deduction in which your taxable income is reduced; instead, it's a dollar-for-dollar subtraction from your tax liability, making it more valuable. The credit reimburses 100 percent of the first $1000 of tuition and 50 percent of the next $1000. Here is how the Hope Credit works.

AMOUNT OF CREDIT

The maximum credit per year is $1500 per student. If you have more than one family member (such as yourself, your spouse, or your child) in college, you can take more than one Hope Credit.

The credit may only be taken twice per eligible student and has to be taken before the end of the second year of college. However, if the student has advanced standing because he or she got academic credit through Advanced Placement (AP), International Bacclaurate (IB), or other proficiency exams, then that academic credit is not counted for the purposes of the tax credit. Note that most students complete their first two years of college during three different calendar years. Thus, if a student started college in September of 2002, then the second year of college might be completed in June of 2004. Usually, the Hope Credit would be taken in tax years 2002 and 2003, for a maximum credit of $3000 per student.

ELIGIBILITY

The student must be in a degree program attending at least half-time. The student also must have no felony drug convictions.

The credit starts to phase out between $40,000 and $50,000 of the modified adjusted gross income (MAGI) for those taxpayers who file as single, head of household, or qualifying widow(er). The credit phases out between $80,000 and $100,000 of the MAGI for those taxpayers who file their taxes jointly. You are not eligible for the credit if your MAGI is above $50,000 ($100,000 for a joint return). You are also not eligible for the credit if your filing status is married filing separately.

The parents (or whoever is claiming the student as a dependent) usually take the tax credit. However, if the parents are not eligible to take the credit (for example, because of the income requirement), then the student can take the credit on his or her tax return, provided the parents don't claim the student as a dependent. This can only occur if the child is able to claim that he or she provided the majority of his or her own support (see more about this in the second and third examples below). Does it make sense for parents to not claim their child as a dependent in order to let the student take the Hope Credit? The answer is "sometimes." Here are three examples:

EXAMPLE 1: Bill and Mary have adjusted gross income of $110,000, which makes them ineligible to take the Hope Credit for their 18-year-old daughter, Alyssa. Alyssa earned $5000 working in a restaurant last year and an additional $200 in interest income. If Bill and Mary claim Alyssa as a dependent, Alyssa will have tax liability of $51 for the year. If Bill and Mary don't claim Alyssa as a dependent, then Alyssa will have no tax liability, but Bill and Mary will have a tax increase of $900 because they would not be able to get the $3000 exemption for Alyssa. This ends up not being cost-effective. Besides,

Alyssa would have to claim that she provided more than half of her own support in order to make Bill and Mary ineligible to claim their daughter as a dependent. This would be unlikely since as a high school senior, Alyssa lived in her parent's home and banked her earnings while driving her parents' car.

EXAMPLE 2: Ken and Tracey earn $750,000 per year and are not eligible to take the Hope Credit. Their 18-year-old son, Jeremy, has a $300,000 stock portfolio that generates dividend income of $10,000. During his senior year of high school, Jeremy earned an additional $8000 working in the family business, for a total income of $18,000. If Ken and Tracey take Jeremy as a dependent, Jeremy has tax liability of $1699. If Ken and Tracey decide not to claim Jeremy as a dependent, their tax liability remains unchanged. That's because their dependent allowances have already been phased out (the phase-out for a married couple is adjusted gross income of between $206,000 and $328,500). Jeremy, however, has been able to completely wipe out his tax liability. His tax bill would be zero. With the help of a standard deduction of $4700, an exemption allowance of $3000, and the $1500 Hope Credit, Jeremy eliminated his tax liability while Ken and Tracey were no worse off. Note, though, that in order to get the dependent allowance, Jeremy has to claim that he is providing more than half his own support. Otherwise, the IRS could claim that Jeremy was actually Ken and Tracey's dependent. You can't take the dependent allowance for yourself when someone else is entitled to take you as a dependent. This remains true even if the other taxpayer chooses not to claim the dependency allowance. Jeremy may be able to demonstrate that he is providing the majority of his support by paying the full amount of his college education from his own resources

EXAMPLE 3: Jane is a single Mom who earns $52,000 and is not eligible for the Hope Credit. Her 18-year-old son, Jimmy, worked all through his senior year of high school and through the summer. He also worked through the fall of his freshman year of college. All told,

Jimmy earned $10,000 for the year. If Jane claims Jimmy as her dependent on her tax filing, Jimmy's tax liability will be $533. This tax liability would be wiped out if Jane doesn't claim Jimmy as a dependent. Jimmy's taxes would drop to $231 from being able to take a dependency allowance and the remainder would be covered by the Hope Credit. (Again, Jimmy would have to claim that he was providing the majority of his own support). However, Jane's taxes will be increased by $810 from the loss of the dependent allowance. It ends up being best for all concerned to keep Jimmy as Jane's dependent on her tax return and to forgo the Hope Credit.

In these three examples, it only made sense to forgo the dependent benefits in one case. Ironically, the family that was by far the most well to do (Ken, Tracey, and Jeremy) was the only family able to benefit from the Hope Credit, a tax benefit designed to help poor and middle-income students get a head start in college. The lesson here is to do the math and don't just assume you can't benefit from a certain tax deduction or credit. The second lesson is to not only look at the tax savings involved. Before voluntarily removing your child as a dependent on your tax return, make sure that you are not losing any employee or government benefit such as health insurance that you might otherwise be entitled to. By the way, many of these benefit plans require that the child be dependent on you for support, not that you claim the child as your dependent on your tax return. That's a subtle but important difference. For most people, not claiming the dependency of a child on a tax return should have no effect on coverage. However, you should consult with your employee benefits manager, your insurance carrier, and perhaps an attorney before deciding how to proceed.

QUALIFYING EXPENSES

Expenses that qualify for the Hope Credit are (1) tuition and fees and (2) books and supplies if the costs of such items are paid directly to the school and are a condition of attendance. Room and board, student health fees, and transportation are not qualifying expenses.

Lifetime Learning Credit

Requirements for the Lifetime Learning Credit are similar to those for the Hope Credit. The income requirements are the same and the expenses that qualify are the same. The Hope Credit is only for the first two years of undergraduate education, while the Lifetime Learning Credit is available for all years of undergraduate and graduate education. Because the Hope Credit is more generous than the Lifetime Learning Credit, most people who qualify use the Hope Credit for the first two years of college and the Lifetime Learning Credit for the remainder of their college education.

The Lifetime Learning Credit is also available for part-time students and is available for those students not enrolled in a degree program. In addition, the rule disqualifying students who have a felony drug conviction from the Hope Credit does not apply to the Lifetime Learning Credit.

The Lifetime Learning Credit is computed by taking 20 percent of the first $10,000 of tuition expenses, for a maximum credit of $2000 per year. This amount is applicable to tax year 2003 and beyond. Previously, the maximum Lifetime Learning Credit was $1000. These amounts are per tax return not per student. If a family has more than one student in college, these amounts can be split among various students.

Tuition Tax Deduction

Starting with tax year 2002, it is possible to deduct up to $3000 per year of tuition for yourself or a dependent. This new deduction is instead of, not in addition to, the Hope Credit or Lifetime Learning Credit. You can't take the deduction in a year you take one of the tax credits. The income requirements for the tuition tax deduction are somewhat higher than for the tax credits. The deduction is available to those taxpayers with incomes up to $65,000 for single, head of household, and qualified widow(er), and up to $130,000 for those taxpayers filing jointly. The deduction rises to $4000 in 2004 and 2005 before expiring at the end of 2005. In tax years 2004 and 2005, taxpayers with an MAGI of between $65,001 and $80,000 ($130,001 and

$160,000 for a joint return) may deduct $2000 of tuition expense. Unlike other tax deductions, you don't have to itemize your deductions on your tax return to qualify for the Tuition Tax Deduction.

Like the situation for tax credits, you can't use funds distributed from a 529 plan account or a Coverdell ESA or tax-free U.S. Savings Bonds and take the Tuition Tax Deduction. You have to use funds saved on a taxable basis or funds you have borrowed to make the tuition payment to qualify. If you are using tax-advantaged funds from a 529 plan account or Coverdell ESA or tax-free Savings Bonds, you must either forgo the deduction or withdraw the funds on a non-qualified taxable basis. Remember, the taxes and penalties are computed only on the earnings, not on the entire withdrawal. So, it will usually pay to take an unqualified distribution of $3000 in order to get a tax deduction of $3000.

Tax Treatment of 529 Distributions

When the time comes to take a distribution from a 529 account, you generally ask the plan for a form. In many of the plans, the form can be printed online. The plan will generally ask if the distribution is qualified. Most of the plans won't ask for documentation. However, you need to save all the college bills to document the expenses in case the IRS wants to audit the distributions. If the distribution is not qualified, the plan will want to know if this is a situation that allows for waiver of the 10 percent additional tax penalty. These situations include death of the beneficiary or receipt of a scholarship for the beneficiary.

When a nonqualified distribution is made, the plan will report this on form 1099Q and the distribution will be divided between return of principal and earnings. The earnings are prorated in the case of a partial distribution. For example, if $10,000 is deposited into a 529 savings plan account and over five years it grows to $15,000, then a $1500 distribution would be $1000 return of principal and $500 would be earnings. If the distribution were nonqualified and subject to the 10 percent penalty, then the tax would be $135 (assuming a 27 percent tax bracket) plus a $50 penalty. When taking a nonqualified distribution, you need to be aware of state tax treatment. In states that offer a tax deduction for contributions, there will probably be a "recapture" of the deduction when the distribution is nonqualified.

Putting It All Together

Now that you've seen some of the rules for tax credits and deductions for education, how do you construct a savings strategy that maximizes your tax benefits? You want to balance the tax benefit of tax-free savings with the tax benefit of credits and deductions. Here are some steps to take:

1. Figure out which credits and deductions you are likely to be eligible for. Keep in mind that your eligibility will be based on the level of income during the year the money will be spent on college, not income in the current year.

2. Figure out whether some of the college expenses are likely to be financed with loans.

3. If your income qualifies you for deductions and credits, try to save the amount needed to receive these tax benefits outside the tax-advantaged plans, while saving the rest in 529 accounts or Coverdell ESAs. You would subtract the amount of planned borrowing from the amount saved outside tax-advantaged plans.

An Example of How One Family Put It Together

Joe and Mary have $10,000 in savings for their daughter Susan. The funds are currently in a taxable bank account. Susan is 15 years old and will be starting college in the fall of 2004. The parents know that they would like to consider a private school for Susan but will certainly not have saved the total $130,000 cost of some of the schools by time the payments are due. With a combined income of $85,000, Joe and Mary know that some combination of need-based grants, loans, and student employment will be required to get Susan through school.

When Susan goes through the admissions process, she selects a school has a total cost of attendance of $32,500 per year. Let's assume that this represents $25,000 for tuition and $7500 for room and board. Joe and Mary find that the private school, using institutional methodology, determined that the college would offer a financial aid package consisting of $11,800 of grants and $4000 of low-interest loans. Joe, Mary, and Susan will pay the remaining $16,700 per year. This $16,700 represents the expected family contribution (There will be more discussion on the institutional methodology and the expected family contribution in Chapter 7).

Table 6-1 shows the tax credits that Joe and Mary qualify for during the time Susan will be attending college.

TABLE 6-1. Tax Credits Available for One Child's Undergraduate Education

Tax Year	Type of Credit	Maximum Qualifying Expenditure ($)	Amount of Tax savings ($)
2004	Hope Credit	2,000	1500
2005	Hope Credit	2,000	1500
2006	Lifetime Learning Credit	10,000	2000
2007	Lifetime Learning Credit	10,000	2000
2008	Lifetime Learning Credit	10,000	2000
		34,000	**9000**

The first thing you'll probably notice is that there are five years in the example. That's because Susan starts school in the fall of 2004 and graduates in May of 2008. There are five calendar years in which Susan will be enrolled in college at least part of the year.

In order to receive the $9000 in total tax savings, $34,000 will have to come from nontax-advantaged sources. This includes the $16,000 in low-interest loans that were part of the financial aid package. Thus, $18,000 should be in investments such as mutual funds, bank accounts, and other taxable investments. Since $10,000 has already been saved in the bank, that amount will presumably grow over the next few years. So, less than $8000 needs to be saved outside tax-advantaged savings plans in order to bring the final balance up to $18,000. Any additional savings can be in 529 accounts, Coverdell ESAs, and tax-exempt Savings Bonds.

Of course, the total $18,000 saved is not going to be enough to send Susan to college. Since the first-year parental contribution is $16,700, there is likely to be at least a total expense of $66,800 for the four years of school. Even after subtracting the $18,000 saved and the $9000 in federal tax benefits received, Joe, Mary and Susan will have to come up with an additional $39,800 to complete Susan's undergraduate education. Hopefully this demonstrates why 529 plans and Coverdell accounts can be an important part of a college savings plan even for those families that qualify for both federal tax benefits and need-based financial aid. There will be more detailed information on how 529 accounts and Coverdell ESAs interact with the need-based financial aid process in the Chapter 7.

Financial Aid Formulas

I t seems that there is a great deal more mystery and misinformation in the need-based financial aid formulas than is necessary. To some extent, it's unavoidable because of the patchwork quilt of federal, state, and private aid programs. On the other hand though, colleges don't always help as much as they could in educating parents about how financial aid formulas work. I've spoken with many financial aid professionals who have grave concern that if the methodology for computing aid is too transparent, then there will be those who "game the system" and make themselves look poorer than they really are and siphon financial aid away from the truly needy. I have some sympathy for that argument, but I have even more sympathy for those who lose out because they are in the dark about how colleges determine need-based financial aid. It's not so much that the financial aid officer at your local college is deliberately keeping the "formulas" a secret; it's just that he or she is concerned that parents and students will view the formulas as gospel, when in fact, there are many elements beyond a formula that determine the amount of financial aid.

Financial aid formulas are the starting point for determining how much aid will be ultimately granted. However, these formulas don't always generate the results most people expect. Here are some examples:

EXAMPLE 1: Sam and Rebecca earn a combined $75,000 per year. They live in San Francisco and pay rent of $2000 per month for their two-bedroom apartment. Their take-home pay after taxes is $4750 per month. They also have $35,000 in credit card bills that have a minimum monthly payment of $1000. After spending $1200 a month on food, clothing, and utilities, there are only a few hundred dollars left for discretionary items. They have never been able to save more than $1000 for their son's education. Thus, they expect when it becomes time for college that they won't have to pay more than $5000 a year for school. How could they possibly afford more? Well, guess again.

The federal financial aid formulas say that Sam and Rebecca should be able to pay about $12,600 per year for their son's education. Does this sound fair? Perhaps; perhaps not.

EXAMPLE 2: John worked for 26 years as an executive for a large corporation. He has not worked for the last 18 months due to injuries he received in a car accident. He receives $2000 per month in disability payments. He also has a pending lawsuit against the driver of the other car. His 401(k) balance is $1,175,000. His son receives need-based financial aid at the private school he attends, which covers $28,000 of the $37,000 total cost.

EXAMPLE 3: Sally is a single parent who earns $12,000 a year. Her son Michael would like to become a physician and has strong grades in high school. Her ex-husband, Bill, pays no alimony but does pay $10,000 per year in child support for Michael. The divorce decree requires Bill to pay this amount until Michael is 21. The divorce decree also states that Bill can claim Michael as a dependent on his tax return (even though he is the noncustodial parent). Bill earns $600,000 per year. Bill is up-to-date on his support payments, but Sally and Michael have not seen Bill in 10 years. When Michael applies to three different schools, he gets three very different financial aid results. At the state university, he is told that the annual out-of-pocket cost will be only $1000. A second school, a private university awarded Michael a $32,000 need-based aid package and said his contribution would only be $2500. A third school (also private) only provided an $8000 package on the $35,000 total cost. That third school said that Bill and Sally would be responsible for the remaining $27,000.

EXAMPLE 4: Max and Fred are brothers. Last year, the two brothers claimed equal ownership of the winning ticket in the state lottery and split the $10 million lump-sum prize. After federal, state, and local taxes, each received a check for $3 million and immediately quit their respective jobs. Max took the funds and paid off his $200,000 mortgage, gave his son a gift of $200,000 to use for college and put the remaining $2.6 million in a bond fund that generates $160,000 of annual taxable income. When Max's son, Roger, went to a private college, Roger wrote a check for the $33,000 annual expense. Fred, on the other hand, bought a new home for $1 million cash, and put $750,000 in a variable life insurance policy that invests in the stock market. He also put $250,000 into a 48-month CD that pays $10,000 of taxable income. The remaining $1 million was put into a portfolio of municipal bonds that generate $50,000 of tax-free income. Since Fred has only $10,000 of taxable income, he can file his taxes with form 1040-A. When his daughter Cindy applies to the state university, the financial aid office offers her a financial aid package covering $11,000 of the $13,000 total cost.

You can (and perhaps should) debate the fairness of these examples. And it should be pointed out that many financial aid officers around the country, when faced with difficult situations can and do make adjustments from the established formulas. As one financial aid officer told me, "None of us got into this business because we love paperwork. We really want to make the resources available so that needy students can go to the best school they possibly can." It should also be pointed out that most of the examples above are extreme cases. Most of the time, the formulas track actual need better. However, the fact that these extreme examples can exist is enough to make my point that parents and students need to be enlightened on how these formulas work. As you can see from the examples, need-based financial aid by its very nature can be arbitrary. Someone has to make a decision on how much of your bank account can be used for college. Then someone has to make a decision on how much of your home equity, your retirement account, your children's bank account, and finally, how much of your current income, can be used to pay the bill.

Methodologies for Calculating Financial Aid

The Federal Methodology

The federal methodology, which is established by the U.S. Department of Education and approved by Congress, is the primary methodology for establishing eligibility for virtually all of the federal financial aid programs. These programs include Federal Pell Grants, subsidized Federal Direct Stafford/Ford Loans (made under the Direct Loan Program); subsidized Federal Stafford Loans [made under the Federal Family Education Loan (FFEL) program]; and assistance from "campus-based" programs, including Federal Supplemental Educational Opportunity Grants (FSEOG), Federal Perkins Loans, and Federal Work Study.

In order to qualify for financial aid at almost every public and private college in the United States, you need to fill out the FAFSA (Free Application for Federal Student Aid), the federal financial aid form. The form can be found at www.fafsa.ed.gov. Often at public colleges and universities, the FAFSA is the only form that needs to be submitted. When the form is submitted, the Department of Education computes the expected family contribution (EFC). According to the Department of Education, the EFC is exactly what it says: It's the amount that is expected to be paid by the student and his or her family for college costs. However, another way of looking at this is that the EFC represents the determination of what the feds won't allow aid to cover.

The Institutional Methodology

In addition to the federal methodology, private schools can calculate financial need using a set of formulas designed by the College Board, known as the institutional methodology. Moreover, schools may deviate somewhat from the standard institutional methodology depending on their own resources and individual policies. The form used for the institutional methodology is the CSS (College Scholarship Service) PROFILE. The form can be filled out online at www.collegeboard.com. Unlike the FAFSA, the CSS PROFILE is not free. When you fill out the CSS PROFILE you designate the schools you want the form to go to. You then are charged a fee (currently $17) per school. At that time you also are presented with a set of additional questions about your finances that are unique to the schools that you are applying to.

Both the FAFSA and CSS PROFILE have preapplication worksheets at their Web sites. It's a good idea to review these worksheets before sitting down to complete the forms.

Information Required on the FAFSA

When filling out the FAFSA, you will need a copy of your latest tax return and all bank and investment account statements.

The data needed to complete the FAFSA includes:

➤ Adjusted gross income from the tax return.

➤ Earned income from wages, salaries, tips etc.

➤ Nontaxable benefits including earned income credit, child tax credit, welfare benefits (doesn't include food stamps or subsidized housing), and nontaxed Social Security benefits.

➤ Nontaxable income including payments to tax-deferred pension and savings plans, IRA deductions, payments to SEP, SIMPLE and Keogh plans, child support received, tax-exempt interest, foreign income exclusion, untaxed pensions or IRA distributions, and housing, food, or other living allowances paid to the military or clergy.

➤ Deductions from income for FAFSA purposes including Hope and Lifetime Learning tax credits, child support paid because of divorce or separation, taxable earnings from Federal Work Study or other need-based work programs, or any scholarship, fellowship, or AmeriCorps award that was taxable.

➤ Number of exemptions on tax return.

➤ Net worth of investments. Investments include: real estate (but not the home you live in), trust funds, money market funds, mutual funds, CDs, stocks, stock options, bonds, other securities, Coverdell ESAs, 529 savings plans, installment and land sale contracts (including mortgages held). Investments don't include: the home in which you live, the present value of life insurance and retirement plans, or the value of prepaid tuition plans.

➤ Net worth of owned businesses and/or investment farms (does not include a farm that you live on and operate).

➤ Current balance of cash, savings, or checking accounts. (Make sure this figure is not double counted with the investment balance.)

The FAFSA collects this data for the student and custodial parents. If both parents are living and married to each other, then the FAFSA requires information from the student and both parents. If the parent is widowed or single, then the FAFSA requires data from both the student and the parent. If a widowed parent has remarried, then data is required from the student, the parent, and the parent's new spouse.

In case of divorce or separation, the FAFSA requires information from both the student and the parent with whom the student lived the majority of the time. If the student lived with both parents equally, then the parent who provided the majority of support should fill out the form. If the parent filling out the form has remarried, then FAFSA requires data on both the parent and that parent's spouse. The federal assumption is that the household in which the student lives bears the first responsibility for financing college.

Information Required on the CSS PROFILE

The CSS PROFILE requires all the information contained in the FAFSA and then some. Additional information needed includes:

➤ The value of the parent's home and amount owed on the home.

➤ Funds paid for private elementary, junior high, and high school tuition for dependent children.

➤ Savings and investments held in the name of the student's siblings who are under 19 and not in college.

➤ The name and address of the noncustodial parent and whether there is a court order requiring support. In addition the form asks if there is a formal agreement that the noncustodial parent will be paying for education.

➤ After all the required questions are answered on the PROFILE, there are then the supplemental questions that individual schools will ask to better assess financial need, and also quite frankly, to verify some of the data reported elsewhere in the CSS PROFILE. The supplemental information may include:

➤ The year in which your home was purchased and its original purchase cost.

➤ The year and model of any vehicles owned.

➤ The current value of your IRA, 401(k), or other pension plans.

➤ A supplemental form asking for income and assets of the noncustodial parent.

Basic Financial Aid Tenets

When organizing your finances, keep in mind some basic tenets of financial aid calculations:

➤ Assets in the student's name are expected to be spent more heavily on college expenses than parent's assets. Thus, student assets are "assessed" (or "taxed") more heavily.

➤ Assets are not all treated equally. For example, the federal methodology completely ignores funds in a retirement account or funds used as part of home equity.

➤ Debt doesn't always help. On the FAFSA, there is no place to indicate any debt payments. On the CSS PROFILE, mortgage payments and student loan payments (paid by parents) are an adjustment to the calculation. The calculation does not include the expense of car loans, car leases, credit card debt, or other consumer debt. However, sometimes a college may consider high consumer debt if it occurred for a reason thought to be beyond the family's control. Families who have high consumer debt as a result of unemployment or medical expense should indicate that to colleges.

➤ Not every dollar of income or assets is considered. Only income and assets above a certain threshold are considered. These thresholds are computed based on the levels of state and local taxes where you live, whether there are one or two working parents, and the age of the older parent. For example, using the federal methodology, a working couple in Oregon earning $55,000 per year would have $3000 subtracted from their income for "employment expense," $4950 for state and local tax, $4207 for Social Security tax, $5700 for federal income tax, and $16,450 for the "income protection allowance." This leaves $20,693 to be considered as available income. This amount is then subject to a percentage assessment. When looking at assets, if the older parent is 45, then the "asset protection allowance" is $38,600, meaning that assets below $38,600 are not part of the federal calculations.

➤ Sometimes it doesn't matter what your assets are. If parents earn $49,999 or less and both student and parents are eligible to file their taxes using form 1040-A or form 1040-EZ then FAFSA doesn't ask any questions about assets.

Major Differences Between Federal and Institutional Methodologies

There are some major differences between the federal and institutional methodologies:

➤ The federal methodology does not consider home equity, while the institutional methodology does.

➤ The federal methodology does not consider the value of retirement accounts, while the institutional methodology sometimes does. (There are optional questions on the CSS PROFILE that individual schools can ask if they so choose—one of those questions concerns the value of retirement plans).

➤ The federal methodology has the simplified calculation for those who file form 1040-A. Those individuals do not have to list assets. The institutional methodology continues to count assets for all applicants.

All of this leads us back to the four examples at the beginning of the chapter and how it led to some surprising results. Let's review these examples and see how some of these outcomes occurred:

In the first example, Sam and Rebecca, the couple in San Francisco, have fairly high living expenses in relation to their income. They also have high consumer debt levels with $35,000 in credit card debt. The financial aid formulas may slightly adjust for higher cost of living areas. However, they rarely adjust for high levels of consumer debt. There is no easy solution for this situation, but if Sam and Rebecca had been aware of the financial aid formulas, they could have been more frugal in the years leading to Susan's college years. They could have even considered living in a less expensive area.

The lesson here is clear: Avoid consumer debt like the plague. It drains your resources and gives you no extra benefit when financial aid calculations are being made.

In the second example, John's son will be receiving substantial financial aid despite the fact that John is a millionaire. The formulas take into consideration his low income after becoming disabled. However, the formulas don't consider the value of the pension plan and don't consider that John might eventually collect a substantial sum after he settles with the auto insurers as a result of his car accident. All that matters is that he has a low current income. This is especially true with the federal methodology.

The lesson here is that making maximum contributions to your retirement plan helps to secure your long-term financial future while having little or no impact on most financial aid formulas. Both the

FAFSA and PROFILE don't ask about retirement plans. (More private colleges are looking at retirement plans in supplemental questions on the PROFILE and in their formulas, but many still don't ask about them.)

In the third example, Sally, the single parent, doesn't expect much help from her ex-husband in paying for college, even though her ex can well afford to pay. Here she gets some inconsistent treatment from various schools because of the differences between methodologies at various schools. The noncustodial parent's income is not even reported on the FAFSA form, so that the state school, which exclusively uses FAFSA, only considers Sally's modest income. The first private school, which usually asks for a supplemental financial statement from the noncustodial parent, decides that they won't require it in this case. The school accepts the explanation from the child's guidance counselor that father and son have had no contact for a decade. The third school, which is aware of the father's resources, opts not to be as generous and decides that the noncustodial parent's income should be a significant factor in the aid package it awards. This third school takes the position that the college should not act in *loco parentis* financially. In effect, people can divorce their spouse, but not their offspring.

The lesson here is that you can't necessarily predict how a college will interpret your unique situation. It pays to compare award packages from various schools. If you're in a situation where you are depending on financial aid and your finances can be subject to interpretation, make sure you apply to a variety of schools.

In the fourth example, two equally wealthy individuals who had set up their finances differently received a profound difference in financial aid treatment. One brother qualified for no aid for his son, but the other brother got substantial aid for his daughter. Why? The second brother, Fred sheltered his assets in his new home and a large life insurance contract. Both of these assets are excluded from consideration on the FAFSA. Fred has substantial income from his municipal bond portfolio and this information would have to be indicated on the FAFSA. However, because Fred's *taxable* income is so low, two things happen on his daughter's aid application: (1) Fred doesn't have to disclose the level of his assets and (2) because Fred's taxable income is below $13,000, he qualifies for automatic determination that the expected family contribution (EFC) is zero. The CSS PROFILE using institutional methodology wouldn't give this same result, because there would be questions on home equity and the municipal bond portfolio would be disclosed. However, since Cindy is going to a state university, only the FAFSA was filed and the extensive aid package was awarded. To add insult to injury, the first brother, Max was told by his accountant a year later that because he gave his son such a large gift, he would either have to pay gift tax or permanently reduce the amount of his estate tax exclusion.

The unfortunate lesson here is that sometimes need-based financial aid is a reward for shrewd planning as opposed to genuine financial need.

Calculating the Expected Family Contribution

See the section earlier in this chapter describing the information needed for FAFSA. Determine whether you will be using the regular worksheet or the simplified worksheet. (The simplified worksheet is used when both parents and students can file their taxes using form 1040-A or 1040-EZ). Use the worksheets and tables of Figure 7-1 (pages 89–100) to determine your EFC.

Comparing Treatment of Parent and Student Assets

As you perform some of the calculations in the EFC worksheet, it becomes clear that assets and income that belong to the student are treated far differently from those that belong to the parent.

Consider the extreme example of a two-parent family where the only assets are the equity in the family home, a $50,000 retirement fund, and a $50,000 college savings fund. Since the home equity and the retirement fund are excluded from consideration in the federal methodology, only the $50,000 college savings fund is part of the asset calculation. Assuming there are two parents, and the older parent is 45 years old, then the asset protection allowance is $42,200.

The remaining $7800 is then multiplied by 12 percent for a contribution from assets of $936. If we assume that the parents have available income (after allowances) of $25,000, then that $936 would be multiplied by an income-dependent factor of 47 percent for a total contribution from the $50,000 fund of $439.92. This represents only 5.64 percent "tax" on the excess $7800 and only 0.9 percent of the total $50,000.

If, however, the parents decided each year to provide a gift to their child of $10,000, and the child now owned the same $50,000, take a look at what the result would be. The child would enter $50,000 on line 45 and then at line 49, the amount would be multiplied by 35 percent for a result of $17,500. There is no asset protection allowance for students. The underlying philosophy behind this different treatment of assets is that student-owned assets are more available for education than parental assets. So, the simple decision of where and under whose name to put the $50,000 could result in the asset component of the EFC amounting to either $440 or $17,500! *This simple decision could be the difference between getting an aid package for college and getting no financial aid at all.*

To recap the different treatment of parent and student income and assets:

➤ Once after-tax (federal, state, and Social Security) student income exceeds an income protection allowance of $2380 (for calendar year 2002), then income is assessed at a 50 percent rate.

➤ For parental income the maximum rate is 47 percent of after-tax income, but parental income first has to exceed an employment expense allowance of up to $3000 and an income protection allowance that can range from $13,470 for a single-parent household to $28,580 for a family of six.

➤ Student assets are assessed at 35 percent in the federal methodology (25 percent using institutional methodology).

➤ Parental assets are assessed at a maximum of 5.64 percent in the federal methodology. However, before assets are considered at all they must exceed an asset protection allowance that ranges from $12,400 for a single-parent household where the parent is 35 to $74,000 for a two-parent household where the older parent is at least 65 years old.

➤ The parental contribution is divided by the number of children in college. Thus, parents who get turned down for aid when the oldest child starts school, may get a substantial aid package once a younger sibling starts college if both are in college at the same time.

Financial Aid Treatment of Various Savings Vehicles

Various savings vehicles have very different treatments when it comes to financial aid. Much depends on who the "owner" of the funds is, how the tax laws treat the savings vehicle, and how the FAFSA and CSS PROFILE treat the account.

UNIFORM GIFT TO MINORS ACT/UNIFORM TRANSFER TO MINORS ACT: The rules on UGMA/UTMA accounts are very clear. These funds are owned by the student. Hence the balance of the account is included in student assets while interest and capital gains are included in student income. Thus 35 percent (25 percent using institutional methodology) of these funds will be allocated to the expected family contribution when the financial aid award is computed.

SAVINGS BONDS: Again, look to see who owns the bonds. If the bonds are in the child's name, they count as the child's asset. If they are in the parent's name, they count as the parent's asset. When redeemed, the interest is taxable to the owner. Therefore, the income will be included for either the parent or the student (depending on who is the owner). Of course, after the bonds are cashed in, they are no longer reported as an asset. If the bonds qualify for tax-free treatment, then what? Keep in mind that in order to qualify for tax-free treatment, the bonds have to have been purchased by an individual at least 24 years old on the day the bond was issued (see Chapter 4 for more information). As a result, the parent will usually be the owner of the bond. However, what about the tax-free interest? The FAFSA gives no guidance for this situation, but one senior official at the Department of Education said that the tax-free income from qualified Savings Bonds should be included in parental tax-exempt income (worksheet B) on the FAFSA. Interestingly, the Department of Education has a different view of the tax-free income from 529 savings plans.

COVERDELL ESAs: One of the distinctions of the Coverdell ESA is that it constitutes an immediate transfer of fund ownership to the beneficiary. Thus, for financial aid purposes, a Coverdell account is considered an asset of the student. If the student would have otherwise qualified for financial aid, a vehicle that keeps the ownership in the parent's name is superior from a financial aid standpoint.

529 PREPAID PLANS: Currently, prepaid plans have a unique place in the federal financial aid formulas. They are excluded from the asset calculations and withdrawals are not counted as income. Instead, any withdrawal is counted as a *resource*. What that means is that the funds withdrawn from a prepaid plan reduce the aid package dollar for dollar. In other words, there is a 100 percent financial aid "tax" on the withdrawals from these plans. Unless these federal rules change (and they might by late 2003) prepaid plans are not savings vehicles that interact well with financial aid programs.

529 SAVINGS PLANS: Unlike Coverdell ESAs, 529 savings plans are owned by the contributor of the funds, usually the parent. That's because the funds can be withdrawn by the account owner on a non-qualified basis. If the account owner is the parent, then the present value of the 529 savings plan becomes a parental asset for financial aid purposes. Remember, the parental asset is assessed in the federal financial aid formulas at a maximum 5.64 percent instead of 35 percent. In the 2002–2003 financial aid forms (which were based on

2001 tax returns), the earnings portion of a 529 savings plan (which was taxable in 2001) was included as part of income on the FAFSA. Now that the earnings portion of 529 savings plans are tax-free, what is the treatment of those earnings on the 2003–2004 FAFSA? *A decision was made during the summer of 2002 to exclude the earnings portion 529 savings plans from inclusion in student or parental income when filling out the 2003–2004 FAFSA.* This is great news for savers, since it removes one of the major concerns that parents had with 529 savings plans.

Going Forward

The financial aid formulas on the FAFSA are covered by statute and approved by Congress and the President every five years. The current statute was signed into law during the fall of 1998 during the Clinton Administration. These formulas will be up for renewal sometime during late 2003, but final reauthoriztion of the Higher Education Act is not expected until early 2004. What changes will be made? At this point, no one knows for sure. However, participants in the process have expressed concern over the very different treatment that 529 prepaid plans receive in financial aid calculations when compared with 529 savings plans. There is a fair amount of confusion as to why the treatment of 529 savings plans and 529 prepaid plans are treated so differently in the federal financial aid formulas. The reason is fairly simple. The rules covering prepaid plans are covered by statute, but those same rules make no mention of the more recently created 529 savings plans. As a result, the Department of Education was able to use its discretion in the absence of any mention in the law. Hopefully, the Education Department and the Congress will unify the treatment of the two types of plans and end the practice of treating proceeds from prepaid plans as a resource.

What other things might be on the table? Some are concerned about the wide disparity (particularly in the federal methodology) between the treatment of parental assets and income and student assets and income. In many families, the fact that a student has a great deal of assets doesn't represent anything more than assets given to a child by parents or another relative. In general, policy-makers need to strike a balance between providing aid for the truly needy and making sure that the formulas continue to provide a strong incentive for families to save for education.

FIGURE 7-1

2003-2004 EFC FORMULA ■ : DEPENDENT STUDENT

1. Parents' Adjusted Gross Income (FAFSA/SAR #74) (If negative, enter zero.)

2. **a.** Father's income earned from work (FAFSA/SAR #77) _____

2. **b.** Mother's income earned from work (FAFSA/SAR #78) + _____

Total parents' income earned from work =

3. Parents' Taxable Income (If tax filers, enter the amount from line 1 above. If non-tax filers, enter the amount from line 2.)*

4. Untaxed income and benefits:

- Total from FAFSA Worksheet A (FAFSA/SAR #79) _____

- Total from FAFSA Worksheet B (FAFSA/SAR #80) + _____

Total untaxed income and benefits =

5. Taxable and untaxed income (sum of line 3 and line 4)

6. Total from FAFSA Worksheet C (FAFSA/SAR #81) -

7. **TOTAL INCOME** (line 5 minus line 6) May be a negative number. =

8. 2002 U.S. income tax paid (FAFSA/SAR #75) (tax filers only); if negative, enter zero.

9. State and other tax allowance (Table A1. If negative, enter zero.) +

10. Father's Social Security tax allow. (Table A2) +

11. Mother's Social Security tax allow. (Table A2) +

12. Income protection allowance (Table A3) +

13. Employment expense allowance:

- Two working parents: 35% of the lesser of the earned incomes, or $3,000, whichever is less

- One-parent families: 35% of earned income, or $3,000, whichever is less

- Two-parent families, one working parent: enter zero +

14. **TOTAL ALLOWANCES** =

Total income (from line 7)

Total allowances (from line 14) -

15. **AVAILABLE INCOME (AI)** May be a negative number. =

*STOP HERE if **both** of the following are true: line 3 is $15,000 or less, **plus** the student **and** parents are eligible to file a 2002 IRS Form 1040A or 1040EZ (they are not required to file a 2002 Form 1040), or they are not required to file any income tax return. If both circumstances are true, the Expected Family Contribution is automatically zero.

16. Net worth of investments** (FAFSA/SAR #82) If negative, enter zero.

17. Net worth of business and/or investment farm (FAFSA/SAR #83) If negative, enter zero.

18. Adjusted net worth of business/farm (Calculate using Table A4.) +

19. Cash, savings, & checking (FAFSA/SAR #84) +

20. **Net worth** (sum of lines 16, 18, and 19) =

21. Education savings and asset protection allowance (Table A5) -

22. Discretionary net worth (line 20 minus line 21) =

23. Asset conversion rate X .12

24. **CONTRIBUTION FROM ASSETS** If negative, enter zero. =

Available Income (AI) (from line 15)

Contribution from assets (from line 24) +

25. **Adjusted Available Income (AAI)** May be a negative number. =

26. **Total parents' contribution from AAI** (Calculate using Table A6; if negative, enter zero.)

27. **Number in college in 2003-2004** (Exclude parents) (FAFSA/SAR #66) ÷

28. **PARENTS' CONTRIBUTION** (standard contribution for 9-month enrollment)*** If negative, enter zero. =

**Do not include the family's home.

***To calculate the parents' contribution for other than 9-month enrollment, see worksheet page 4.

FIGURE 7-1 (continued)

REGULAR
WORKSHEET
Page 2

29. Adjusted Gross Income (FAFSA/SAR #39) (If negative, enter zero.)	
30. Income earned from work (FAFSA/SAR #42)	
31. Taxable Income (If tax filer, enter the amount from line 29. If non-tax filer, enter the amount from line 30.)	
32. Untaxed income and benefits:	
Total from FAFSA Worksheet A FAFSA/SAR #44)	
Total from FAFSA Worksheet B (FAFSA/SAR #45) +	
Total untaxed income and benefits =	
33. Taxable and untaxed income (sum of line 31 and line 32)	
34. Total from FAFSA Worksheet C (FAFSA/SAR #46) -	
35. TOTAL INCOME (line 33 minus line 34) May be a negative number. =	

36. 2002 U.S. income tax paid (FAFSA/SAR #40) (tax filers only); if negative, enter zero.		
37. State and other tax allowance (Table A7. If negative, enter zero.) +		
38. Social Security tax allowance (Table A2) +		
39. Income protection allowance +	2,380	
40. Allowance for parents' negative Adjusted Available Income (If line 25 is negative, enter line 25 as a positive number in line 40. If line 25 is zero or positive, enter zero in line 40.) +		
41. TOTAL ALLOWANCES =		

Total income (from line 35)		
Total allowances (from line 41) -		
42. Available income (AI) =		
43. Assessment of AI X	.50	
44. STUDENT'S CONTRIBUTION FROM AI = If negative, enter zero.		

45. Net worth of investments* (FAFSA/SAR #47) If negative, enter zero.		
46. Net worth of business and/or investment farm (FAFSA/SAR #48) If negative, enter zero. +		
47. Cash, savings, & checking (FAFSA/SAR #49) +		
48. Net worth (sum of lines 45 through 47) =		
49. Assessment rate X	.35	
50. STUDENT'S CONTRIBUTION FROM ASSETS =		

PARENTS' CONTRIBUTION (from line 28)	
STUDENT'S CONTRIBUTION FROM AI (from line 44) +	
STUDENT'S CONTRIBUTION FROM ASSETS (from line 50) +	
51. EXPECTED FAMILY CONTRIBUTION (standard contribution for 9-month enrollment)** If negative, enter zero. =	

*Do not include the student's home.

** To calculate the EFC for other than 9-month enrollment, see the next page.

FIGURE 7-1 (continued)

NOTE: *Use this additional page to prorate the EFC only if the student will be enrolled for other than 9 months and only to determine the student's need for campus-based aid, a subsidized Federal Stafford Loan, or a subsidized Federal Direct Stafford/Ford Loan. Do not use this page to prorate the EFC for a Federal Pell Grant. The EFC for the Federal Pell Grant Program is the 9-month EFC used in conjunction with the cost of attendance to determine a Federal Pell Grant award from the Payment or Disbursement Schedule.*

REGULAR
WORKSHEET
Page 3

A1. Parents' contribution (standard contribution for 9-month enrollment, from line 28)		
A2. Divide by 9	÷	9
A3. Parents' contribution per month	=	
A4. Multiply by number of months of enrollment	X	
A5. Parents' contribution for LESS than 9-month enrollment	=	
B1. Parents' Adjusted Available Income (AAI) (from line 25—may be a negative number)		
B2. Difference between the income protection allowance for a family of four and a family of five, with one in college	+	3,730
B3. Alternate parents' AAI for more than 9-month enrollment (line B1 + line B2)	=	
B4. Total parents' contribution from alternate AAI (calculate using Table A6)		
B5. Number in college (FAFSA/SAR #66)	÷	
B6. Alternate parents' contribution for student (line B4 divided by line B5)	=	
B7. Standard parents' contribution for the student for 9-month enrollment (from line 28)	-	
B8. Difference (line B6 minus line B7)	=	
B9. Divide line B8 by 12 months	÷	12
B10. Parents' contribution per month	=	
B11. Number of months student will be enrolled that exceed 9	X	
B12. Adjustment to parents' contribution for months that exceed 9 (multiply line B10 by line B11)	=	
B13. Standard parents' contribution for 9-month enrollment (from line 28)	+	
B14. Parents' contribution for MORE than 9-month enrollment	=	
C1. Student's contribution from AI (standard contribution for 9-month enrollment, from line 44)		
C2. Divide by 9	÷	9
C3. Student's contribution from AI per month	=	
C4. Multiply by number of months of enrollment	X	
C5. Student's contribution from AI for LESS than 9-month enrollment	=	

*For students enrolled more than 9 months, the standard contribution from AI is used (the amount from line 44).

Use next page to calculate total EFC for enrollment periods other than 9 months

FIGURE 7-1 (continued)

REGULAR
WORKSHEET
Page 4

Parents' Contribution—use ONE appropriate amount from previous page: • Enter amount from line A5 for enrollment periods less than 9 months **OR** • Enter amount from line B14 for enrollment periods greater than 9 months	
Student's Contribution from Available Income—use ONE appropriate amount from previous page: • Enter amount from line C5 for enrollment periods less than 9 months **OR** • Enter amount from line 44 for enrollment periods greater than 9 months +	
Student's Contribution from Assets • Enter amount from line 50 +	
Expected Family Contribution for periods of enrollment other than 9 months =	

FIGURE 7-1 (continued)

2003-2004 EFC FORMULA ▓ : DEPENDENT STUDENT

SIMPLIFIED
WORKSHEET
Page 1

1. Parents' Adjusted Gross Income (FAFSA/SAR #74)
    (If negative, enter zero.)

2. a. Father's income earned from work
    (FAFSA/SAR #77)

2. b. Mother's income earned from work
    (FAFSA/SAR #78)   +_____

    Total parents' income earned from work   =

3. Parents' Taxable Income
    (If tax filers, enter the amount from line 1 above.
    If non-tax filers, enter the amount from line 2.)*

4. Untaxed income and benefits:

    • Total from FAFSA Worksheet A
      (FAFSA/SAR #79)   _____

    • Total from FAFSA Worksheet B
      (FAFSA/SAR #80)   +_____

    Total untaxed income and benefits   =

5. Taxable and untaxed income (sum of line 3 and line 4)

6. Total from FAFSA Worksheet C (FAFSA/SAR #81)   -

7. **TOTAL INCOME**
    (line 5 minus line 6) May be a negative number. =

8. 2002 U.S. income tax paid (FAFSA/SAR #75)
    (tax filers only); if negative, enter zero.

9. State and other tax allowance
    (Table A1. If negative, enter zero.)   +

10. Father's Social Security tax allow. (Table A2) +

11. Mother's Social Security tax allow. (Table A2) +

12. Income protection allowance (Table A3)   +

13. Employment expense allowance:

    • Two working parents: 35% of the lesser of the
      earned incomes, or $3,000, whichever is less
    • One-parent families: 35% of earned income,
      or $3,000, whichever is less
    • Two-parent families, one working
      parent: enter zero   +

14. **TOTAL ALLOWANCES**   =

Total income (from line 7)

Total allowances (from line 14)   -

15. **AVAILABLE INCOME (AI)**
    May be a negative number.   =

*STOP HERE if **both** of the following are true: line 3 is $15,000 or less,
plus the student **and** parents are eligible to file a 2002 IRS Form
1040A or 1040EZ (they are not required to file a 2002 Form 1040), or
they are not required to file any income tax return. If both circumstances are true, the Expected Family Contribution is automatically
zero.

16. Net worth of investments**
    (FAFSA/SAR #82)
    If negative, enter zero.

17. Net worth of business and/or investment farm
    (FAFSA/SAR #83)
    If negative, enter zero.

18. Adjusted net worth of business/farm
    (Calculate using Table A4.)   +

19. Cash, savings, & checking (FAFSA/SAR #84) +

20. Net worth (sum of lines 16, 18, and 19)   =

21. Education savings and asset
    protection allowance (Table A5)   -

22. Discretionary net worth
    (line 20 minus line 21)   =

23. Asset conversion rate   X   .12

24. **CONTRIBUTION FROM ASSETS**
    If negative, enter zero.   =

Available Income (AI) (from line 15)

Contribution from assets (from line 24)   +

25. **Adjusted Available Income (AAI)**
    May be a negative number.   =

26. **Total parents' contribution from AAI**
    (Calculate using Table A6; if negative, enter zero.)

27. **Number in college in 2003-2004**
    (Exclude parents) (FAFSA/SAR #66)   ÷

28. **PARENTS' CONTRIBUTION** (standard
    contribution for 9-month enrollment)***
    If negative, enter zero.   =

**Do not include the family's home.
***To calculate the parents' contribution for other than 9-
    month enrollment, see simplified worksheet page 3.

*NOTE: Do NOT complete the shaded areas;
asset information is not required in the simplified formula.*

FIGURE 7-1 (continued)

SIMPLIFIED
WORKSHEET
Page 2

29.	Adjusted Gross Income (FAFSA/SAR #39) (If negative, enter zero.)	
30.	Income earned from work (FAFSA/SAR #42)	
31.	Taxable Income (If tax filer, enter the amount from line 29. If non-tax filer, enter the amount from line 30.)	
32.	Untaxed income and benefits: Total from FAFSA Worksheet A FAFSA/SAR #44) Total from FAFSA Worksheet B (FAFSA/SAR #45) + Total untaxed income and benefits =	
33.	Taxable and untaxed income (sum of line 31 and line 32)	
34.	Total from FAFSA Worksheet C (FAFSA/SAR #46) -	
35.	**TOTAL INCOME** (line 33 minus line 34) May be a negative number. =	

36.	2002 U.S. income tax paid (FAFSA/SAR #40) (tax filers only); if negative, enter zero.	
37.	State and other tax allowance (Table A7. If negative, enter zero.) +	
38.	Social Security tax allowance (Table A2) +	
39.	Income protection allowance +	2,380
40.	Allowance for parents' negative Adjusted Available Income (If line 25 is negative, enter line 25 as a positive number in line 40. If line 25 is zero or positive, enter zero in line 40.) +	
41.	**TOTAL ALLOWANCES** =	

Total income (from line 35)		
Total allowances (from line 41) -		
42.	Available income (AI) =	
43.	Assessment of AI X	.50
44.	**STUDENT'S CONTRIBUTION FROM AI** If negative, enter zero. =	

45.	Net worth of investments* (FAFSA/SAR #47) If negative, enter zero.	
46.	Net worth of business and/or investment farm (FAFSA/SAR #48) If negative, enter zero. +	
47.	Cash, savings, & checking (FAFSA/SAR #49) +	
48.	**Net worth** (sum of lines 45 through 47) =	
49.	Assessment rate X	.35
50.	**STUDENT'S CONTRIBUTION FROM ASSETS =**	

PARENTS' CONTRIBUTION (from line 28)	
STUDENT'S CONTRIBUTION FROM AI (from line 44) +	
STUDENT'S CONTRIBUTION FROM ASSETS (from line 50) +	
51. EXPECTED FAMILY CONTRIBUTION standard contribution for 9-month enrollment** (If negative, enter zero.) =	

*Do not include the student's home.

** To calculate the EFC for other than 9-month enrollment, see the next page.

NOTE: Do NOT complete the shaded areas; asset information is not required in the simplified formula.

FIGURE 7-1 (continued)

NOTE: *Use this additional page to prorate the EFC only if the student will be enrolled for other than 9 months and only to determine the student's need for campus-based aid, a subsidized Federal Stafford Loan, or a subsidized Federal Direct Stafford/Ford Loan. Do not use this page to prorate the EFC for a Federal Pell Grant. The EFC for the Federal Pell Grant Program is the 9-month EFC used in conjunction with the cost of attendance to determine a Federal Pell Grant award from the Payment or Disbursement Schedule.*

		SIMPLIFIED WORKSHEET Page 3
A1. Parents' contribution (standard contribution for 9-month enrollment, from line 28)		
A2. Divide by 9	÷	9
A3. Parents' contribution per month	=	
A4. Multiply by number of months of enrollment	X	
A5. Parents' contribution for LESS than 9-month enrollment	=	
B1. Parents' Adjusted Available Income (AAI) (from line 25—may be a negative number)		
B2. Difference between the income protection allowance for a family of four and a family of five, with one in college	+	3,730
B3. Alternate parents' AAI for more than 9-month enrollment (line B1 + line B2)	=	
B4. Total parents' contribution from alternate AAI (calculate using Table A6)		
B5. Number in college (FAFSA/SAR #66)	÷	
B6. Alternate parents' contribution for student (line B4 divided by line B5)	=	
B7. Standard parents' contribution for the student for 9-month enrollment (from line 28)	-	
B8. Difference (line B6 minus line B7)	=	
B9. Divide line B8 by 12 months	÷	12
B10. Parents' contribution per month	=	
B11. Number of months student will be enrolled that exceed 9	X	
B12. Adjustment to parents' contribution for months that exceed 9 (multiply line B10 by line B11)	=	
B13. Standard parents' contribution for 9-month enrollment (from line 28)	+	
B14. Parents' contribution for MORE than 9-month enrollment	=	
C1. Student's contribution from AI (standard contribution for 9-month enrollment, from line 44)		
C2. Divide by 9	÷	9
C3. Student's contribution from AI per month	=	
C4. Multiply by number of months of enrollment	X	
C5. Student's contribution from AI for LESS than 9-month enrollment	=	

*For students enrolled more than 9 months, the standard contribution from AI is used (the amount from line 44).

Use next page to calculate total EFC for enrollment periods other than 9 months

FIGURE 7-1 (continued)

SIMPLIFIED
WORKSHEET
Page 4

Parents' Contribution—use ONE appropriate amount from previous page: • Enter amount from line A5 for enrollment periods less than 9 months **OR** • Enter amount from line B14 for enrollment periods greather than 9 months	
Student's Contribution from Available Income—use ONE appropriate amount from previous page: • Enter amount from line C5 for enrollment periods less than 9 months **OR** + • Enter amount from line 44 for enrollment periods greater than 9 months	
Expected Family Contribution for periods of enrollment other than 9 months =	

FIGURE 7-1 (continued)

Table A1: State and Other Tax Allowance
for Worksheet A (parents only)

STATE	PERCENT OF TOTAL INCOME		STATE	PERCENT OF TOTAL INCOME	
	$0-14,999	$15,000 or more		$0-14,999	$15,000 or more
Alabama	5%	4%	Missouri	6%	5%
Alaska	3%	2%	Montana	8%	7%
American Samoa	4%	3%	Nebraska	8%	7%
Arizona	6%	5%	Nevada	3%	2%
Arkansas	6%	5%	New Hampshire	7%	6%
California	8%	7%	New Jersey	8%	7%
Canada	4%	3%	New Mexico	6%	5%
Colorado	7%	6%	New York	11%	10%
Connecticut	6%	5%	North Carolina	8%	7%
Delaware	8%	7%	North Dakota	6%	5%
District of Columbia	10%	9%	Northern Mariana Islands	4%	3%
Federated States of Micronesia	4%	3%	Ohio	8%	7%
Florida	4%	3%	Oklahoma	6%	5%
Georgia	7%	6%	Oregon	10%	9%
Guam	4%	3%	Palau	4%	3%
Hawaii	8%	7%	Pennsylvania	7%	6%
Idaho	7%	6%	Puerto Rico	4%	3%
Illinois	6%	5%	Rhode Island	9%	8%
Indiana	6%	5%	South Carolina	8%	7%
Iowa	8%	7%	South Dakota	4%	3%
Kansas	7%	6%	Tennessee	3%	2%
Kentucky	7%	6%	Texas	3%	2%
Louisiana	4%	3%	Utah	8%	7%
Maine	9%	8%	Vermont	8%	7%
Marshall Islands	4%	3%	Virgin Islands	4%	3%
Maryland	9%	8%	Virginia	8%	7%
Massachusetts	9%	8%	Washington	4%	3%
Mexico	4%	3%	West Virginia	6%	5%
Michigan	9%	8%	Wisconsin	10%	9%
Minnesota	9%	8%	Wyoming	3%	2%
Mississippi	5%	4%	Blank or Invalid State	4%	3%
			OTHER	4%	3%

Multiply parents' total income (EFC Worksheet A, line 7) by the appropriate rate from the table above to get the "state and other tax allowance" (Worksheet A, line 9). Use the parents' *state of legal residence* (FAFSA/SAR #67). If this item is blank or invalid, use the student's *state of legal residence* (FAFSA/SAR #24). If both items are blank or invalid, use the *state* in the student's mailing address (FAFSA/SAR #6). If all three items are blank or invalid, use the rate for a blank or invalid state above.

FIGURE 7-1 (continued)

Table A2: Social Security Tax

Calculate separately the Social Security tax of father, mother, and student.

Income Earned from Work*	Social Security Tax
$0 - $84,900	7.65% of income
$84,901 or greater	$6,494.85 + 1.45% of amount over $84,900

*Father's 2002 income earned from work is FAFSA/SAR #77.
Mother's 2002 income earned from work is FAFSA/SAR #78.
Student's 2002 income earned from work is FAFSA/SAR #42.
Social Security tax will never be less than zero.

Table A3: Income Protection Allowance

Number in parents' household, including student (FAFSA/SAR #65)	Number of college students in household (FAFSA/SAR #66)				
	1	2	3	4	5
2	$13,470	$11,160	———	———	———
3	16,770	14,480	$12,170	———	———
4	20,710	18,410	16,120	$13,810	———
5	24,440	22,130	19,840	17,540	$15,240
6	28,580	26,280	23,990	21,680	19,390

NOTE: For each additional family member, add $3,230.
For each additional college student (except parents), subtract $2,290.

Table A4: Business/Farm Net Worth Adjustment
for EFC Formula Worksheet A (parents only)

If the net worth of a business or farm is—	Then the adjusted net worth is—
Less than $1	$0
$1 to $95,000	40% of net worth of business/farm
$95,001 to $290,000	$ 38,000 + 50% of excess over $95,000
$290,001 to $480,000	$135,500 + 60% of excess over $290,000
$480,001 or more	$249,500 + 100% of excess over $480,000

FIGURE 7-1 (continued)

Table A5: Education Savings and Asset Protection Allowance
for EFC Formula Worksheet A (parents only)

Age of older parent*	Allowance if there are two parents	Allowance if there is only one parent	Age of older parent*	Allowance if there are two parents	Allowance if there is only one parent
25 or less..	0	0	45	42,200	20,700
26	2,500	1,200	46	43,300	21,100
27	5,000	2,500	47	44,300	21,600
28	7,500	3,700	48	45,400	22,200
29	9,900	5,000	49	46,600	22,600
30	12,400	6,200	50	47,700	23,100
31	14,900	7,400	51	49,200	23,700
32	17,400	8,700	52	50,400	24,200
33	19,900	9,900	53	51,700	24,800
34	22,400	11,200	54	53,200	25,400
35	24,900	12,400	55	54,500	26,200
36	27,400	13,600	56	56,200	26,800
37	29,800	14,900	57	57,900	27,400
38	32,300	16,100	58	59,600	28,200
39	34,800	17,400	59	61,400	28,900
40	37,300	18,600	60	63,200	29,700
41	38,200	19,000	61	65,100	30,500
42	39,200	19,400	62	67,300	31,200
43	40,200	19,800	63	69,200	32,100
44	41,200	20,300	64	71,600	33,100
			65 or more	74,000	34,100

*If age of older parent (FAFSA/SAR #70) is blank, use age 45 on the table.

Table A6: Parents' Contribution From AAI

If parents' AAI is—	The parents' contribution from AAI is—
-$3,410 or less	-$750
-$3,409 to $12,000	22% of AAI
$12,001 to $15,100	$2,640 + 25% of AAI over $12,000
$15,101 to $18,200	$3,415 + 29% of AAI over $15,100
$18,201 to $21,200	$4,314 + 34% of AAI over $18,200
$21,201 to $24,300	$5,334 + 40% of AAI over $21,200
$24,301 or more	$6,574 + 47% of AAI over $24,300

FIGURE 7-1 (continued)

Table A7: State and Other Tax Allowance
for Worksheet A (student only)

Alabama	3%	Missouri	3%
Alaska	0%	Montana	5%
American Samoa	2%	Nebraska	4%
Arizona	3%	Nevada	0%
Arkansas	4%	New Hampshire	1%
California	5%	New Jersey	3%
Canada	2%	New Mexico	4%
Colorado	4%	New York	7%
Connecticut	2%	North Carolina	5%
Delaware	5%	North Dakota	2%
District of Columbia	7%	Northern Mariana Islands	2%
Federated States		Ohio	5%
of Micronesia	2%	Oklahoma	4%
Florida	1%	Oregon	6%
Georgia	4%	Palau	2%
Guam	2%	Pennsylvania	3%
Hawaii	6%	Puerto Rico	2%
Idaho	5%	Rhode Island	4%
Illinois	2%	South Carolina	5%
Indiana	4%	South Dakota	0%
Iowa	5%	Tennessee	0%
Kansas	4%	Texas	0%
Kentucky	5%	Utah	5%
Louisiana	2%	Vermont	4%
Maine	5%	Virgin Islands	2%
Marshall Islands	2%	Virginia	4%
Maryland	6%	Washington	0%
Massachusetts	5%	West Virginia	4%
Mexico	2%	Wisconsin	5%
Michigan	4%	Wyoming	0%
Minnesota	6%	Blank or Invalid State	2%
Mississippi	3%	OTHER	2%

Multiply the total income of student (EFC Worksheet A, line 35) by the appropriate rate from the table above to get the "state and other tax allowance" (Worksheet A, line 37). Use the student's *state of legal residence* (FAFSA/SAR #24). If this item is blank or invalid, use the *state* in the student's mailing address (FAFSA/SAR #6). If both items are blank or invalid, use the parents' *state of legal residence* (FAFSA/SAR #67). If all three items are blank or invalid, use the rate for a blank or invalid state above.

CHAPTER 8

Adding Up Grants, Loans, and Student Employment

The financial aid forms are filled out. The college acceptances have now arrived, and after the excitement of the acceptance has subsided, it's time to look at the financial aid package. The college may charge $35,000 per year, but it said you're eligible for a $20,000 financial aid package. Does this mean that the school just takes $20,000 off the top and you pay the rest? Not usually. The financial aid package usually has a loan component, a work component, and then, finally, a grant component.

The final package is often a huge surprise to many parents and students. They were under the impression that financial aid meant a reduction in the bill right off the top with no strings attached. However, that's not the case at most schools. It's usually expected that financial aid means a part-time campus job and loan payments that can go on for many years after graduation.

This is probably as good a time as any to reiterate some of the philosophy behind this book. The purpose is to encourage you to save and invest for college education. The argument that it doesn't pay to save because it reduces eligibility for financial aid misses the point. If you divert your current income to, say, buying a car and don't save for college instead, some extra aid might come your way. However, keep in mind that part of that package will be diverting some of the student's (and possibly the parents') *future* income to paying back loans.

Also, virtually every financial aid professional points out that the formulas discussed in Chapter 7 are primarily driven by *income*. The level of assets is usually a less important factor in the aid award calculation. Finally, many financial aid professionals talk about *flexibility of choice*. What that means is that the family who has saved substantially for college is likely to have a variety of choices when it comes to deciding which college to attend. Not saving assumes that there will be financial aid available at the school of choice. In a period in which college endowments have declined along with the financial markets, that may be a big assumption and a potential limitation of choice. Those who have saved less will have to decide between various available financial aid packages. As we saw in the previous chapter, because of the way in which the financial aid formulas work, some families are not always going to be able to choose their "first choice" college. This may be especially true of those families that have high living expenses or high consumer debt.

The same flexibility argument occurs after college graduation. The student whose family was able to save substantially will have more flexibility in deciding which career path to take. I know of one graduate who felt forced to leave a secure, well-paying job in the financial community for one that paid more in the short run, but entailed substantial risk of being let go. He took this risk, in part because he had over $100,000 in student loans and felt a great deal of pressure paying these loans back. As it turns out, his new firm had substantial layoffs after the terrorist attacks of September 11, 2001. A year after being let go, he had not yet found a new job. While there is nothing wrong with some moderate level of student loans, high levels of student debt can steer students away from jobs that may have low starting salaries but good long-term potential. It can also contribute to a delay of other long-term financial and personal goals, such as getting married, buying a home, and of course, saving for the next generation's educational needs.

Let's compare two hypothetical families to illustrate the point. Both families had a child who was born in the spring of 1985 and will start college in August 2003. Both families had $40,000 of income in 1985 and earn $75,000 in 2003. Family A saved $2000 per year, while family B saved nothing. In 2003, Family A had a college savings nest egg of $75,000. Now, both families are contemplating sending their child to the same school that has a total cost of $35,000 per year.

When the financial aid department evaluates both families, the award will take into account the $75,000 put away for college. Assuming that this is the parents' only savings, the federal financial aid formula will first subtract the asset protection allowance of $42,200 (assuming a two-parent family with the older parent age 45), leaving $32,800 to be assessed at 5.64 percent. This means that the contribution from assets for Family A will be calculated at $1850 per year. Because of the difference in savings, a typical aid package might be $16,000 per year for family A and $18,000 for family B.

This means that Family A will have to come up with $19,000 per year, or $76,000 for four years, while Family B will have to come up with $17,000 per year or $68,000 for four years. Now you tell me, which position would you prefer to be in: Would you rather have to pay $76,000 when you have $75,000 in the bank or would you rather pay $68,000 when you have no money saved? The bottom line is that Family A is actually going to be able to pay the $19,000 per year out of their pocket, while Family B is almost certainly going to have to borrow substantially beyond the loan component that is embedded in the financial aid package. We'll expand on this loan component in the next section.

Behind the Financial Aid Award

In the vast majority of cases, the financial aid office "packages" the financial aid award in layers. Most schools start with a layer they call *self-help*. Self-help might include a student loan or a campus job. In some cases it might only be the "assumption" that there will be some outside employment. When that happens, the award is at least partially, and sometimes fully, reduced by the assumed income to be earned during the summer and during the school year.

It is only after that top layer of self-help that grants are received. Grants, of course, represent the most desirable part of financial aid, the part that requires no additional employment or repayment.

Instead of layering the award with self-help first and then providing grant aid, some colleges will "sandwich" the aid package with a small layer of grant aid first, followed by self-help and finally, the bulk of the grant aid. This provides those families who have more modest levels of need with the ability to receive some grant aid. Schools that do this tend to be among the schools with larger endowments. These schools have the financial ability to provide somewhat more competitive aid packages to their students.

Now let's take a look at the total financial aid package offered to the two families in the above example, one that saved and the other that didn't. As a reminder, both now earn $75,000 and Family A has $75,000 in college savings, while Family B doesn't have any savings.

Financial Aid Package for Family A

Stafford loan	$2,625
Work-study employment	$1,500
Grants	$11,875
Total	$16,000

Financial Aid Package for Family B

Stafford loan	$2,625
Work-study employment	$1,500
Grants	$13,875
Total	$18,000

Assume for the moment that Family A, which has been saving $2000 per year all along, can now boost its college expenditures to $4000. This family might be able to bypass the loan component of the financial aid package and, in addition, take the $19,000 out of its savings each year. If all goes as planned, the student might then be debt free at the end of college.

On the other hand, if family B also spends $4000 per year on college, they not only will have to borrow $2625 per year as part of the loan package, they will also have to borrow an additional $12,000 per year to pay the expected family contribution of $17,000 per year. At the end of four years, the student (as part of the financial aid package) might have a loan balance of $20,000 (including accrued interest and origination fees). The student's loan balance is that high because as the student progresses through college, higher Stafford loan limits replace grant aid. In addition, the parents (or perhaps the student) might have a loan balance of an additional $52,000 (including accrued interest). Assuming for the moment, that the total of $72,000 of loans can be repaid at an average rate of 4.5 percent over a 10-year period, the monthly payment will be $746.20. This will result in over $89,500 of total payments. All of that could have been avoided if family B had saved $2000 per year for 18 years. That $36,000 expenditure avoids a future $89,500 expenditure even after factoring in $8000 in additional financial aid. So don't make financial aid an excuse not to save.

Front Loading

The above example is typical for a first-year student. In subsequent years, the proportion of loan aid often rises while the proportion of grant aid goes down. There are several reasons for this. The first reason is that the loan limits in most federally subsidized loan programs rise through the college years, allowing more debt to fall under that umbrella. The second reason is that students are more likely to leave school early in their college career; therefore, many college aid programs prefer not to saddle students with debt unless it seems likely that the student will be getting a degree and have the increased earning power to make the loan payments. A third possible reason is that with the first-year aid award, parents and students are comparing aid packages from several schools. Some speculate that this competition provides an incentive for schools to offer their best package for the first year.

Princeton's Financial Aid Package

In 2001, Princeton University, one of the wealthiest universities in the United States with an endowment of $8 billion, revamped its financial aid procedures. The major change was an end to including loans as part of their financial aid packages. All Princeton aid is now in the form of grants. The calculation of aid is somewhat different than most private schools with no consideration of home equity and somewhat larger asset protection allowances. Princeton also increased the asset protection allowance for families that rent by at least $140,000 to offset the value of the equity in a typical home. Princeton also requires financial statements from both parents in the case of divorce or separation (with some limited exceptions for individual family circumstance).

In 2002, the school assumed a student contribution of $2050 from summer employment. Princeton also expected a student contribution from assets of only 5 percent compared with the standard 35 percent found in the federal methodology. Princeton has a calculator on their Web site (www.princeton.edu) that can give an early indication of the college's assessment of financial need.

The combination of strong academics and somewhat more generous aid packages has created excess demand for a Princeton education. Perhaps the number 1 ranking in the *U.S. News & World Report* college rankings hasn't hurt either. In addition, because of Princeton's approach to need-based financial aid, the magazine ranks the school a "best buy." Despite a total price approaching $38,000 in 2002–2003, Princeton now sends the thin letter of rejection to more than 90 percent of those applying.

Princeton is not alone in its financial aid formulas. Other Ivy League schools, including Harvard and Yale (which have even larger endowments than Princeton), now have approaches to similar Princeton's in calculating financial aid.

Early-Decision Programs

Most colleges allow the applicant to designate their school as a first choice by promising that they will attend if admitted. On the face of it, the program sounds like a great idea. Students get to apply to only one school, while colleges get to accept students that they know are going to attend. Students also often believe that an early decision application can improve the odds of acceptance. Some admissions officers deny there is an admissions edge to an early application, while others acknowledge a slight advantage. This, of course, is school dependent. In any event, early admissions are a good deal for the college itself because from the school's perspective, it raises the percentage of admitted students that attend the college. This helps raise the college's standing in most rankings, although *U.S. News & World Report* recently stopped using "yield" as a criteria.

The reality for students is somewhat different. Often the student can't apply just to his or her early-decision school because the regular application deadlines at many schools come at about the same time that the response is coming from the early-decision school. There simply wouldn't be enough time to write the essays and get the recommendations together for other schools if the early decision-school did not accept the student. As a result, most early-decision students end up readying their applications for a variety of schools even when they apply for an early decision.

However, the real reason for concern about early-decision programs is financial. When a student is accepted on an early-decision basis, the ability to compare a variety of financial aid packages is lost. I know of students who have applied for an early decision to an elite school, have been rejected or deferred, only to find that they have received a substantial merit scholarship or a very different need-based package at one of their other college choices. Had they received an early-decision acceptance, they would not have known what other colleges would have put in their aid package.

Thus, early-decision programs are a viable option for students who:

➤ Have identified a particular school that is far and away a first choice

➤ Might not qualify for need-based financial aid

➤ Are willing to take the chance of a less competitive aid package in exchange for admittance at the school of their choice

I've been to several college information sessions where someone asks what happens when the early-decision acceptance arrives and the financial aid award is inadequate. The school representative usually responds that the student is not going to be forced to attend and the family will not be held to its commitment. However, this is not a situation that anyone would want to be in. You will then have to explain this situation not only to the school that accepted the student, but also to the other schools that the student is applying to as well as to the high school counselor who has already received notification of the early acceptance. As a result, there are some situations in which bypassing the early-decision route might be a wise idea. These include:

➤ When you're asking a private school not to consider the income and assets of a noncustodial parent

➤ When there is a large difference between the calculation of need under the federal methodology and the institutional methodology and the student is considering both private and public schools

➤ When the student's preference between schools isn't strong and the student might qualify for merit aid at some of his or her college choices

Comparing Financial Aid Awards at Different Schools

The financial aid award letter usually arrives at the same time or within a few days of the acceptance letter. There are several things to consider when evaluating the offer of financial aid.

➤ Does the aid package meet 100 percent of documented need? In other words, is the sum of the expected family contribution plus the aid package enough to cover the cost of attendance? (Not every school meets 100 percent of need, so it's the first thing you should check). Then look at the net cost of attending the school after taking the gross cost of attendance less the self-help component and grant aid. Is the result an affordable amount for the family?

➤ Is this a final offer or is the school requesting further documentation before finalizing their offer?

➤ Is the entire offer based on need or is there a merit portion to the award?

➤ How much of the award is represented by grants and how much is represented by loans and student employment?

➤ If there are loans included as part of the package, what is the interest rate? Is there an origination fee for the loan? Is interest on the loan payable during the school years? If interest is not payable, does the interest accrue during the years the student is enrolled in school? Is the loan offer a better deal than what could be obtained from an outside lender? It pays to discuss this with the financial aid officer. When comparing the packages from two or more schools, don't necessarily assume that the terms of the loan are the same.

➤ Find out whether the grant or merit portion of the aid package is renewable. How does the aid award get calculated in subsequent enrollment years?

If the offers from various schools are dramatically different, it may be possible to inquire at the school with the less generous offer if they would consider reevaluating their offer. However, before dealing with the school there are some ground rules to consider:

First, take a look at the school's calculation of expected family contribution. If one school calculated an EFC substantially higher than other schools, it's fair game to ask why their calculation seems to be different.

If, on the other hand, two schools calculated EFC in similar fashion, but one school provided a larger proportion of grants, it is fair game to ask the school if it could reconsider how it packaged the aid award.

In general, you will be taken seriously when you compare awards at similar types of schools. An elite private school may not be particularly interested in how a public school evaluated your need. However, they might be very interested to know that a similar private school calculated your EFC $3000 lower than they did.

What schools especially don't want to do is to get into a discussion mixing apples and oranges. Specifically, don't bother calling an Ivy League school asking them to match the $20,000 merit scholarship that another school gave your son or daughter because your son or daughter would prefer to attend their school. In almost every case, a school that has a policy of need-based scholarships only will not negotiate based on another school's merit award.

Keep in mind that when all is said and done, some financial aid packages may be better than others. These differences may go into the final decision as to where the student ultimately goes to college. I can't stress enough that saving early and saving often for higher education gives families more flexibility during the college admissions process *and* for the years following graduation.

CHAPTER 9

The Mystery of Merit-Based Aid

In addition to the need-based financial aid system discussed in the previous two chapters, there is a second financial aid apparatus that provides significant funding for higher education. It's the merit-based scholarship system.

Merit aid is just what it sounds like. Without regard to financial circumstance, aid is provided to certain students because of what they bring to a particular college campus. Students may get aid because of their ability in a particular sport or for their ability as an artist or a musician. In many cases, students get aid because their grades were high or because of their score on one of the college entrance exams.

There is a fair amount of controversy over merit aid. When I've visited colleges, I've generally found that the financial aid office strongly dislikes the concept of merit aid, while admissions officers and many senior-level college administrators are supportive of the concept.

Many financial aid professionals take the stance that the amount of resources that a school has for financial aid is limited and merit aid only makes it that much more difficult to provide funding for needy students. They're dismayed that sometimes a needy student is not able to go to the college of his or her choice while aid is being funneled to students of middle- or upper-income families.

Administrators outside the financial aid office take the view that in order to attract a strong student body, many schools are going to have to provide scholarships to certain students. It may be that a college sees its average SAT score hovering around 1000. As a strategic move, the school may decide to provide scholarships to those applicants with scores above 1400 or 1500 for the ultimate reason of attracting more students with scores of 1100 or 1200 who pay their own way. Thus, they may find that handing out some selective scholarships is a financial investment worth making. The extreme case of this type of strategy is college sports. Look at any school that regularly competes in the NCAA men's division I basketball tournament. These colleges make substantial money from their basketball program and consider the awarding of a free college education to that seven-foot center a wise investment. In some cases, the value of the scholarships for the team is less than the cost of the coaching staff. The argument is that providing these merit athletic scholarships provides a positive return, not only on a tangible basis, but also on an intangible basis through name recognition. In effect, the schools get free advertising as they compete in a bowl game or in "March Madness."

More and more schools are becoming less shy about awarding academic scholarships. There are perhaps 150 research universities that would like to someday be listed among the top 50 universities in the *U.S. News & World Report* annual rankings of colleges. There are perhaps another 100 small liberal arts colleges that would also like to be in the top 50. As a result, you typically find that schools that are at the very top of the rankings, such as Princeton, Harvard, and Yale in the research university list, and Amherst and Pomona at the top of the liberal arts list tend not to give any merit aid. However, schools just a bit lower down on both top-50 lists often offer merit packages to their top applicants. In addition, some very fine schools that are not currently in the very top rankings offer merit aid. The trick is to see if you can identify a school in which the student might be in the upper 10 percent of the applicant pool.

As straightforward as that sounds, most people concentrate on doing the reverse. They apply to schools where they are in the lower half of the applicant pool in hopes that they will gain acceptance on the strength of their essay or recommendations. Sometimes that works; lightning strikes, and an offer of admission is received. However, students ought to put as much effort into the application sent to schools at the lower end of their application spectrum. That's because, again, lightning might strike and the offer of a merit scholarship might be received.

As earlier mentioned, some colleges that offer merit aid are top-notch private schools. For example:

Emory University through its Emory Scholars program, offers up to 150 scholarships each year. Seventy-five students receive awards of two-thirds tuition while 50 will receive full tuition. Finally, 25 highly qualified students will receive an award covering both tuition and room and board. Students need to be nominated by their high school and go through a separate application procedure to qualify for the program.

University of Rochester awards up to $10,000 scholarships for those students who score high on the SAT I. The current cutoff is a score of 1350. Students who are New York State residents get a $5000 reduction in cost if they scored below the 1350 mark. In addition, the university awards up to 10 Renaissance scholarships to outstanding applicants. This amounts to four years of full tuition.

Smith College offers up to 10 admitted applicants half-tuition awards. In addition, a limited number of full-tuition scholarships are awarded to highly qualified women who plan to obtain a degree from Smith's engineering program.

About 100 of Duke University's incoming 1500 undergraduates each year get merit aid awards of as much as full tuition. Criteria include academics and leadership. There are a variety of programs and students are automatically considered when they apply for admission.

Rice University already has tuition and expenses far below that of other comparable private schools. However, Rice also offers merit aid that can reduce the cost of education even further. Rice offers up to full-tuition scholarships to those "impact people" who tend to be "outstanding scholars who have been recognized for their personal achievements at the state, national and international level." All applicants are automatically considered for merit aid.

Washington University in St. Louis has an extensive program of merit aid. Most are annual awards of $2500, but some awards are for half or even full tuition. Many of these scholarships require separate application.

This is just a sample of the merit aid available at some of the most competitive schools in the United States. These merit aid programs are not just available at schools that are tough to get accepted to. Plenty of schools that typically accept average students provide merit aid to their best applicants. Literally hundreds of private colleges have some sort of merit aid plan.

Some of the biggest growth in merit programs over the last several years has come from public colleges and from state and local governments. More than 20 states currently have merit aid programs.

Some of the larger programs include the one administered by the state of Georgia, which was among the first states to start such a program in 1993. The Georgia Hope Scholarship (not to be confused with the federal Hope Tax Credit) pays full tuition at a state school or up to $3000 per year at a private school in the state of Georgia. Students have to graduate from a Georgia high school with at least a B average. In Alaska, those students in the top 10 percent of their high school class can get a scholarship at the University of Alaska of $2750 per year.

In New York, programs vary from campus to campus of the State University of New York. At the campuses at Albany and Stony Brook for example, presidential scholarships ranging up to full tuition are available for those students who are in the upper 10 percent of their high school class and have commensurate scores on the SAT.

In Florida, Students with a B average or better can qualify for a 75 percent tuition reduction at the University of Florida. The Florida Bright Futures program also provides aid for private colleges in Florida. In all, about one of every three Florida high school graduates qualifies for at least some aid from the Bright Futures program.

If you want to see if the college you're interested in offers merit aid, it's fairly simple to find out. Just look at some of the college's brochures or go to their Web site. At almost every school, you would click on the section of the Web site devoted to admissions and then look at the section for financial aid. Most colleges make a big deal out of their merit aid programs because it helps them market the school. Even those schools that may have 3000 applicants, only to hand out six scholarships will often heavily promote merit aid. The probability of getting an award might be 0.2 percent, but the college will try to make sure you at least hear about the program.

Qualifying for Merit Aid

The following actions, which you should consider anyway when applying for college, take on added importance when considering merit aid qualification:

➤ Study for and take various college entrance exams including PSAT, SAT I, SAT II, and ACT.

➤ Take the most challenging courses offered at high school.

➤ Cultivate high school teachers for recommendations.

➤ Participate in after-school activities that may lead to aid. This includes sports, music, community service organizations, and religious groups.

➤ Focus on one or two activities where you can show a passion for the activity and perhaps a leadership role as opposed to participating in dozens of activities with only a superficial role in each.

➤ Keep in touch with the high school guidance office, which may have information on a variety of merit aid opportunities.

➤ Make sure you're aware of merit programs run by your home state or local government.

➤ Search for merit aid opportunities in the public library or online.

Merit Scholarship Programs

One of the first contacts that most high school students have with merit aid programs is when they take the PSAT. In addition to its traditional role as a "warm up" exam for the SAT I, the PSAT is also a qualifying exam for the National Merit Scholarship Program.

The PSAT is a three-part examination consisting of a verbal, math, and writing test. Each of the three sections is scored on a 20 to 80 scale, so 240 is the maximum "index" score. Approximately one million high school juniors take the exam each year in October. By Thanksgiving, scores are released, and subsequently the top 50,000 scorers are identified and commended. The following fall, the National Merit Scholarship program names about 15,000 semifinalists based on their PSAT scores and that number is later reduced to about 13,000 finalists. About 8000 of these students ultimately are awarded funding through the National Merit Scholarship Program and its sponsoring corporations and colleges. Many of the winners of National Merit Scholarships get the funding by virtue of attending a school that is a sponsor of the program or having some relationship to one of the corporate sponsors (typically a child of an employee). Scholarships vary depending on the sponsor, but are generally $500 to $2000 per year depending on cost of school and financial need.

National Merit finalists often find themselves the recipient of various offers from many of the top state universities around the nation. Schools such as Arizona State University, Iowa State University, the University of Oklahoma, and the State University of New York at Albany all have merit scholarship programs for National Merit finalists. These scholarships tend to be fairly generous, with most of these schools covering most or all of tuition and some even also covering room and board. Many other schools have programs for National Merit finalists so be sure to check if you or your child happens to be in this group. More information on the National Merit Program can be found at www.nationalmerit.org.

The Coca-Cola Scholars Foundation supports students with strong academic records and a commitment to community service.

The foundation awards 50 national scholarships totaling $20,000 over four years. In addition, there are 200 regional scholars named who receive $4000 over four years. More information can be found at www.coca-colascholars.org.

The DiscoverCard Tribute Scholarship recognizes high school juniors of promise. Criteria include strong academic achievement, community service, and overcoming adversity. The program awards up to nine scholarships in each state and the District of Columbia of $2500 each. There are also up to nine national awards of $25,000. More information can be found at www.aasa.org/discover.htm.

The Intel Science Talent Search tries to identify some of the nation's most promising science students. About 1500 students around the country literally spend years designing projects for this competition. The program ultimately selects 300 semifinalists. This is narrowed down to 40 finalists and then 10 winners. The grand prize winner gets a $100,000 scholarship, while the 2nd through 10th place winners get prizes ranging from $20,000 to $75,000. The 30 remaining finalists each receive a $5000 prize. Nevertheless, all 300 semifinalists are often sought after and become eligible for additional merit aid at a variety of schools. More information on the Science Talent Search can be found at www.intel.com/education/sts/.

The Military

No discussion of merit aid would be complete without mentioning the U.S. military. Over the years, literally millions of Americans have been educated using military and veterans' benefits. There are several ways one can tap the educational benefits of the U.S. military.

➤ Get educated at one of the military service academies: a top-notch education without charge can be had at the military service academies located at West Point (Army), Annapolis (Navy), Colorado Springs (Air Force), and New London (Coast Guard). In exchange, there is usually a five- to eight-year service commitment. Admission is extremely competitive and nomination by a member of Congress is required.

➤ ROTC: Many schools offer this program, which can provide up to $17,000 per year for tuition plus a monthly stipend of $250 for freshmen and sophomores, $300 for juniors, and $350 for seniors. ROTC can be "tried out" as a class in many schools without obligation. However, once a scholarship program is contracted for, military obligations can be for up to eight years after graduation.

➤ Enlist in active service after high school and then use veterans' benefits for college. Programs include the Montgomery GI Bill (MGIB). Under the MGIB, you contribute $100 per month for a total of $1200. In return, full-time military personnel get up to $28,800 in educational support. Each service also has programs that supplement the MGIB. For example, the Army College Fund (ACF) provides supplemental educational funds.

➤ Enlist in active service after college and have the military assist in student loan repayment. Active military personnel can get a third of their loans paid or $1500 (whichever is more) for each year of active duty. The loan must be in a federally insured program including Stafford, Perkins, ALAS, GSL, PLUS, FISL, NDSL or SLS. Repayments can total up to $65,000. In addition, those with at least 60 college credits who enter the armed forces can obtain enlistment bonuses of $8000.

➤ Join the reserves or National Guard while in college. The Army reserves have a program called Concurrent Admissions Program (ConAP). This is a joint program between the Army and over 1500 two- and four-year colleges. The National Guard Tuition Assistance funds up to 75 percent of tuition costs with a cap of 15 semester hours per year and up to $3500 of reimbursement per year. In addition, the National Guard also offers benefits under the Montgomery GI Bill Selected Reserve (MGIB-SR). This benefit can pay $272 per month for full-time college enrollment for up to 36 months. MGIB-SR benefits may not be used with National Guard Tuition Assistance to pay for the same course.

Scratching Beneath the Scholarship Surface

The scholarships listed above are but a tiny sample of the various scholarship programs available. There are a variety of scholarships open to residents of various regions of the United States. Also, if you are a member of a fraternal organization, an organized religion, or a labor union, you may qualify for a scholarship.

There are a variety of services that charge fees to help search for scholarships. There is probably no need for that. I've been fairly impressed with www.fastweb.com. There is no charge for the service and once the student inputs his or her interests and qualifications, the system responds with a variety of scholarship opportunities. The service also reminds the student about upcoming deadlines for various scholarship programs.

Don't go overboard though in trying to apply for every scholarship. Many of these programs require essays and recommendations that can be extremely time-consuming to apply for. On the other hand, don't just automatically assume that you or your child will never qualify for anything. Many students get some merit aid so why not try?

How Merit Awards Interact with Other Aid and Calculations

Need-Based Aid

At many colleges that meet 100 percent of documented need, getting merit-based aid ends up reducing the need-based package. That's the bad news. However, the good news is that getting merit aid often reduces the loan and student employment (self-help) portion first, before reducing the school's grant aid. Here's an example:

If the initial financial aid package consisted of:

Loan	$2625
Student employment	$1750
Grant aid	$8000

And the student were to receive a $5000 merit scholarship, the aid package would become:

Loan	$0
Student employment	$0
Grant aid	$7375

This doesn't mean that the student still can't take out a loan or have a job, it just means that now the proceeds from loans or employment can go directly to the student, either to help pay the expected family contribution or toward the student's own funds.

Expected Family Contribution

Often a private school will calculate through its institutional methodology a higher EFC than would be calculated under the federal methodology. In that case, the school will often first eliminate the self-help part of the aid package when an outside scholarship is received. Then, before touching grant aid, the school will allow the EFC to be reduced to the federal level. Thus, in the example above, if the federal EFC were $18,000 and the schools EFC based on institutional methodology was $20,000 then many schools would keep the grant aid at the original $8000. These policies can make a difference, so make sure you're aware of what the policies regarding outside scholarships are before the final decision to enroll in a particular school is made.

529 Prepaid Plans

In Chapter 7, we covered the financial aid treatment of 529 prepaid plans. Most financial aid formulas treat 529 prepaid plans as a resource, similarly to outside merit aid. So, the examples above where the self-help portion of an aid award is reduced first also apply if you are dealing with the proceeds from a prepaid plan.

CHAPTER 10

Beyond Undergrad

When people think about saving for college, you hear time and time again that they need to save for two or four years. That's true for many, if not most, students. However, an increasing proportion of students now get advanced degrees.

Saving may be even more important for students who intend to go to graduate schools than for students who intend to make their associate's or bachelor's degree the completion of their formal education. There are a number of reasons for this:

➤ Tuition is often higher in graduate and professional programs than would be the case in undergraduate programs.

➤ Financial aid is usually skewed toward self-help; that is, loans make up the bulk of aid packages combined with campus employment (often teaching positions). Grant aid is often much more scarce than in undergraduate programs.

➤ Living expenses are usually higher. The freshman dorm that was an enjoyable experience for an 18-year-old is usually not suitable for graduate students. Many graduate students opt for more expensive campus apartments or higher-priced off-campus housing.

➤ The opportunity for summer employment may be limited since many graduate and professional programs entail research projects or thesis preparations that consume large amounts of time.

Financial Aid for Graduate Programs

There's good news and bad news on the financial aid front for graduate students: The good news is that the calculation of financial aid for grad students is usually based on the student's own assets and income. It is far easier to designate the graduate student as independent than is the case for an undergraduate student. The bad news is that many graduate aid programs are heavily weighted toward assisting the student in getting loans. It is not uncommon for students who are studying law or medicine or are in a top business or engineering school to end up with loan balances that reach or exceed $100,000. It should be noted that much depends on the type of graduate program the student is entering. In general, PhD programs in the arts and sciences are more likely to have more access to merit aid than professional programs in law, business, or medicine.

Students in the arts and sciences will often have the ability to get teaching fellowships that in many cases can completely offset the tuition in graduate school. At most schools however, these fellowships are for doctoral-level programs, not master's programs.

Loans

There is usually good availability of credit for most students in graduate programs. The Stafford loan limits expand to $18,500 annually ($8500 with subsidized interest, $10,000 with unsubsidized interest).

Speaking of loans, when one nears the end of graduate school, it may also be time to consider consolidating all of the student loans that have been accumulated through the undergraduate and graduate years. It might be tempting since interest rates are at historical lows. However, the reduction in interest rate usually also comes with the ability to lengthen the maturity of the loan. Students who originally had 10 years to pay may in many cases be able to pay over 20 years. For students with crushing loan balances this may seem to be a bonanza since the loan payments can drop dramatically. However, keep in mind that the consolidation can also mean thousands more in interest payments over the longer life of the loan. For the one-year period ending July 1, 2003, loans can be consolidated at 4.06 percent if they were issued after July 1, 1998. For loans issued before July 1, 1998, the rate is 4.86 percent. If you are a new graduate you can get a special 3.46 percent rate if consolidation takes place during the six-month grace period before repayment starts.

Consolidation can only be done once, so the best time to consider this transaction is during the months of May and June, when the rates for the next year are set. That way you can see if the rates that will be implemented in July might be even lower. In any event, consider consolidating the loans to get the lower rate, but resist the urge to extend the payments. If you can possibly afford it, try to stick to the original payment schedule so that you're done paying for college before it's time to pay for the next generation's education!

Graduate students can sometimes reduce the cost of their education by getting a job in the same or similar field and then going to school part-time. Some employers may provide a benefit package that pays some or all of the educational cost. For 2002, if that amount was $5250 or less, the benefit is tax-free. Additional amounts are taxable income. If however, the employer doesn't pay, there is still an important tax benefit. If courses are taken to maintain or improve the student's current employment, then the expenses are deductible as a miscellaneous deduction. For example, if you are employed as a teacher earning $50,000 and you take courses leading to a master's degree with a tuition cost of $10,000, the entire cost (less 2 percent of adjusted gross income) can be deducted. In this example, 2 percent of $50,000 is $1000, so $10,000 – $1000, or $9000, can be deducted. Assuming a 27 percent federal income tax bracket, taxes are reduced by $2430.

Now, what if the employment is not related to the educational program or you're in a much lower tax bracket? Remember the Lifetime Learning Credit from Chapter 6? You're still eligible even in graduate school. The Lifetime Learning Credit pays up to $2000 (20 percent of up to $10,000 of educational expenses). Even those expenses paid for with borrowed money are eligible. However, expenses paid for with proceeds from a 529 or Coverdell ESA are not eligible for the tax credit. As a reminder, eligibility for the credit phases out between $40,000 and $50,000 of adjusted gross income for single tax-payers ($80,000–$100,000 for joint returns).

Merit Aid

Depending on the specific graduate program, there may be merit aid available. Usually the best resources to find these programs are at the graduate or professional school that will be attended as well as the school the student attended as an undergraduate. Don't just stop at the financial aid office though. Sometimes the career development office may be plugged in to some opportunities for graduate merit aid.

In addition, it's not a bad idea to check out some of the federal aid programs that might be available. One Web site that may be helpful is www.students.gov. This is a general Web site, but it has links to some of the federal programs that provide aid to graduate students.

Military Aid

Also, don't forget about some of the options (mentioned in the previous chapter) the military offers for those who are already college graduates. This includes up to $65,000 in loan repayments over a three-year period. There are additional benefits for those who have training in the legal and health care professions.

Saving

After investigating all the need-based aid, merit-based aid, and loan programs, it will probably be clear that there is still no substitute for saving for graduate school. Most of the same savings vehicles that were useful for undergraduate education can also be used for graduate work. Additional funds can be placed in a 529 savings plan, in Coverdell ESAs, or in other financial instruments such as mutual funds.

As I described before, saving additional funds through the years leading up to college may somewhat reduce the amount of financial aid that is available during the undergraduate years, but provides tremendous flexibility and benefits in the long run if substantial borrowing can be avoided.

Since most financial aid for graduate school is based on the assumption that the student is independent, there usually will be no further reduction in need-based aid if the parents happen to have additional funds saved for graduate school.

CHAPTER 11

A College Saving Guide for Students and Their Grandparents

So far, most of this book has been oriented toward parents who are saving for their children's college education. However, it may take more than just the parents' funding to make a college education a reality. Depending on family circumstances, grandparents and the students themselves may have some role in providing education funding.

The Grandparents' Role

Grandparents can play a unique role in providing for their grandchildren's education. When a new grandchild is born, it may be that the grandparents are better off financially than the parents. Often at this stage, grandparents are well established in their jobs and may have substantial home equity or savings. *Provided retirement savings are not being compromised*, there may be funds available for future educational savings. Putting money away years before the child is ready for school is an opportunity to buy an education at a discount instead of paying future higher prices and paying interest for years on top of those higher prices.

The question is how to best provide for the child and avoid pit-falls. There is, of course, no perfect solution. Some grandparents decide that the best approach is to save money under their own name, and when the time comes to pay the bill at the college, they pay the college directly. There is some advantage to this since the payment of tuition is a specific exclusion to the gift tax laws. In other words, if you pay $24,000 of tuition for your grandchild, it does not constitute a taxable gift and is not subject to the $11,000 gift tax limitation. The other advantage is that there is not likely to be any financial aid impact. Any assets that have been set aside would be in the grandparents' name and as such, are not usually part of the financial aid calculation (provided the grandparents are not currently serving as the custodial parents).

There is one problem with this simple approach. If at the outset, the grandparents announce that "We'll be paying for college, just send us the bill," it's entirely possible that some event such as death, illness, divorce, or financial difficulties makes fulfillment of the pledge impossible. This may be a great way of going about things if a grandchild is already in college and there are insufficient savings to pay the expenses. However, for a young child who is many years away from college, some precautions should be taken to ensure that there would be sufficient funds to pay for school.

If the goal is to keep the funds in the grandparents' name until the child is in college, then some provision should be made to address some of the things that can go wrong with that plan. The grandparents should consider providing for the grandchild in their will or purchasing life insurance with the grandchild as a beneficiary. In addition, the grandparents should consider protecting their assets with a long-term care insurance policy.

The life insurance option may make sense if a grandparent is in very good health and can qualify for preferred rates. For example, a very healthy, nonsmoking male 60-year-old grandparent can insure himself for $100,000, for an annual premium of about $900. That premium would be unchanged for up to 20 years. When it comes time for college, the grandparent can discontinue the premiums and start paying for college. However, if the grandparent dies before college begins then there is the assurance that the funds are available for education.

The option of using life insurance makes the most sense when the grandparents are gradually saving for their grandchildren under their own name. The insurance policy helps assure that the savings plan will ultimately be completed.

If, on the other hand, the grandparents already have sufficient assets in place to send a child to college, life insurance may not be necessary. Instead, all that is needed is to make sure that the child is provided for in the grandparents' will and that there is sufficient long term care insurance. The grandparents may still want to keep these assets in their own name because they want to have those assets continue to generate income for them. It may also be that these assets have substantial long-term capital gains and that the best thing from a financial planning standpoint is to leave the ownership intact so that the heirs can benefit from a "step-up" in cost basis when they are inherited.

In most situations, however, a simpler approach is all that is needed. Grandparents, too, can set up 529 savings plans for their grandchildren. While contributing to a 529 doesn't have the same advantage of unlimited gift and estate tax exclusion that a direct payment to a college has, there are significant advantages to using a 529 savings plan. For example, a contribution to a 529 savings plan is considered a completed gift to the beneficiary for estate tax purposes. Thus, if a grandparent sets aside $100,000 in his or her own name for a grandchild and then dies before the grandchild goes to college, the $100,000 would be part of the grandparent's estate and could be taxable. However, if the $100,000 were contributed to a 529 savings plan, those funds would be outside the estate.

Grandparents can contribute up to $11,000 each per year for each grandchild. In other words, a grandmother and grandfather with two grandchildren can contribute up to $44,000 per year without incurring any gift tax liability. In order to do this, the grandmother would set up a 529 savings plan for each grandchild and the grandfather could set up an account for each grandchild as well. Also, each grandparent can contribute up to $55,000 in a single year for each beneficiary, and elect that the gift occurred over a five-year period for gift tax purposes. If, however, the donor dies prior to the beginning of the fifth calendar year following the gift, the portion of the gift allocated to the years following the donor's death goes back into the donor's estate.

Grandparents who want to go beyond a contribution of $55,000 may also find favorable tax treatment. Grandparents can use a portion of their lifetime exemption from the generation-skipping transfer tax. This exemption is $1 million in 2002 and is scheduled to be increased over the next several years. Ultimately, the federal estate tax is scheduled to be eliminated by 2010. The estate tax is scheduled to reappear in 2011, but Congress may decide to make the elimination of the federal estate tax permanent. You may want to check with a tax advisor before making a gift beyond the $55,000 limits.

Don't confuse the "completed gift" rules for estate tax purposes with the idea that depositing money into a 529 savings plan represents an irrevocable gift. It does not. Grandparents can still maintain control over the funds and can retrieve the funds if the need occurs. There will be taxes and penalties if a nonqualified withdrawal is made, but those taxes and penalties will be assessed only on the accumulated earnings, not on the original contributed principal.

As a result of the "control issue," grandparents contributing to a 529 savings plan should also consider long-term care insurance to protect against at least one type of major unforeseen expense. Without such coverage, it's entirely possible that the money put away into a 529 savings plan would become part of the donor's asset base when it comes time to pay for assisted living or nursing home care.

An alternative approach is to make an irrevocable gift to the child through a Uniform Gift to Minors Act/ Uniform Transfer to Minors Act account. The grandparent as the donor can still guide the investments and not worry that because of unforeseen circumstances the funds never reach the intended child. However, the disadvantage is that these funds will then be assessed for financial aid purposes later on. The other perhaps larger disadvantage is that the funds don't necessarily have to be used for education. When the grandchild becomes an adult, he or she will have full discretion over the funds and that discretion may not include spending the funds on college.

There is no perfect solution. However, the best solutions usually include when possible, a frank and open discussion between the student's grandparents, parents, and if old enough, the student as well.

The Student's Role

Up to now we haven't mentioned the role the student plays in providing the best possible education for himself or herself at a reasonable out-of-pocket cost to his or her family. The student might be asking at this point, what can I do? I can't save $100,000 for school, that's up to my parents. Well maybe you can't save a substantial sum, but that doesn't mean you have no role.

First and foremost, the student's responsibility is to get the best possible grades in line with his or her capabilities. In addition, the student needs to take advantage of as many extracurricular and community activities as possible, and on a leadership level if possible. This doesn't mean that the student has to be captain of the football team and editor of the school newspaper at the same time. However, if you're hanging out or watching TV every day after school maybe you should consider one of the clubs or teams your school offers. Not for you? Then how about getting involved in some community group? Perhaps a local hospital, community center, food pantry, or soup kitchen needs help. Maybe your clergyman has some ideas in this regard. Still not interested? If you're old enough, maybe a part-time job is for you? Getting the best possible grades and being active in *something* leads to the highest probability that you will have an assortment of possibilities when it comes time to apply to college and you and your family will have the opportunity to compare various schools with various costs.

Consider taking advanced placement or international baccalaureate programs if they are available. They can give you college-level credit. This credit can be used to take higher-level classes and in some cases can lead to an earlier graduation, which at some schools can significantly lower the cost of college. While an early graduation is not the most common outcome, just taking such advanced courses is likely to help you gain more college acceptances and give you a wider array of college choices.

Be realistic when choosing a college. When you're in college, do what you can to graduate from college in four years instead of five or six.

Apply for scholarships. Ask your guidance counselor, as well as contacts you may have in any athletic, community, religious, or fraternal groups that you're involved in for all such information. Also take a look at Internet scholarship sites. Sites include www. fastweb.com, www.finaid.org, www.collegeboard.com, and www. scholarships.salliemae.com.

Save your best schoolwork—you may need it to help you with college or scholarship applications.

Save money where ever you can: Are there things you can do without in high school in order to reduce the amount you might have pay in student loans when you're in your thirties?

Consider a part-time job. Not only can the extra money help with college expenses, some of the experiences that you have while working can provide interesting material for your college essay. Keep in mind, that tax rates are usually much lower for students than they are for parents. As a result, students get to keep much more of their income than their parents would. On the other hand, also keep in mind that income earned by the student will have an impact on financial aid calculations.

A part-time job may have other benefits. Some employers even have scholarship programs for their teenage workers. For example, McDonald's Corporation offers a $1000 scholarship to an outstanding employee in each state who is also a high school senior and works at least 15 hours per week. Some McDonald's owner-operators have supplemental scholarship programs. One employee in the United States will get the "McScholar of the year" award, which includes a $5000 scholarship.

CHAPTER 12

College Rebates

O ver the past few years, you may have seen various offers that say you can earn thousands of dollars toward college savings by doing nothing more than buying many of the same brand-name products and shopping in many of the same stores that you already may be patronizing. Does this sound too good to be true? We'll take a closer look.

While there have been several educational rebate offers that have popped up over the last few years the two that have received the most attention have been Upromise and Babymint. A third program, edexpress, is also in operation but has gained somewhat less attention. While there are operational differences between the three programs, the essence is the same. Each program has lists of participating merchants, service providers, and products that have partnered with these firms. If you make one of these purchases, you receive a rebate in your account.

For example, at Upromise if you buy a new General Motors vehicle, you can register the VIN (vehicle identification number) on the Upromise Web site and you will be credited with $150. Sell your home using a Century 21, Coldwell Banker, or ERA office and collect 0.33 percent of the purchase price. The sale of a $300,000 home can net you $1000. However, these transactions are few and far between. More commonly, buy 15 gallons of regular gasoline at a Mobil or Exxon station and $0.15 is on its way to your account. Spend $20 on office supplies at Staples and you'll get $0.40.

At Babymint, you can get 5 percent rebates on your purchases at such major retailers as the Gap and Macy's. You can also get rebates on such services as Tru-Green Chemlawn, and Merry Maids.

Both Babymint and Upromise also offer a no-fee credit card that rebates 1 percent of your purchases back to you. Babymint offers a card issued by MBNA America, while Upromise has a card issued by Citibank. There is no current credit card arrangement with edexpress.

How the Rebates Work

Why are Babymint, Upromise, and edexpress willing to just give my family money for college? There must be some catch. The catch is that the companies that have partnered with Babymint and Upromise are putting up the cash in the hope that you will know that you can get a rebate from a particular partner and incorporate that into your buying decision. In essence, Bed Bath and Beyond, or Exxon Mobil hope that you will divert more of your purchases to them and become a more loyal customer. In effect, they're willing to pay to buy some customer loyalty.

All three programs start with an online registration. For Upromise, the Web address is www.upromise.com. For Babymint, it's www.babymint.com. Edexpress is at www.edexpress.com. After the initial registration, the programs are a bit different.

Upromise

After you've registered online, you register your credit card. Upromise is then able to access your credit card account and figure out whether you've made an eligible purchase. Participating merchants include Circuit City, Staples, Exxon Mobil, and Lands' End. In addition, a variety of regional supermarket and drug store chains participate in the program. In that case, you register the supermarket's frequent purchase card and when an eligible item is purchased in the supermarket or drug store you get a rebate.

Upromise has also signed up hundreds of restaurants around the country to participate in the plan. You look up the area in which you live on the Upromise Web site and get a list of restaurants in your area.

Not every participating restaurant offers a rebate every night of the week, so you need to check the listings. When you visit a participating restaurant, all you have to do is pay the bill with your registered credit card and a 10 percent rebate will be credited to your Upromise account.

As your rebates grow, Upromise asks you to designate a student beneficiary of the rebates. The rebates are then held in an account run by Upromise Investments, a registered broker-dealer. Ultimately you are encouraged (but not required) to open a 529 plan account with a participating operator of 529 savings plans. The lineup of participating managers has changed over time. Currently, the plans available for use with Upromise are: Citigroup Global Markets, which operates plans in Colorado and Illinois; New York Life, which operates the CollegeSense plan with Schoolhouse Capital in New Mexico; Vanguard, which operates a plan in Nevada; or Upromise itself, which also operates a plan in Nevada (in conjunction with Vanguard and Strong). Starting in November 2003, Upromise will become the new program manager of the 529 savings plan in New York (with Vanguard and Columbia Management). One caution, however, if you are going to open a 529 savings plan only to be a repository for Upromise rebates, each plan with the exception of the Illinois Bright Start plan and the Nevada Vanguard plan (for accounts over $3000) charge an annual fee that can wipe out a significant portion of the rebates. Normally after the 529 account is opened, rebates are added to your account quarterly once they reach a certain amount (usually $50).

Upromise doesn't heavily promote this fact, but it's possible to ask that the accrued rebates be directly sent out in the form of a check. After you make a written request, with a signature guaranteed by a bank, they will send you the money.

Babymint

Babymint works the same way as Upromise in that you accrue rebates from a variety of retailers. However, you accrue some of your rebates by buying gift certificates for these retailers. The list of retailers includes Gap and Macy's. There seem to be, however, fewer opportunities for large rebates such as from General Motors or Century 21/Coldwell Banker/ERA. However, if you were making a big-ticket purchase at a participating retailer, the savings could start to add up. The grocery program works a bit differently than Upromise as well. Before you go shopping you check the Babymint Web site and there are a variety of coupons available. These coupons provide a variety of savings. For example, there might be a coupon for $1 off a Healthy Choice deli item. You hand the coupon in at the store and you receive 10 cents off the item at the register. Later on, after the store sends the coupon for redemption, you get an additional $1 added to your Babymint account. There are also a variety of retailers that issue a rebate when you use the Babymint credit card for purchases. Those rebates are in addition to the 1% earned from the credit card purchases. Finally, there is an extensive list of online retailers that offer Babymint rebates when an item is purchased after using the link in the Babymint Web site.

Once the rebates are accrued at Babymint, the funds are then distributed. Because Babymint is not a bank or a broker-dealer, the funds can't be retained there. In this regard, Babymint provides a bit more flexibility, allowing members to have their rebates contributed to *any* 529 plan. In addition, through a simple checkbox, Babymint gives members the option of having the rebate sent to the member in the form of a check.

Another twist to Babymint is the relationship with Sage Scholars. If one were to sign up with Sage's 529 plan offering and then attend a select list of colleges (all private schools), Sage offers to match all of the accumulated rebates.

Edexpress

Edexpress works similarly to the other two plans, but in many cases the rebate levels are slightly higher. However, a $24.95 annual fee may offset some of that benefit. The fee can be deducted monthly from your rebates at $2.08 per month. According to the edexpress Web site, the fee is risk-free for the first year. In other words they won't deduct more than the earned rebates.

If you are a big spender at some of edexpress's partners, you may be able to offset the monthly charge. Many of the partners can also be found in the lists of Babymint or Upromise. For example, edexpress provides a 5 percent rebate on online purchases at Lands' End, while Upromise offers 3 percent. Thus, it would take at least a $104 purchase to break even on one month's fee. If you spend more, you're ahead of the game.

Edexpress then takes your rebates (called edbucks) and deposits them into a municipal bond account at a broker. The funds can be withdrawn and made payable to an educational institution or to a student lender. There may be state tax consequences to having an edexpress account since you may be getting interest on out-of-state municipal bonds. This interest is tax exempt at the federal level, but taxable at the state level. Edexpress now allows you to transfer the funds to a 529 savings plan or a Coverdell account. For most families, moving the funds to either a 529 account or Coverdell ESA is probably superior to leaving it in the muni bond account.

The Credit Cards

As mentioned earlier, both Upromise and Babymint have relationships with credit card issuers that provide 1 percent rebates on purchases. Neither card has a fee, but both have a limit on the maximum rebate that can be received per year. In both cases, you can't get more than a $300 rebate per year. That translates into a maximum of $30,000 of eligible spending on the card.

The Significance of the Rebates

While some families might accumulate thousands of dollars over a decade using these rebate plans, the average family will probably find their savings to be substantially less. I'm currently a member of both Upromise and Babymint. Over the course of a year, I was able to accumulate about $200 in my Upromise account. Of that sum $150 came from the purchase of a GM vehicle and $14 came from a rebate at a restaurant where my son had a birthday party. It takes a long time to accumulate anything substantial when you're getting individual rebates of 10 and 20 cents.

Still, there's no charge to join Babymint or Upromise, and getting something is better than getting nothing. If one were to join both programs and sign up for the rebate credit cards and accumulate $500 a year in rebates, that's not bad. If you were to place that $500 in to a 529 savings plan account each year for 15 years and get an 8 percent annual return, you would end up with over $13,500. That won't pay for an entire college education, but it could represent a substantial supplement to your other savings.

One caution is in order here. These rebate programs can be helpful to your college savings plan as long as you're getting rebates on items you would have bought anyway. It's counterproductive if you are spending more to get the rebate. If you can avoid the purchase altogether and save the proceeds for education, you've helped your cause more than any rebate possibly could.

Participants at Upromise

In order to receive these rebates you must either register your credit card, supermarket card, or order online through the Upromise Web site. Some offers have special conditions. See the Upromise Web site for further details.

Grocery, Services, Stores, and Restaurants

1-800-FLOWERS.COM 3.5%
AAMCO Transmissions 5%
Accent 3%
ADT $1 per month
AIR WICK by WIZARD 3%
American AAdvantage $50
Anthony's 3%
Aquafresh 5%
AT&T 4%
Auto Driveaway Co. 5%
Avis 5%
Bed Bath & Beyond 2%
BIC 3%
Caltrate 3%

Cascade Complete 4%
Other Cascade Products 3%
Cendant Mortgage $300
All Centrum 3%
Century 21 1/3% up to $3000
Century 21 Mortgage $300
Circuit City 2%
Citi 1%
Coca-Cola Soft Drinks 1%
Coldwell Banker 1/3% Up to
     $3000
Coldwell Banker Mortgage $300
Colorific 3%
Cottonelle 5%
Countrywide Home Loans 0.2%
Dean Dips 3%

Depend 3%
Disney Hundred Acre Wood 1%
Disney Xtreme! Coolers 1%
Eggo 3%
ERA Mortgage $300
ERA Real Estate 1/3% up to
    $3000
Expo 3%
Exxon 1 cent per gallon
First Warranty Group 7%
Fisher Chef's Naturals
    Ingredient Nuts 3%
Fisher Snack Nuts 3%
Fisher Snack Mixes 3%
All Funny Bagels Combination
    Lunches 3%
Fujifilm 3%
Garelick Farms 4%
General Motors $150
Glad 3%
Glass Plus 3%
GM Motor Club $5
GoodNites 3%
Gorton's Seafood 3%
Huggies 3%
Keebler Cookies 3%
Keebler Crackers 3%
    & Ice Cream Cones 3%
Kellogg's Cereals 3%
Kellogg's Snacks 3%
KitchenAid $15
Kleenex 5%
Kotex 5%
Lehigh Valley Dairies 3%
Liquid Paper 3%
Lysol 3%
Maaco 4%

McDonald's 3%
Marie's Dips 3%
Marie's Salad Dressing 3%
Minute Maid Beverages 1%%
Mobil 1 cent per gallon
Monro Muffler/Brake &Service
    10%
Mrs. Grass 3%
Mueller's 3%
Murray Cookies 3%
The Neat Sheet Ground Cover
    3%
Nestle Ice Cream Bars
    & Frozen Novelties 3%
New York Life Insurance $25
    or $40
Pennsylvania Dutch 3%
Olay 3%
Old English 3%
Old Spice 3%
PaperMate 3%
Pep Boys 4%
Poise 3%
Polident 5%
Pop-Tarts 3%
Pull-Ups 3%
all R&F 3%
all Ronco 3%
Safelite AutoGlass 4%
Scott 5%
Sensodyne 5%
The Sharper Image 5%
SkippyPeanut Butter 3%
Speedy Auto Service 10%
Spiegel 5%
Staples 2%
Sunshine Crackers 3%

Snyder's of Hanover 3%
Spray N Wash 3%
Super PoliGrip 5%
Terminix 4%
Tide 3%
Tylenol 4%
Viva 5%
Warranty Gold 3%
Welch's Fruit Spreads 4%
Whirlpool $5-$35
Zest 3%

Online Companies

1-800 CONTACTS 3%
1-800-FLOWERS.COM 3.5%
Ann Taylor 3%
ashford.com 4%
Avis 5%
Avon.com 5%
babygap.com 3%
TheBabyOutlet 4%
Bass Pro Shops 2%
bedbathandbeyond.com 2%
BIGDOGS.com 5%
Blair 5%
Blair Clearance 5%
blue nile 3%
Bluelight.com 2%
Bose 2%
Brylane Home 3%
Buy.com 2%
Cabelas.com
CATHERINES 3%
Chadwick's of Boston 3%
Chef's 5%
Childcraft 3%

Circuit City 2%
Coldwater Creek 3%
Collectibles Today 6%
The Container Store 3%
Cooking.com 5%
Crayola.com
Critics Choice Video 5%
David's Cookies 10%
Day-Timer 3%
Delias.com 3%
Dell.com 2%
Discovery Store 3%
DisneyStore.com 4%
Domestications 4%
Duncraft 5%
DunhamsSports.com 2%
eBags.com 3%
Eddie Bauer 3%
Eddie Bauer Outlet 2%
Elisabeth by Liz Claiborne 4%
eToys.com
Expedia 1%
Famous Footwear 5%
Fannie May Candies 4%
Fossil Watches 10%
FragrenceNet.com 5%
frenchtoast.com 3%
gap.com 3%
gapkids.com 3%
gapmaternity.com 3%
Gardener's Supply Company 5%
Garnet Hill 4%
Gateway.com 2%
GiftBaskets.com 7%
GiftCertificates.com 4%
The Golf Warehouse 3%

H2O+ 4%
H&R Block 10%
Hallmark Flowers 7%
Handspring 3%
Harry and David 5%
HearthSong 5%
Hickory Farms 5%
The Home Marketplace 8%
Horchow 3%
Hotwire 1%
HSN 3%
Ice.com 4%
Illuminations 4%
Jackson & Perkins 5%
JC Penney 3%
JCrew.com 2%
Jessica London 3%
jjill.com 3%
Johnston & Murphy 4%
Joann.com 4%
Jos. A. Bank 4%
KaBloom 3.5%
Kaplan Test Prep 2%
Kbtoys.com 3%
King Size Direct 3%
Kohl's 2%
Lane Bryant 3%
LeapsAndBounds 5%
Lerner Catalog 3%
Lids.com 6%
Lilian Vernon 3.5%
L.L.Bean $3 per order
Lands' End 3%
Lands' End Overstock 3%
Magazines.com 25%
Magellan's 5%

MarthaStewart.com 3%
Microsoft 5%
Mikasa 2%
MrsFieldsCookies.com 4%
The New York Times $10 per
    subscription
Neiman Marcus 3%
Newport News 3%
Niketown.com 3%
Nordstrom.com 3%
oldnavy.com 3%
Omaha Steaks 5%
OneHanesPlace 3%
OneStepAhead 5%
Oreck 4%
Oriental Trading Company 3%
Orvis 6%
OshKosh B'Gosh 5%
Oshmans.com 2%
Overstock.com 4%
Overtons.com 2%
PacSun 4%
Palm Store 3%
Paul Fredrick 6%
Patagonia 5%
Payless Shoe Source 3%
PC Connection 2%
Performance Bike 3%
Personal Creations 4%
PETsMART.com 5%
Priceline.com 2%
QVC.com 3%
RedEnvelope 3.5%
REI.com 3%
REI-Outlet.com 3%
Road Runner Sports 3%

Roaman's 3%

Ross-Simons 3%

Scholastic $6.50 per order

Scholastic Store 3%

Sephora.com 3%

The Sharper Image 5%

Shoes.com 6%

SierraTradingPost 3%

SmartBargains 4%

Smith + Noble 4%

Spiegel.com 5%

TheSportsAuthority.com 2%

Staples.com 2%

Sunglass Hut 3%

Things Remembered 3%

Tom's of Maine 4%

Tupperware 5%

ULTA.com 3%

USA Today $10 per subscription

ValueMags.com 25%

VitaminShoppe.com 5%

Walmart.com 2%

West Marine 2%

White Flower Farm 6%

Wilsons Leather 3%

Woolrich 3%

Yankee Candle 4%

Participants at Babymint

Online Companies

1-800 Contacts 4%

1-800-Flowers.com 7.0%

A Pea in the Pod 4%

Activa Sports 5%

Adidas 5%

Aerosoles 3%

Allergy Buyers 3%

Ashford.com 5%

Atlanta Falcons Online Store 2%

Avenue.com 4%

Avon 5%

Azzurra Cellulite Treatment 6%

Baby Songs Videos & Audios 6%

BabyAge.com 4%

BabyCenter.com 5%

BabyGap 3%

babystyle—baby 5%

babystyle—maternity 5%

Barnes & Noble.com 3%

Bass Pro Shops 4%

BestBuy.com 1%

BigDogs.com 6%

Blair 6%

Blindsgalore 4%

BlueDolphin.com 25%

BODEGA Fudge & Chocolates, Inc. 10%

Bose 2%

Brooks Brothers 3%

Brookstone.com 2%

Brylane Home 4%

Brylane Kitchen 3%

Business Cards 2%

Buy.com 1%

CallingCards.com 5%

Chadwick's of Boston 3%

CheapAirlines.com $4

CHEF'S 4%
ChildCraft 4%
ColdWater Creek 5%
Collectibles Today 7.0%
CompUSA 2%
Computers4sure 2%
Cooking.com 5%
CornerHardware.com 2%
Crayola.com 4%
David's Cookies 4%
Day-Timer 4%
Dell Business 2%
Dell Home Systems 1%
Delta Air Lines $2
DERMAdoctor.com 4%
DiabetesStore.com 4%
Diamond.com 4%
Disney Store 4%
Dollar Rent A Car 3%
Domestications 5%
DrugStore.com 6%
DVDPlanet 3%
eBags 6%
EddieBauer.com 4%
EddieBauer.com—Home 4%
EddieBauer.com—Women's 4%
EddieBauerOutlet.com 4%
Edwin Watts Golf 3%
Enterprise Rent-A-Car 1%
Equifax Consumer Services 10%
Expedia.com $1
Florist.com 10%
Floweria.com 8%
Flying Noodle 6%
Fossil 11%
FragranceNet.com 6%

Frames Direct & Contacts 4%
FranklinCovey.com 5%
FrenchToast.com 4%
FTD.COM 4%
Gap.com 3%
Gap.com 3%
GapKids 3%
GapMaternity 3%
Gardener's Supply Company 6%
Gateway 1%
GiftBaskets.com 8%
Giftwrap.com 10%
Golfsmith.com 3%
GoodGuys.com 3%
GTC Telecom 5%
H&R Block 10%
Hallmark.com 8%
HammacherSchlemmer.com 6%
Handspring 3%
Harry and David 5%
Hat World Lids.com 5%
Hearthsong.com 6%
Hickory Farms 6%
Hotwire 1%
Houston Texans Online Store 2%
HSN 3%
Ice.com 6%
Illuminations.com 5%
iNest $10
InkJetUSA.com 16%
InterstateBatteries.com 4%
JCPenney.com 3%
Jessica London 3%
Jordan Marie Baby Boutique 6%
Jos. A Bank.com 4%

JustFlowers.com 9%

JustMySize.com 3%

Kaplan Test Preparation 2%

KBToys.com 3%

KingSizeDirect.com 3%

Kohls.com 2%

Lands' End 3%

LandscapeUSA.com 4%

LaneBryant 4%

Leaps and Bounds 4%

Lensmart 5%

Lillian Vernon Online 4%

Limoges Jewelry 6%

Linenplace.com 7.0%

Linens 'n Things 3%

LL Bean $3

M&M's Colorworks 5%

magazines.com—children's 25%

magazines.com—men's 25%

magazines.com—women's 25%

Marshall Field's Direct 3%

Martha Stewart 3%

Microsoft 6%

MiMi Maternity 4%

MLB.com 5%

Motherwear 4%

Motorola 4%

Mrs. Fields Original Cookies, Inc 4%

MusicSpace.com—50's and 60's 4%

MusicSpace.com—70's 4%

MusicSpace.com—80's 4%

MusicSpace.com—90s 4%

Name It Golf 3%

National Pet Pharmacy 4%

NetFlix $6

Nickelodeon Store 3%

Nordstrom.com 3%

Northern Tool and Equipment 3%

OfficeDepot.com 2%

OfficeMax.com 2%

OldNavy.com 3%

OmahaSteaks.com, Inc. 5%

OneHanesPlace.com 3%

OneShare.com $5

OneStepAhead 4%

OrderDSL.net $25

Oreck.com 4%

Oriental Trading Co 4%

Orvis 7.0%

OshKosh B'Gosh 5%

Oshmans.com 3%

Overstock.com, Inc. 4%

Pacific Sunwear 5%

Palm 4%

PartsAmerica.com 5%

Performance Products 5%

Perfumania 5%

Pet Food Direct.com 4%

Petco 4%

PetSmart.com 6%

Priceline.com 1%

Prime Wine 5%

RadioShack 3%

Radisson Hotels & Resorts 1%

Real Goods 4%

RedEnvelope 7.0%

Reebok 3%

REI 3%

REI-Outlet.com—Men's 3%

REI-Outlet.com—Women's 3%
Relax The Back 3%
Road Runner Sports 5%
Roaman's 4%
Ross-Simons 4%
RX-web.com 6%
SeaBear Smokehouse 4%
Sears Home Center 4%
Sears Room for Kids 4%
Sears ShowPlace 4%
Sephora.com, Inc. 4%
Shoes.com 7.0%
Sierra Trading Post 5%
SimplyWireless.com $20
Smart Bargains 3%
SnoopyStore.com 6%
Sony Music Direct 5%
Sony Style Stores 2%
SpaFinder.com 4%
SpaWish 4%
Springhill Nursery 8%
Standard Deviants 10%
Sunglass Hut and Watch Station 4%
SunnyCell.com 9%
T-Mobile $25
Target 3%
The Container Store 4%
The Golf Warehouse 3%
The New York Times $15
The Tire Rack 3%
The Vermont Country Store 5%
The Wine Messenger 5%
TheBabyOutlet 4%
TheSportsAuthority.com 3%
Tiger Direct 2%

Tom's of Maine 5%
ToolKing.com 4%
Travelocity.com $1
Tupperware.com, Inc. 5%
Upper Deck Sports Memorabilia 7.0%
USA Today $9
ValueMags.com 20%
Verizon Online DSL $30
Verizon Wireless $5
Vermont Teddy Bear Co. 5%
VitaCost.com 5%
VitaminShoppe.com 6%
Waddell & Reed Inc.
Wall Street Journal 40%
Walmart—Electronics 3%
Walmart—Grills 3%
Western Union $3
World of Watches 4%
Yankee Candle 5%

The following companies offer 5 percent rebates when gift certificates are purchased through Babymint (check the Babymint Web site for details):

Amazon.com 5%
AMC Theaters 5%
American Home Shield 5%
BabyGap 5%
Blockbuster Video 5%
FurnitureMedic 5%
Gap 5%
GiftCertificates.com Super Certificates 5%

Jiffy Lube 5%

Loews Cineplex 5%

Macy's 5%

Merry Maids 5%

Olive Garden® 5%

Pegnato & Pegnato 5%

Red Lobster 5%

Regal Cinemas 5%

Rescue Rooter 5%

ServiceMasterClean 5%

Starbucks 5%

Terminix 5%

TruGreen ChemLawn 5%

Universal Gift Certificate 5%

Participants at edexpress

The following companies participate in edexpress. Some rebates are accessed through your registered credit card; other rebates are accessed through online shopping through the edexpress Web site. More details are available on the edexpress Web site.

00inkjets.com 30%

1-800-FLOWERS.COM 8%

1-800-Patches, Inc. 10%

1-800-Petmeds 9%

123lasertoner 20%

123Posters.com 18%

800Wine.com 8%

A Trendy Home 8%

A&E/The History Channel 10%

AAA Balloons 18%

AAA Fruit Baskets 15%

Aaron Baby Basket 13%

ABirdsWorld.com 10%

Abundant Earth 8%

Academic Superstore 5%

Adagio Teas 10%

AKA Gourmet 12%

Alexblake.com 10%

Alibris 7%

All Together Leather 7%

All WineBaskets 8%

All Worth Press 15%

Allergy Be Gone 8%

Allergy Control Begins at Home 10%

Almond Plaza 7%

Altrec.com Outdoors 7%

Andante 7%

Applian Technologies 20%

AreYouGame.com 7%

Art & Artifact 7%

Art From Montana LLC 15%

ARTinaClick 15%

Ashley Skin Nutrition 15%

Atlanta Falcons 5%

Authentic Styles 6%

AutoPartsGiant.com 8%

Avon 8%

Babies Can't Read 5%

BabyBazaar.com 8%

BabyCenter,LLC 10%

Back Country 6%

Bags For Less 20%

Bare Necessities.com 8%

Bargin Outfitters 7%

Barnesandnoble.com 5%

Baseball Warehouse 8%

Bass Pro Shops 5%

Beadroom.com 10%

BeautyTrends 15%

Bellacor.com 10%

BestBuy.com 1%

Big Yank Sports 7%

BigFitness.net 7%

Bikeshop.com 1%

Binoculars.com 5%

Bissell Corporation 8%

Blair 9%

Blindsgalore 5%

bloomingblub.com 11%

Bluelight.com 3%

BODEGA Fudge & Chocolates 10%

Bodybuilding-Qfac 15%

BodyTrends 5%

Bonsai Boy of New York 5%

BookCloseouts.com 10%

BooksonTape 15%

Bose 3%

brecks 15%

Bride Name Change Kit 20%

British Food & Scottish Food Delivered Worldwide 10%

Brooks Brothers 5%

Brookstone 4%

BrushstrokesArt.com 10%

Buy.com 1%

BuyCostumes.com 6%

CallingCards 10%

Candlemart.com 15%

Candlesjustonline.com 10%

CandyWarehouse 10%

Car Toys 7%

Chadwick's of Boston 5%

CheaperThanDirt.com 5%

Chef's Catalog 5%

Children's Christian Videos, Games and Software 9%

Cinema Studio Store 10%

Classic Closouts 9%

CleanAir4Life 15%

Cobra Electronics 6%

CoffeeA.M.com 10%

Coldwater Creek 5%

Colorado Pen Company 8%

Complete Tax 20%

CompUSA 3%

Computers4SURE 3%

Consumer Direct Warehouse 5%

cooking.com 5%

CouponClearingHouse.com 10%

CrossToy.com 8%

Cutepcs.com 7%

CyberEdit and EssayEdge 20%

Cyberguys!® Program 10%

CZJewelry.com 10%

Danit's 7%

David's Cookies 8%

Day-Timer 5%

dELiA*s 5%

Dell Home Systems 1%

Denver Broncos 5%

DietPower 15%

DiningWare.com 13%

Directly Home 5%

Discount Jogging Strollers 10%

Discovery.com 8%

Disney Movie Club 5%

Disney Store 5%

Dogs Health 15%

DogToys.com 10%

Domestications 8%

E-HairLoss 25%

eBay.co.uk 4%

ECampus 5%

Eddie Bauer 6%

Efootware.com 5%

eHobbies.com 3%

ElephantBooks.com 12%

eLuxury 7%

Emode 30%

EthnicGrocer.com 10%

eToys 5%

Etronics.com 2%

Expedia.com 2%

EyeColor 7%

eyeglasses.com 8%

EZ Weightloss.com 10%

Falk Culinair Copper Cookware 10%

Femail Creations 8%

Fine Jewelers.com 8%

Florist.com 16%

Flowerfarm.com 10%

Flowers Across America 12%

Fogdog Sports 5%

Fonts.com 15%

FootAction 4%

Footsmart 8%

ForSaleByOwner.com 20%

Fossil.Com 15%

FragranceX.com 10%

Frame Place 10%

FramesDirect.com 15%

Franklin Mint 6%

FTD.COM 6%

FUGAWI 10%

Furniture Domain 10%

Furniture Online 5%

Gadget Universe.com 12%

Gaiam.com 8%

Gallery Collection by PRU 10%

Gap.com 5%

Gardener's Supply Company 8%

Gear Software 15%

genetree.com 25%

Gevalia 9%

GiftBaskets.com, Inc. 10%

GiftCertificates.com 5%

GiftTree 12%

Giftwrap.com 20%

GigaGolf.com 8%

Global Gallery 10%

GoCollect.com 12%

Goldenmine.com 10%

Goldspeed.com 7%

GoodGuys.com 5%

GTC Telecom 10%

Guiding Light Video 9%

Guild.com 10%

Gumey's Nursery 15%

Hale Indian River Groves 6%

Hallmark.com 12%

HandSpring 5%

Happy Feet 8%

Harry and David 6%

Health4her.com 10%
Healthypooch.com 12%
Heavenly Treasures 10%
Henry Fields Nursery 15%
Hickory Farms 7%
Hit Me Now.com 7%
Hobbytron.com 10%
Hollywood Mega Store 10%
Home Shopping Network 10%
HomeVisions.com 10%
HotelDiscounts.net 5%
Hotwire.com 1%
Houston Texans 5%
HRBLOCK.COM (By H&R
    Block) 7%
I See ME 10%
ICE.com Inc 8%
IceJerseys.com 6%
iGourmet.com 8%
Illuminations.com, Inc 6%
Imagine the Challenge 15%
Import Parts Bin 10%
Inkjets.com 25%
Integrity Music 10%
International Jock 8%
International Male 6%
International Star Registry 20%
Iomega 3%
irock!Digital Audio 12%
Ironman Home Gym 10%
JC Whitney .com 6%
JenniferAnn.com 15%
Jewelry Network 6%
Jewelry Spotlight 10%
Jigsaw Puzzles 25%
Joann.com 8%

Joann.com 8%
Jos. A Bank 8%
Journeys 7%
JustFlowers.com 18%
Kalyx.com 20%
Kaplan Test Prep 3%
Karate Depot 10%
Kays 4%
KBtoys.com 5%
Kitchen Etcetera 10%
Kitchen Home Gadgets 5%
Kmart.com 3%
kohls 4%
Krupps.com 13%
Lands' End Inc 5%
LaParfumerie.com 10%
Learning Strategies 10%
Leeps and Bounds 8%
Lerner 5%
Lillian Vernon 6%
Linenplace.com 11%
Linens'n Things 5%
Linguaphone 10%
Liz Claiborne 12%
Love Scent Pheromone 10%
Luggage OnLine 8%
Made in Firenze 10%
Magazine.com 30%
Magellan's 10%
McAfee 10%
MCSports.com 4%
Medifocus 5%
Merlite Jewelry 10%
MexGrocer.com 10%
Michigan Bulb 15%
Micro Warehouse,Inc. 5%

Micro Warehouse,Inc. 5%

Mikasa 4%

Modem Max 30%

MotherNature.com 12%

Multiple Trends 10%

Music123.com 5%

Nabisco Gifts 10%

Natural Golf 10%

Net Nanny 12%

net2phone 10%

New Line Cinema 10%

NewBargins.com 10%

Newport News 5%

NGA Garden Shop 10%

Nickelodeon Store 6%

Nirvana Chocolates 10%

Nisim International 25%

Nutri Systems 15%

NutriCounter.com 25%

Office Depot, Inc 2%

OfficeMax.com 6%

Oldnavy.com 4%

Omaha Steaks 7%

One Great Family.com 20%

One Step Ahead 8%

Oriental Trading Co. 5%

Orvis 12%

OshKoshB'Gosh 7%

Oshmans.com 7%

OutdoorDecor.com 15%

Overtons 4%

Pacific Sunwear 5%

Palm 5%

Pargolfgear.com 10%

Parts Express 7%

Peepers.com 5%

Performance Bicycle 5%

Perfumania 1%

Perfumes America 10%

Personal Creations 8%

Personalized Golf 6%

Petfooddirect.com 8%

Petscriptions.com 7%

Pfaelzer Brothers 7%

PhoneShark.com 15%

Pinatas.com 15%

Playcentric 5%

PokeOrder 5%

Pop's Unfinsihed Furniture 3%

Posters Now 21%

Power-Glide 30%

Prime Wine 10%

PrintPal 20%

ProSports 10%

Quadratec Inc. 5%

Raffaello Ties 12%

Red Wagons 5%

RedEnvelope 8%

Reeds Jewelers 7%

REI 5%

Relax the Back 5%

Ringos Leather 8%

Road Runner Sports 10%

Robeez 8%

Rochester Big &Tall 7%

Rooms to Go 2%

Rooms to Go Kids 2%

Ross-Simons 5%

Rugman 12%

RugsUSA.com 10%

SafetyZone.com 5%

San Diego Chargers 5%

Scholarship Experts 10%

SeaBear Smokehouse 8%

Sears Home Center 7%

Sears Room for Kids 7%

Sears Show Place 7%

Securitall.com 10%

Select Comfort 5%

Selfhelpworks 20%

Sensational Beginnings 6%

Sephora 5%

Sharper Image 10%

Shindigz 10%

Shoes.com 10%

Shop At Home 30%

Sierra Club 15%

Sierra Trading Post 5%

Silhouettes 6%

Simply Dresses 7%

SitStay.com 10%

SizeAppeal 10%

Smallflower 10%

Smart Home 8%

SmartBargains 8%

Smarter Kids 6%

SmoothFitness.com 7%

SnoreMD 10%

SoftMoc 13%

Softwarefirst.com 7%

Sony Music Direct 10%

Sony Style Stores 2%

Sovietski Collections 15%

SpaWish.com 6%

Spiegel 5%

Spilsbury.com 10%

Sports Jewelry Super Store 6%

Sportsman's Guide 7%

Springhill Nursery 15%

StacksandStacks 7%

Stonewall Kitchen 8%

Stress Less 12%

SunWear 7%

Superfabulous 5%

Sure Fit Slipcovers 10%

T.Shipley 10%

Tabasco Store 12%

TackleDirect 6%

Target 6%

Teacher Created Materials 10%

Team Store 7%

terrysvillage.com 5%

Teva 7%

textbookx.com 5%

Textileshop 10%

The Company Store 5%

The Eastwood Company 6%

The Golf Channel Store 5%

The Golf Warehouse 5%

The Home Marketplace 15%

The Internet's Flooring Store 3%

The Kids Window 8%

The Lighter Side Co. 10%

The Popcorn Factory 12%

The SkinStore,Inc. 12%

The Space Store 7%

The Sports Authority 7%

The Wall Street Journal 15%

The Wine Messenger 10%

The Wright Stuff 10%

TheBabyOutlet 8%

Things From Another World 7%

Things Remembered 6%

TinyMonkey cards 10%

TodoFut Soccer 10%

Tom's of Maine 8%

Tool King 10%

Total Campus 5%

TotalOfficeSupply 5%

Tower Records 4%

Travelocity.com 1%

Tupperware 7%

Tweeter.com 3%

Ulla Popken Limited Partners 10%

Ulta.com 10%

Ultra Hair Away 15%

Undergear.com 8%

Unitedshades.com 10%

Universal Gear 7%

Vacuumcleanersetc 5%

ValueMags 30%

ValueZone.com 10%

Vapir 15%

Vikingop.com 3%

VitaCost.com 10%

VitaminLab.com 5%

VitaminShoppe.com 10%

Walmart.com 5%

Walter Drake 15%

Warner Bros 10%

Warner Bros 10%

Weather Affects 10%

Webclothes.com 8%

What on Earth Catalog 7%

Wicks End 5%

Wide Awake Coffee 5%

Widerview Village 5%

Willygoat Toyland 4%

Wilson Leather 5%

Wind & Weather Catalog 12%

Windowbox.com 12%

Wine Messenger 10%

wine.com 6%

WineAccents.com 10%

Wonderfulbuys.com 5%

WonderfullyWacky.com 10%

Woolrich 6%

Yves Rocher 15%

Zappos.com 15%

ZapTel 20%

zChocolate.com 20%

Zirh Skin Nutrition 12%

Zoobooks 8%

CHAPTER 13

A Closer Look at Six 529 Plans

I'll approach the next-to-last chapter of this book by taking an in-depth look at six popular 529 plans. In Chapter 14, we'll incorporate some of those plans into a cohesive college savings plan taking into consideration taxes, financial aid, and investment risk.

First, Table 13-1 shows performance figures for the first five plans that we'll be discussing in this chapter. In each case, the table shows 2002 returns for an allocation designed for a two-year-old child born in

TABLE 13-1. Managed Allocation Returns (2002)	
New York's College Savings Plan	−16.5 percent
Bright Start Savings (Illinois)	−18.4 percent
College America (Virginia)	−11.4 percent*
	−16.1 percent*
	(after sales charges)
College Savings Plan of Nebraska	−20.7 percent
	(aggressive allocation)
	−16.1 percent*
Unique College Investing Plan (New Hampshire)	−18.2 percent
	(portfolio 2018)

Note: Not surprisingly, each of these plans reported a negative return for 2002. However, to put this in perspective, the S&P 500 had a total return (including dividends) of −22.10 percent in 2002. Thus, all of the plans listed above provided a better return than a passive investment in the S&P 500. That's little comfort to those who watched their investment decline during 2002.

*Aggressive allocation designed by Standard & Poor's.

2000. The allocations were either the age-based allocations available in the program or a custom allocation designed by Standard and Poor's.

New York's College Savings Program

New York's 529 savings plan is currently in transition. It had been administered since 1998 by TIAA-CREF, which also operates plans located in California, Connecticut, Georgia, Idaho, Kentucky, Michigan, Minnesota, Michigan, Missouri, Oklahoma, Tennessee, and Vermont. Starting in mid-November 2003, the New York plan will be administered by Upromise Investments. The Upromise group will include investment options managed by Vanguard Group and Fleet Bank's Columbia Management Group. Most of the discussion about TIAA-CREF (except for New York tax provisions) is applicable to the 12 other state plans administered by the firm.

Regardless of the administrator used, the most notable feature of New York's plan is the tax deduction available for New York resident taxpayers. Contributions up to $5000 for an individual and contributions for joint returns up to $10,000 are deductible from income on a New York State income tax return. These deductions also apply to those New York taxpayers who are subject to local income tax (primarily residents of the City of New York or Yonkers).

Accounts can be opened by requesting an application over the phone at 1-877 NYSAVES (1-877-697-2837). You can also open an account online at www.nysaves.com. Accounts opened before mid-November 2003 can remain invested with TIAA-CREF for up to five years. However, no additional funds can be deposited after that date with TIAA-CREF. Upromise/Vanguard/Columbia would manage all new deposits. Current account holders will have the option of converting their accounts to the Vanguard or Columbia options during the five-year transition period. It is expected that the options offered by Columbia will be advisor-sold.

The TIAA-CREF plan has four primary investment options:

➤ Guaranteed option

➤ Age-based option

➤ Aggressive age-based option

➤ High equity option

The guaranteed option represents an obligation of TIAA life insurance, which guarantees the principal and a pre-established level of return. The return during 2002 was 5.2 percent. By mid 2003, that rate had declined to 3.8 percent.

The age-based option provides a blend between a TIAA-CREF Russell 3000 Equity Index Fund and a TIAA Fixed-Income Fund. The Russell 3000 contains the 3000 largest companies in the United States. This blend varies with the age of the beneficiary. Younger beneficiaries get more stocks, and as the beneficiary gets older, there is some movement into the fixed-income fund. The aggressive age-based option blends the same funds, but consistently provides a higher allocation to stocks over the years.

The high equity option provides a fully invested position (depending on market conditions). This option uses the same Russell 3000 Index Fund. An account owner could opt to make his or her own allocation between the high equity and guaranteed option. This has some merit, since the bond portion of the age-based portfolio has tended to underperform the guaranteed option, with higher volatility.

Unfortunately, the performance of the two age-based options has been abysmal over the last few years. Much of this has been because up until November 2002, TIAA-CREF opted to use a growth stock index fund instead of the current Russell 3000 fund. Going forward, the equity portion of the age-based portfolios will be more diversified. Account owners can also take a do-it-yourself approach and create a blend between the high equity and guaranteed options.

One thing that TIAA-CREF has going for it is below-average expenses. This 529 Savings plan has an 0.60 percent expense ratio. During the bidding process, New York State officials stressed that they wanted to keep expenses low. Thus, it's reasonable to expect that going forward, Upromise/Vanguard/Columbia will also have below average expenses. In Nevada, for example, the program that Upromise runs using Vanguard and Strong funds has an expense ratio of 0.65 percent plus a $20 annual fee for the passive Vanguard funds. As this book went to press, the fee arrangements in New York had not been finalized. However, press reports indicate that the Upromise/Vanguard expenses will be lower than the TIAA-CREF expenses.

The New York college savings plan has some unique provisions: First is its penalty for early withdrawals. There is a penalty of 10 percent of earnings if a withdrawal is made less than 36 months after the account has been opened. Keep in mind that the funds don't have to remain in the plan for 36 months, just that the account has been opened for that length of time. For example, if an account is opened in October of 2003, with a $25 initial deposit and $10,000 is deposited in January 2006, then a qualified withdrawal of $9000 made in December 2006 would have no penalty. That's because the account has been open more than 36 months, even though the bulk of the funds were left on deposit for less than a year.

Even after the penalty, the New York college savings plan could be a smart idea for New York residents looking for a short-term savings vehicle. For example: George and Maria live in New York City and have a daughter attending a college in Missouri. They are considering opening a CD for $10,000 paying 2.0 percent to pay their daughter's college expenses due in six months. Instead, they could deposit the funds into New York's College Savings Plan and get a tax deduction for the $10,000 deposit. Six months later, George and Maria request a qualified distribution to pay their daughter's expenses. Because this account has not been open for three years, it would be considered an early withdrawal and subject to the 10 percent earnings penalty. Assuming that George and Maria are in the 6.85 percent maximum state tax bracket, are in the 3.648 percent New York City tax bracket, and receive a return of 0.58 percent for the six months the funds were invested in the Vanguard income option, George and Maria would receive the following:

➤ A reduction of $685 on their New York State taxes,

➤ A reduction of $365 on their New York City taxes,

➤ Earnings of $58 for the six months the funds were on deposit

➤ A penalty of $5.80 for early withdrawal (10 percent of $58)

This is far superior to the $100 of taxable interest that George and Maria would have received had they opened the CD instead.

Another, less favorable provision of the New York college savings plan is the tax treatment applied to the plan if assets are rolled over to another state's plan. In late 2002, New York's Tax Department announced that starting in 2003, it would consider a transfer to another qualified tuition program as a nonqualified withdrawal for New York tax purposes. This means that the earnings portion of the distribution would be taxable by New York, and in addition, if the taxpayer took a tax deduction for the contribution, that contribution would also then be taxable by New York State upon withdrawal. This could effectively prevent a New York taxpayer from switching plans since taxes could be payable on both earnings and initial principal.

Bright Start Savings (Illinois)

This 529 savings plan is run by Citigroup Global Markets, a unit of Citigroup. The plan can be reached by phone at 877-BRIGHTSTART or online at www.brightstartsavings.com.

Bright Start offers a variety of investment options including age-based portfolio allocations, an all-equity option, a fixed-income option and a principal-protection option.

Like the New York plan described above, the Illinois Bright Start Savings plan allows for contributions deductible from Illinois state income tax. However, the marginal tax rate in Illinois is 3 percent as opposed to 6.85 percent in New York. This serves to make the tax deduction somewhat less valuable than would be the case in New York. Also, the annual expenses in this 529 savings plan total 0.99 percent, somewhat higher than New York's 0.60 percent. Does that slight difference matter? In a word, yes. As Table 13-2 demonstrates, over time, the difference in fees can completely offset the value of the Illinois state tax deduction.

If an Illinois taxpayer were to deposit $10,000 into either Bright Start or the New York college savings plan he or she would be initially ahead by using the Illinois plan. That's because Illinois provides a tax deduction for its residents while New York gives no such tax break to Illinois

TABLE 13-2. **Effect of Expenses on Returns**

Year	Bright Start with 0.99 Percent in Expenses	New York Plan with 0.60 Percent in Expenses
0	$10,200.00	$10,000.00
1	$10,711.02	$10,540.00
2	$11,247.64	$11,109.16
3	$11,811.15	$11,709.05
4	$12,402.89	$12,341.34
5	$13,024.27	$13,007.78
6	$13,676.79	$13,710.20
7	$14,362.00	$14,450.55
8	$15,081.53	$15,230.88
9	$15,837.12	$16,053.34
10	$16,630.56	$16,920.22
11	$17,463.75	$17,833.92
12	$18,338.68	$18,796.95
13	$19,257.45	$19,811.98
14	$20,222.25	$20,881.83
15	$21,235.38	$22,009.45

residents. Assume for the moment that this taxpayer would receive $300 in Illinois tax benefits for making the contribution, but because this same taxpayer itemizes his or her deductions at the federal level, there is an increase in federal taxes. Let's assume that on a net basis, the deduction is worth $200 to the taxpayer. So, on the day the contribution was made, the taxpayer is $200 ahead with Bright Start. If both the New York college savings plan and Bright Start manage to earn 6.0 percent per year before expenses, look at what happens: For the first eight years after the contribution was made, Bright Start stays ahead. In year nine 9 and beyond, the New York plan pulls ahead and leaves a higher ending balance. After 15 years, you would have $774 more by forgoing the tax deduction and finding a plan with lower fees.

Unfortunately, the story doesn't end there. Illinois tax law makes it more complicated than that. If you are an Illinois resident, and you invest in an out-of-state 529 plan, your earnings are taxable by the state when withdrawn. That's true even if the withdrawal was "qualified" for federal purposes. So, to continue the example above, after 15 years, the earnings the New York plan would have provided, $12,009.45 ($22,009.45 – $10,000), would be subject to the 3 percent Illinois state tax or $360.28. If, after deducting that tax on the federal return, the net cost were, say, $240, you would still be $534 ahead with the New York plan.

More important than the fees is the investment performance. At this stage, it's difficult to assess the long-term performance of most of the Bright Start equity options. Two of the funds that are used in the program, the Smith Barney Large Cap Growth and the Smith Barney Small Cap Core, were established in 1997 and 1996, respectively. However, two of the funds with 10-year performance records have done quite well. The Salomon Brothers Investors Value Fund had a 10-year return of over 11 percent annually (ending 2002). The Smith Barney Investment Grade Fund returned over 8 percent per year for the 10 years ending 2002. During 2002, most of the equity and age-based options fell significantly along with the market. It's interesting to note that when comparing the age-based portfolios at Bright Start versus the age-based portfolios at the New York College Savings Plan, during the depths of the bear market in the second quarter of 2002 there was significantly worse performance in the New York plan even though New York has a lower allocation to stocks. The difference seems to be that Salomon Smith Barney uses a variety of equity funds in its age-based allocations, while at that time, TIAA-CREF used only large-cap growth stocks (since then, TIAA-CREF switched to a broader-based index for its age-based portfolios).

In addition, the allocations to stocks in Bright Start's age-based portfolios tend to be somewhat higher than they are in New York's College Savings Program. That may help in the long run, but was a decided disadvantage during 2002. For the full year 2002, an age-based portfolio invested for a child born in 2000 was down 18.4 percent, while a portfolio invested in the New York college savings plan for the same age child declined 16.5 percent. For a child born in 1986, the Bright Start account was down 4.63 percent, while the New York plan for the same age child was up 0.5 percent.

On July 15, 2002, Bright Start replaced some of the funds that it uses. For example, Bright Start replaced the Smith Barney Large Cap Value Fund with the Salomon Brothers Investors Value Fund. In addition, the MFS Institutional International Research Equity Fund replaced the Smith Barney International All Cap Growth Portfolio. These changes were positive for historical performance. Will this help future performance? Here's what Bright Start itself says at its Web site about its performance: "In evaluating performance information, you should consider that the Bright Start program is relatively new, that the portfolio does not have a long-term operating or investment performance history and that certain of the funds have been replaced." In other words, *Who knows?*

It's significantly easier to compare the new "principal protection" option that Bright Start introduced in July of 2002 with the "guaranteed option" that the New York college savings plan offers. During the second half of 2002, the Bright Start principal protection option was paying just below 3 percent, while the guaranteed option offered in New York paid over 5 percent. During the first quarter of 2003, the New York guaranteed option rate was 3.8 percent, but this was still ahead of Bright Start. That difference very quickly overcomes any tax benefits offered in Illinois.

THE UPROMISE CONNECTION: One of the primary reasons that many families have opened Bright Start Savings accounts has been the plan's connection to Upromise. Until late 2002, Bright Start was the lowest-cost option among the various 529 savings plan programs that accepted direct contributions from the Upromise program. It's likely that Bright Start will see more competition from the plan in Nevada that Upromise is setting up itself using Vanguard Funds.

CUSTOMER SERVICE: It's possible to open a Bright Start account at an array of Illinois banks. When an account is opened in this fashion, bank deposits supplement the equity offerings in the age-based options instead of money market funds. The bank deposits also become part of the fixed-income option. It's also possible to open an account by printing out the application forms from the Internet site and then mailing them in. Bright Start will also send you an account opening kit by mail if you call their toll-free number. Unfortunately, the account opening process can't be completed online. When I attempted to open an account by mail in January 2002, it took more than a month to complete the process.

Bottom line: Bright Start is a reasonable choice for Illinois taxpayers with a short- to medium-term time horizon who want to obtain the state tax deduction. With no annual fee, Bright Start is also a reasonable choice for out-of-state residents who are looking for a repository for their Upromise contributions. However, with some of the funds lacking a 10-year performance record, it's too soon to tell how the performance of the Bright Start investment choices will compare with other actively managed fund offerings. Investors should also keep in mind that while Bright Start's expenses are competitive compared with other actively managed programs, they are still somewhat higher than many passive investment plans, such as the TIAA-CREF offerings in the New York College Savings Program.

College America (Virginia)

The College America Savings Plan is different from the New York and Illinois plans. If you are looking for a low-cost, do-it-yourself 529 savings plan, this is not the choice for you. That's because this program is sold only through brokers and advisors. Thus, this program contains a variety of sales charges that compensate the advisor who is assisting you in this process. We'll talk more about fees in a moment. For now, let's concentrate on the variety of investment alternatives and performance that is available in this program. Unlike the New York college savings plan and the Bright Start savings plan, which offer three to five different investment alternatives, the College America Savings Plan offers 21 different funds that can be built into your own customized asset allocation. Some investors may find it valuable, for example, to decide to put 57 percent into stocks when another state's age-based portfolio might be using 65 percent.

More importantly, though, the College America Savings Plan represents a bet on active management versus passive indexing. All of the funds in the plan are run by American Funds, a well-regarded organization with over $325 billion under management. One of the nicest aspects of the College America Savings Plan is its reliance on existing funds with long track records. This enables the prospective investor to look at the performance history of the funds and get an idea of both how well the funds did and how much risk was taken.

The funds available in the College America 529 Savings Plan include the following:

GROWTH FUNDS

U.S. growth
AMCAP Fund
The Growth Fund of America
The New Economy Fund

International growth
EuroPacific Growth Fund
New Perspective Fund
New World Fund
SMALLCAP World Fund

GROWTH AND INCOME FUNDS
American Mutual Fund
Capital World Growth and Income Fund
Fundamental Investors
The Investment Company of America
Washington Mutual Investors Fund

EQUITY INCOME FUNDS
Capital Income Builder
The Income Fund of America

BALANCED FUND
American Balanced Fund

BOND FUNDS
American High-Income Trust
The Bond Fund of America
Capital World Bond Fund
Intermediate Bond Fund of America
U.S. Government Securities Fund

MONEY MARKET FUND
The Cash Management Trust of America

Figure 13-1 represents a "scatter plot" of the performance of 19 of the College America investment options that have 10 or more years of history. Each point on the diagram represents the annualized return and the annualized standard deviation for the 10 years ended December 31, 2002. In this way, the risk (standard deviation) and the return can be measured for each investment option. You can see that The Growth Fund of America and the Washington Mutual Investors Fund achieved some of the best returns. However, the Capital Income Builder Fund and the American Balanced Fund did nearly as well, but with substantially lower risk.

In the age-old battle between indexing and active management and load versus no load, the American Funds come out very well. For example, in 2002 an investment split between the Washington Mutual Investors Fund and the Growth Fund of America would have lost 23.14 percent after deducting for all expenses and the 5.75 percent class A front-end sales charge. By contrast, an investment in the Vanguard 500 Index Fund was down 22.15 percent. This is not really a fair comparison because it's rare for any load fund to cover the sales charges in the first year. However, on a three-year basis ended December 31, 2002, an investment split between the Washington Mutual Investors fund and the Growth Fund of America would have lost 7.8 percent versus a loss of 14.6 percent for the Vanguard 500

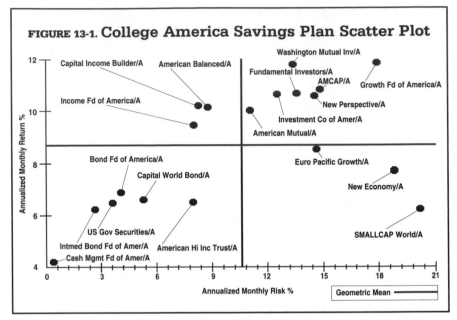

FIGURE 13-1. College America Savings Plan Scatter Plot

Data Source © Standard & Poor's Micropal Inc. (2001)—http://www.micropal.com

Index Fund. Finally, on a 10-year basis, the Washington Mutual/Growth Fund of America would have returned a 10.8 percent positive annual return, versus 9.3 percent for the Vanguard 500 Index Fund. Again, this is after paying the 5.75 percent class A sales charge.

So, the bottom line is that over the last three or 10 years, even after paying all sales charges and expenses you ended up with a higher return than an index fund. Will this continue? Nobody knows for sure. However, even if you don't believe that you can get high enough returns to outperform the market and also compensate an advisor, the College America plan is still worth considering. I think part of this analysis is how you view the sales charges. Some people view the sales charges as a way to gain access to an outperforming fund. However, I prefer to look at these costs as a way to compensate an advisor who is guiding you through the process. This advisor should be helping you figure out your savings goals and should be working with you to allocate your assets based on the amount of risk you are comfortable with. If you're getting this service, paying some fees to compensate the advisor is worthwhile. Of course, if the College America funds keep outperforming after sales charges, you are getting this service at no cost.

Figure 13-2 takes the scatter plot shown in Figure 13-1 and calculates an "efficient frontier." These are the various combinations of portfolios that maximize returns for any given level of risk. What we at Standard & Poor's then did was take the historical risk and return relationships for each fund, consider reasonable balances between various asset classes, and then construct three different portfolios using the choices in the College America program. Those three portfolios are plotted in Figure 13-2. The portfolios are labeled *Aggressive Portfolio*, *Moderate Portfolio*, and *Conservative Portfolio*.

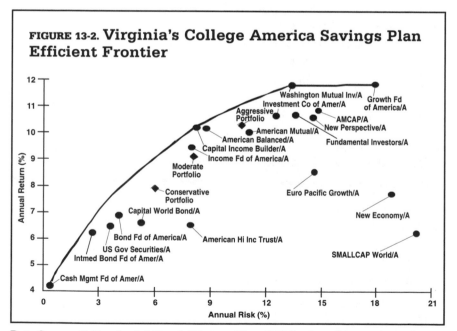

FIGURE 13-2. **Virginia's College America Savings Plan Efficient Frontier**

Data Source © Standard & Poor's Micropal Inc. (2001)—http://www.micropal.com

CONSTRUCTION OF THE AGGRESSIVE PORTFOLIO

Capital Income Builder	5 percent
Growth Fund of America	9 percent
Fundamental Investors	16 percent
Investment Company of America	20 percent
Washington Mutual Investors Fund	30 percent
American High Income Trust	5 percent
Bond Fund of America	15 percent

This portfolio, on a historical basis, had an average annual return of 10.29 percent with a standard deviation of 10.64 for the 10 years ended December 2002. In contrast, an investment in the S&P 500 index would have returned 9.34 percent with a standard deviation of 15.5 percent. Those returns are before sales charges. On an after-sales-charge basis, this portfolio would have returned 9.44 percent. The bottom line is that this portfolio has a slightly higher return than an index fund, but with substantially less risk. We would recommend this allocation for accounts that have a time horizon of 10 years or more.

CONSTRUCTION OF THE MODERATE PORTFOLIO

Capital Income Builder	5 percent
Growth Fund of America	7 percent
Investment Company of America	18 percent
Washington Mutual Investors Fund	30 percent
American High Income Trust	5 percent
Bond Fund of America	20 percent
Cash Management Trust of America	15 percent

This portfolio had an average annual return of 9.11 percent with a standard deviation of 8.14 for the 10 years ended December 2002. On an after-sales-charge basis, this portfolio would have returned 8.37 percent. Note that the Cash Management Trust of America does not have an initial sales charge. We would recommend this allocation for accounts that have a time horizon of four to nine years.

CONSTRUCTION OF THE CONSERVATIVE PORTFOLIO

Growth Fund of America	5 percent
Investment Company of America	10 percent
Washington Mutual Investors Fund	25 percent
American High Income Trust	5 percent
Bond Fund of America	25 percent
Cash Management Trust of America	30 percent

This portfolio had an average annual return of 7.90 percent with a standard deviation of 6.03 percent for the 10 years ended December 2002. On an after-sales-charge basis, this portfolio would have returned 8.37 percent. Note that the Cash Management Trust of America does not have an initial sales charge. We would recommend this allocation for accounts that have a time horizon of two or three years. With a 40 percent allocation to stocks, this portfolio should not be used for investments of less than two years. This allocation, in fact, was down 4.63 percent (before sales charges) during 2002.

If you are selecting an advisor-sold fund, the College America plan should be near the top of your list. Further information about the plan can be found at www.americanfunds.com.

College Savings Plan of Nebraska

This 529 savings plan has a broad array of choices for individuals whothat want a preset savings plan or a do-it-yourself approach. There are four age-based portfolios that gradually shift toward a more conservative investment stance as the beneficiary gets older. There are also six target portfolios that allow the account owner to set a specific risk exposure without regard to the beneficiary's age. Investments in the various portfolios can be reallocated once per year.

In addition to the four age-based and six target portfolios, the College Savings Plan of Nebraska has 22 individual fund portfolios. Here is a list of the funds available in the Individual Fund Portfolio:

MONEY MARKET ASSET CLASS:

Vanguard Prime Money Market Fund

FIXED-INCOME ASSET CLASS:

Vanguard Short-Term Bond Index Fund
Vanguard Intermediate-Term Bond Index Fund
Vanguard Total Bond Market Index Fund
PIMCO Total Return Fund

EQUITY ASSET CLASS:

Vanguard Value Index Fund
Vanguard Century Income and Growth Fund
Vanguard Institutional Index Fund
Vanguard Growth Index Fund
Fidelity Advisor Equity Growth Fund
Vanguard Total Stock Market Index Fund
Vanguard Calvert Social Index Fund
American Century Equity Income Fund
Vanguard Mid-Cap Index Fund
Janus Enterprise Fund
Vanguard Extended Market Index Fund
Vanguard Small-Cap Value Index Fund
Vanguard Small-Cap Index Fund
Vanguard Small-Cap Growth Index Fund

While the list is heavily weighted toward passively managed index funds, The College Savings Plan of Nebraska has some very good actively managed funds as well. Specifically, the PIMCO Total Return Fund, is now the largest bond fund in the United States and has had excellent returns over the last 10 years. In addition, the American Century Income and Growth Fund and Fidelity Advisor Equity Growth Fund also have good long-term records.

Standard & Poor's analysts considered historical risk and return of all the funds available in the College Savings Plan of Nebraska and designed the aggressive asset allocation shown below. Not surprisingly, the well-regarded, actively managed funds are heavily represented in the allocation:

PIMCO Total Return	20 percent
American Century Income and Growth	45 percent
Vanguard Institutional Index	20 percent
Fidelity Advisor Equity Growth Fund	15 percent

This allocation would have been down 15.5 percent in 2002 compared with a loss of 20.7 percent for the age-based aggressive portfolio for a newborn to five-year-old child. However, our this allocation does not include the 0.60 percent management fee, while the age-based portfolio does. So, subtracting an additional 0.60 percent brings us to a loss of approximately 16.1 percent, still better than the 20.7 percent loss in the age-based aggressive portfolio.

Over a 10-year period, the Standard & Poor's designed allocation would have returned 9.26 percent annually (before the 0.60 percent asset management fee). This is just a notch below the aggressive allocation designed by Standard & Poor's for the Virginia College America Program.

Many users of the Nebraska College Savings Plan have chosen the program in order to access the wide array of Vanguard index funds that are available. When you combine the 0.60 percent asset management fee with underlying fund expenses of 0.05% to 0.10 percent, this amounts to a low-cost way to passively invest. Of course, if you use some of the actively managed funds the underlying fees will be higher. There is also a $20 annual fee. Those investors who only want to use index funds may also want to consider two 529 plans in Nevada that make extensive use of Vanguard index funds. One is the Vanguard 529 College Savings Plan (1-866-734-4530, www.vanguard.com). The second is the Upromise College Fund (1-800-587-7305, www.upromisecollegefund.com). Both of these plans may have slightly lower costs for index investments. However, the Nebraska plan provides unbeatable flexibility in combining its assortment of both passive and active funds.

The College Savings Plan of Nebraska can be reached at 888-993-3746 or on the Web at www.planforcollegenow.com.

Unique College Investing Plan (New Hampshire)

This 529 Savings Plan has a wide selection of actively managed funds run by Fidelity Investments, one of the largest mutual fund managers in the United States. Fidelity also runs programs in Delaware and Massachusetts. In addition, Fidelity operates a second plan in New Hampshire that is advisor-sold. However, the Unique College Investing Plan does not require an advisor.

The Unique College Investing Plan offers eight different age-based portfolios. Each portfolio is labeled with a year, approximately corresponding to the point in which the beneficiary will be starting college. Thus Portfolio 2018 is appropriate for a child born in 2000 or 2001. These portfolios will gradually shift from equity to fixed-income securities as the beneficiary approaches college age. For those investors who don't like the allocation indicated for their beneficiary's age, there are also three "static" portfolios that investors can mix and match into the program to meet their own risk preferences. The static portfolios are 100 percent equity, 70 percent equity, and 30 percent bonds, as well as a conservative portfolio that contains 45 percent bonds and 55 percent money market and short-term fixed-income investments. For example, a parent with a child born in 2000 is uncomfortable with the 85 percent allocation to stocks in portfolio 2018 and would prefer a 75 percent allocation to stocks. Let's say an initial $10,000 was being deposited. One choice could be placing $7500 into the 100 percent equity portfolio and $2500 into the conservative portfolio. Another way would be to put $3333 into Portfolio 2018 and $6667 into the 70 percent equity portfolio. This would also achieve a 75 percent overall equity allocation.

UNDERLYING FIDELITY FUNDS

DOMESTIC EQUITY FUNDS
Fidelity Blue Chip Growth Fund
Fidelity Disciplined Equity Fund
Fidelity Fund
Fidelity Growth and Income Portfolio
Fidelity Growth Company Fund
Fidelity OTC Portfolio
Fidelity Small Cap Selector

INTERNATIONAL EQUITY FUNDS
Fidelity Diversified International Fund
Fidelity Overseas Fund

HIGH-YIELD FIXED-INCOME FUND
Fidelity Capital & Income Fund

FIXED-INCOME FUNDS
Fidelity Government Income Fund
Fidelity Intermediate Bond Fund
Fidelity Investment Grade Bond Fund
Fidelity Short Term Bond Fund

MONEY MARKET FUND
Fidelity Cash Reserves

Figure 13-3 shows a scatter plot of the various funds used in the Unique College Investing Plan. This shows risk and return for the funds for the 10 years ended 2002. Among the stars during that period were the Fidelity Growth and Income Portfolio and the Fidelity Equity Income fund. Fidelity's bond funds had credible returns but somewhat below the Smith Barney Investment Grade Fund used in Illinois Bright Start and the PIMCO Total Return Fund that we mentioned in the Nebraska plan.

Fees and expenses amount to a 0.30 percent asset management fee plus the underlying expenses of the funds, which range from 0.90 percent for the College Age Portfolio to 1.10 percent for the 100 percent equity portfolio. In addition there is a $30 annual fee, which is waived if you sign up for either direct deposit or automatic contributions. The fee is also waived once the account reaches $25,000. This expense structure is a notch higher than Illinois Bright Start and is similar to the expense incurred if you invested in some of the active funds offered in the College Savings Plan of Nebraska.

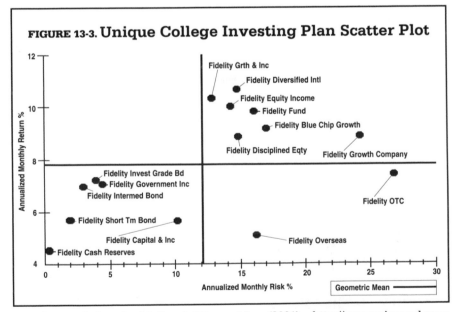

FIGURE 13-3. Unique College Investing Plan Scatter Plot

Data Source © Standard & Poor's Micropal Inc. (2001)—http://www.micropal.com

THE CREDIT CARD: In early 2003, Fidelity established a new credit card loyalty program with MBNA America. This new MBNA card carries no annual fee and rebates 2 percent of purchases into a Fidelity 529 plan account. This program is fairly generous and compares favorably with many other credit card rebate programs including airline and hotel programs. This program alone could help make a significant contribution over time to a 529 account balance. Obviously you don't want to increase your credit card overall spending to get the rebate, but this is a good way to get something back on money you were spending anyway. More details on the credit card can be found on at the Fidelity Web site.

In all, the combination of good long-term performance, moderate fees, and the opportunity to add to your savings with both Upromise and a credit card rebate makes the Unique College Investing Plan one of the top plans worth considering.

The Unique College Investing Plan can be reached at 1-800-544-1722 or at www.fidelity.com/unique.

Texas Guaranteed Tuition Plan

No in-depth discussion of 529 plans would be complete without discussing at least one prepaid plan. Prepaid plans are not for everyone. As we mentioned in Chapter 7, current federal financial aid regulations are less favorable for prepaid plans than for 529 savings plans. In addition, some plans may not be able to easily meet their future obligations. This plan is restricted to Texas residents, but the discussion is applicable to other state prepaid plans.

The reason that many of these prepaid plans could have difficulty meeting future obligations is that tuition increases at state-supported universities have started to skyrocket. The states, facing large budget deficits, are looking to cut the cost of services provided to the public. One of the ways of accomplishing this is shifting some of the cost to those who use the service. As a result, many states have instituted double-digit percentage increases in state university tuition. Texas is no exception to this. In early June of 2003, the Texas state legislature voted to end the practice of small regulated tuition increases and opted instead to deregulate tuition and give the state Board of Regents the ability to set tuition rates.

The Texas Guaranteed Tuition Plan immediately responded that it would close the plan to all new beneficiaries other than infants under one year old. This is not an issue for those who have already invested in the plan. The Texas Guaranteed Tuition Plan should have no problem meeting its future obligations. Contracts issued by the plan are a "full faith and credit" obligation of the State of Texas. This is not true for all prepaid plans and it's one of the first things you should check when considering a prepaid plan.

The first thing to know about the plan is the eligibility requirements. The beneficiary must have not yet graduated from high school and must have been a Texas resident for the 12 months prior to application. A nonresident beneficiary is eligible if the parent is a Texas resident and the parent is the contract purchaser. What's really interesting about the plan is that the beneficiary is considered a Texas resident for purposes of paying tuition when receiving benefits under the plan regardless of the beneficiary's actual residency at the time of college attendance. For example: a family in Houston purchases a contract under the plan covering two years of public college, and then moves to Phoenix when the child is 14. The student later becomes a student at the University of Texas. The student will have his or her first two years covered by the contract at resident rates. However, since benefits under the two-year contract have ended, subsequent years at the University of Texas will be payable at the nonresident rate.

Even though a beneficiary who may have moved out of state would be considered a resident for tuition purposes, he or she would still be considered a nonresident in the admissions process.

There are a variety of contracts that can be purchased under the plan.

Community College: one year, two years

Combined two years Community College plus two years Senior College or University.

Senior College or University (Public): one year, two years, three years, four years, five years

Senior College or University (Private): one year, two years, three years, four years, five years

Obviously there is a wide variance in cost between these contracts. Prices vary depending on the number of years of tuition purchased, the type of institution, and the current age of the beneficiary. For example, a one-year community college contract purchased for a newborn had a lump-sum cost of $1766 in early 2003. At the other extreme, a five-year private college contract was $65,391, when paid as a lump-sum.

The contracts are a bit different when it comes to paying benefits. The private school contracts will pay the average tuition and fees (room and board is not covered) at a private college in Texas. If the beneficiary happens to go to school that is more expensive, the student is responsible for the difference.

The public school contracts will pay all required tuition and fees at any Texas state school. If an out-of-state or private college is selected, then the average cost of a state school is provided. This may or may not work out to be a good deal. Again, keep in mind that this prepaid plan does not cover room and board, books, or any fees that are assessed for a specific program such as lab fees. Also, not every state college in Texas charges the same tuition and fees, so it ends up that those who go to the more expensive schools get a higher return from the plan than those who attend some of the less expensive institutions.

For example, the University of Texas at Austin (among the more expensive institutions) had the following fee schedule per semester (15 hours) for the 2002–2003 academic year: tuition (resident) $1320 plus required fees and charges $655. This would amount to $15,800 for eight semesters (four years).

During early 2003, the plan charged $17,460 for a four-year public college contract where the beneficiary was a newborn. If tuition at the University of Texas at Austin rises 10 percent over the next 20 years, then the out-of-pocket cost of four years of tuition would be $92,658 ($19,965 + $21,962 + $24,158 + $26,573). In effect, $17,460 buys an education with a future value of $92,658. This works out to an annualized return of about 9 percent.

How farfetched is it that we will see many years of double-digit tuition increases? Well, in 2002, Penn State increased tuition 13 percent and in 2003, New York raised tuition 28 percent at its state universities. Other states, including Vermont, Hawaii, West Virginia, Oklahoma, Alabama, Florida, and Utah, have tuition hike proposals. In the 2002–2003 academic year, public school tuition rose an average of 9.6 percent, according to the College Board. Will this continue? With states battling record budget shortfalls, it seems likely that state schools will be hard pressed to keep a lid on tuition.

So, after recognizing that the financial aid treatment of prepaid plans can be negative, the Texas Guaranteed Tuition Plan may be an important component of some families' college savings plans. Specifically the plan is well suited to families who:

➤ Were not likely to be eligible for substantial need-based aid.

➤ Have a preference for a Texas state college or university (particularly a state institution with above-average tuition and fees)

➤ Want to lock in resident rates in case of a move out of state.

The enrollment period each year generally runs from November to May. The plan may also revisit the issue of enrollment for older children once the situation surrounding tuition increases becomes more clear. The plan can be reached at 1-800-445-GRAD or at www.tgtp.org.

CHAPTER 14

Putting It All Together

You've now seen a description of the various ways people can save for college. We've discussed a variety of instruments that can be used for college savings and how they interact with tax law and financial aid. However, you may be asking, How do I sort through all this information to design a savings plan that's right for my situation? In this final chapter, let's take this information and figure out how to customize a plan that fits your particular needs.

Step One

Figure out what you want to accomplish. In Chapter 1, we discussed that you need to decide the type of college you're saving for and that you should try to forecast whether you are likely to be eligible for financial aid. This can be done by using some of the financial aid calculators available online. Also take a look at the federal financial aid formulas displayed in Chapter 7. Once you have figured out what your long-term savings goal is, divide that into a savings goal for the current year.

Step Two

Ask yourself whether your goal is realistic. Just because you may have figured out that you need to save $6000 this year doesn't mean you can. Try to set a goal that you can achieve, keeping in mind that saving for college is one of many financial goals, including saving for retirement, staying out of consumer debt, etc.

Step Three

Determine whether you are likely to be eligible for tax credits and tax deductions. At this point you should go back to Chapter 6 and look at the income requirements for the tax credits and deductions. The Hope and Lifetime Learning credits start to phase out at $40,000 of adjusted gross income for single taxpayers and $80,000 for joint returns. If your income is below that level (when your child is in college), you are likely to qualify.

Step Four

Determine what savings vehicle you want to use. If you are likely to be eligible for tax credits or deductions, you want some money saved outside tax-advantaged plans (such as 529 plans or Coverdell ESAs). However, keep in mind that if you're going to be borrowing funds for college, those funds can be used to qualify for the tax credits and deductions. The example at the end of Chapter 6 discusses how much to save in mutual funds and bank accounts and how the remainder can go into such vehicles as 529 savings plans and Coverdell ESAs.

Step Five

If you determine that you want to open a 529 account, decide which one is right for you. If you live in one of the 25 states listed in Chapter 3 that provide a state tax deduction for contributions to your home state's 529 program, investigate the program in your home state first. However, if you're not satisfied with some provision of the program (such as mediocre performance), then look at the offerings in other states. When looking for a 529 plan account, you should answer the following questions:

➤ Are you are looking for a prepaid plan or a savings plan? If you don't expect to qualify for need-based financial aid and you prefer a state-supported college, a prepaid plan may meet your needs. Otherwise, a 529 savings plan is more likely to be what you're looking for.

➤ How broad is the array of investment choices in the plan? Are you satisfied with the age-based choices or would you like to design your own asset allocation?

➤ What has the historical performance been? How did the plan do in 2002? Keep in mind that equity benchmarks such as the S&P 500 were down sharply that year.

In the beginning of Chapter 13, I posted some 2002 returns for aggressive allocations used for a child born in 2000 for five different 529 savings plans. How does the plan you're considering compare? Also, see if there is a long-term record. Most 529 plans have a rather short performance history. Where the history is brief, see if the plan uses existing mutual funds with a long-term history. In our in-depth plan review in Chapter 13, we found various equity funds that returned over 9 percent per year for the 10 years ended 2002. We also found bond funds that returned over 8 percent for that same 10-year period. How does the plan you're considering compare with those returns?

At this point, let's go through a few examples and see how all of this comes together.

Example 1

Liz and Michael live in New York City and have a combined income of $160,000 per year. They have a one child, a daughter who is two years old. They foresee the child going to a private college and don't expect to qualify for much in the way of need-based financial aid. In going through the step-by-step process above, they realize that they also won't qualify for any of the current tax credits or deductions available for education.

They look first at New York's College Savings Program and realize that the State of New York offers a tax deduction of up to $10,000 for annual contributions into the plan. As New York City residents, they pay a marginal tax rate of 10.5 percent on their income. Even though they believe that active management of their funds might result in slightly higher returns, they decide that the tax deduction is too valuable to pass up and save $10,000 per year in New York's College Savings Program. They also decide that they aren't comfortable with the age-based allocation the plan has so instead, they take 60 percent of the funds and put it into the "high equity option." The remainder is put into the "guaranteed option" which is an obligation of TIAA-CREF Life with a minimum return of 3 percent. In early 2003, that option was paying 3.8 percent. This is a somewhat conservative approach for a beneficiary so young, but it suits Liz and Michael who have the option of becoming more aggressive next year when the plan will be offering Vanguard funds, and they may reconsider the possibility of using an age-based portfolio.

Example 2

Janet is a single mom with a 15-year-old son. She earns $20,000 per year. In early 2002, following the death of her husband, she opted to take the proceeds from his $100,000 life insurance policy and pay off the remaining $30,000 of her mortgage. Her home is currently valued at $130,000. After paying for her husband's funeral and some credit card bills, Janet opened a mutual fund account with $55,000 that is invested half in an equity fund and half in a bond fund. By March of 2003, the account had a value of $50,000. Janet wants to set aside $15,000 for her son's college education and was considering either a custodial account or opening a 529 savings plan account. Either of those choices would probably be a mistake. Since Janet's son is likely to qualify for need-based financial aid and because Janet is likely to qualify for the federal tax credits, it doesn't make sense to switch into either a 529 account or a custodial account that would be considered the son's asset for financial aid purposes.

The best thing Janet can do with regard to saving for her son's college education is nothing. She should instead concentrate on how her retirement will be funded and perhaps having a small portion of her savings in a short-term instrument such as a money market fund or bank account to cover emergencies. By not funding a custodial account she helps maximize the need-based financial aid that her son might receive. Paying off her mortgage last year decreases her available cash but also helps in the calculation of financial aid (particularly under the federal formula). Not starting a 529 plan account helps keep Janet eligible for the Hope and Lifetime Learning Credits. In any event, the fairly short time horizon until Janet's son attends college and her limited tax liability (the Hope Credit will wipe out about virtually all of Janet's tax liability) means that Janet would not get substantial benefit from using a 529 savings plan.

Example 3

Joanne and Chris live in California and earn a combined $85,000 per year. They have a son and a daughter who are five and three years old, respectively. Their goal is to send each child to a private college. They calculate, using some of the online financial aid calculators, that their likely expected family contribution would be $25,000 per year. Thus in today's dollars, they would be likely to be spending $25,000 for each of the six years at least one of their children will be in college, for a total expenditure (in today's dollars) of $150,000. Their first child will be attending college in 13 years and the second child in 15 years. Thus, they would like to complete their savings plan in 14 years. Although they would like to save more, they feel that realistically, the most they can save is $8000 this year.

Since California does not offer a tax deduction for 529 contributions, they decide to open an account with the New Hampshire Unique College Investing Plan, managed by Fidelity Investments. They open an account for each child, and set up an automatic investment plan with $250 per month in each account. That will amount to $6000 for the year, and they also will buy $1000 of savings bonds for each child this year. By setting up an automatic savings plan, Fidelity waives its $30 annual fee for each of the accounts.

Joanne and Chris aren't sure whether they will qualify for federal tax credits and deductions by the time their children are in college, but they qualify based on their current income, so they hedge their bets by putting some of the college savings outside the 529 plan. However, if they want to use the funds from the savings bonds in order to qualify for the educational deductions or tax credits, they won't be able to claim tax-free treatment of the savings bonds. When they set up their accounts in the Unique College Investing Plan, they chose the age-based portfolios. They are concerned about the high allocation to equity in the plan, so the additional funds put into the savings bonds gives them some added protection from downside risk.

Once Joanne and Chris sign up for this savings plan, they also sign up for the credit card that is issued by MBNA and Fidelity that puts 2 percent of their purchases into the 529 accounts. When Joanne purchases the savings bonds, she buys them from the savings-bonds.gov Web site and puts the purchase on her credit card. This helps provide a small supplement to their savings.

Hopefully, these examples demonstrate that while it's not easy to achieve your college savings goals, it's certainly possible. The key to success is often taking a large long-term goal and translating it into a series of short-term goals. Good Luck.

529 Plans by State

The information in this Appendix has been compiled from the plan documents of each state's available 529 plans as of early 2003. All information is subject to change. While we believe the source of this information to be reliable, neither the author nor Standard & Poor's can guarantee its complete accuracy. Before committing to a prepaid tuition contract or opening a 529 savings plan account, you should read all plan disclosures and documents.

STATE OF ALABAMA

Name of plan: Alabama Higher Education 529 Plan

Type of plan: 529 savings plan

Web sites: www.treasury.state.al.us and www.vankampen.com/products/529index.asp

Phone: 866-529-2228

Manager: Van Kampen /State of Alabama

Exclusively broker sold? No.

Are funds guaranteed by the state? No.

Who is eligible to open an account? Anyone 19 or over.

CONTRIBUTION LIMITS

Minimum: $250 initial deposit for state residents; $1000 minimum deposit for nonresidents; subsequent contributions at least $25.

Maximum: No further contributions once all accounts for same beneficiary reach $269,000.

Types of payment plans: Standard payments; automatic contributions available.

Are contributions deductible from income on state tax return? No.

Is the earnings portion of qualified withdrawals subject to state income tax? Yes.

Types of investments available: Age-based portfolios, with Aggressive, Moderate, or Conservative risk profiles. Also, three fixed portfolios: 100% equity, 100% bonds, and a short-term income portfolio invested 50% in government bonds and 50% in money-market instruments. All portfolios managed by Van Kampen.

FEES AND EXPENSES

Annual fee: $10 for Alabama residents; $25 for nonresidents.

Sales charges: None for Alabama residents.

Nonresidents have choice between A shares (2.25%–5.75% sales load plus 0.25% program management fee, 0.10% state administrative fee); B shares (up to 5% deferred sales charge, waived after 5 years, plus 1.00% program management fee and 0.10% state administrative fee); and C shares (1.00% deferred sales charge, waived after 1 year, plus 1.00% program management fee and 0.10% state administration fee).

Expenses: Underlying expense ratio of funds ranges from 0.90% for short-term income fund to 1.24% for equity fund.

Name of plan: Alabama Prepaid Affordable College Tuition (PACT)

Type of plan: 529 prepaid plan

Web site: www.treasury.state.al.us

Phone: 800-252-7228

Manager: State of Alabama

Are funds guaranteed by the state? No.

Who is eligible to open an account? Anyone can open an account. Beneficiary must be in 9th grade or younger. Nonresidents are eligible but contract prices are based on Alabama resident charges at state colleges.

Contributions: Contract prices are dependent on age of beneficiary and length of contract. Contract prices range from $11,413 to $15,629 for four years of tuition. These are lump-sum payments (2002 prices). Installment

payments are also available for four-year contracts ranging from $105–$417 per month.

What do contract payments cover? Tuition and required fees at a four-year Alabama State College. Books and room and board are not covered. However, if the student receives a scholarship, excess funds can be used toward those charges.

Are contributions deductible from income on state tax return? No.

Is the earnings portion of qualified withdrawals subject to state income tax? No.

Can contract benefits be used at private schools or out-of-state schools? Yes, benefit will equal the weighted average and mandatory fees charged by Alabama four-year public colleges. Payments will not exceed actual tuition and fees.

FEES AND EXPENSES

Enrollment fee: $75

Expenses: Interest charges of 8% to 9% are charged to contracts paid by monthly installments.

STATE OF ALASKA

Name of plan: Manulife College Savings

Type of plan: 529 savings plan

Web site: www.manulifecollegesavings.com

Phone: 866-222-7498

Manager: Distributed by Manulife, Multimanager platform (seven firms). T. Rowe Price serves as investment advisor.

Exclusively broker sold? Yes.

Are funds guaranteed by the state? No.

Who is eligible to open an account? Anyone.

CONTRIBUTION LIMITS

Minimum: $500 initial deposit; subsequent contributions at least $50.

Maximum: No further contributions once all accounts for same beneficiary reach $250,000.

Types of payment plans: Standard payments; automatic contributions available.

Are contributions deductible from income on state tax return? No. (Alaska has no income tax.)

Is the earnings portion of qualified withdrawals subject to state income tax? No.

Types of investments available: Age-based portfolios (called enroll-ment-based option); static option where asset allocation stays fixed over the life of the investment with allocation available to five different portfolios. Each of the five portfolios has allocations to funds managed by T. Rowe Price, PIMCO, MFS, Davis Advisors, Franklin-Templeton, Oppenheimer, and AIM Funds. In addition, there is an individual option, with the opportunity to allocate assets to four individual funds managed by AIM, Templeton, or T. Rowe Price (two funds).

FEES AND EXPENSES

Annual fee: $30, waived once assets reach $25,000 or if automatic deposit program is chosen.

Sales charges: Choice between A shares (3.5% sales load plus 0.75% management fee) and C shares (no sales charge, plus 1.05% program management fee).

Expenses: Underlying expense ratio of funds ranges from 0.45% for cash reserves fund to 1.39% for international fund.

Name of plan: T. Rowe Price College Savings Plan

Type of plan: 529 savings plan

Website: www.troweprice.com/collegesavings

Phone: 800-369-3641

Manager: T. Rowe Price

Exclusively broker sold? No.

Are funds guaranteed by the state? No.

Who is eligible to open an account? Anyone.

CONTRIBUTION LIMITS

Minimum: $250 initial deposit; subsequent contributions at least $50.

Maximum: No further contributions once all accounts for same beneficiary reach $250,000.

Types of payment plans: Standard payments; automatic contributions available.

Are contributions deductible from income on state tax return? No. (Alaska has no income tax.)

Is the earnings portion of qualified withdrawals subject to state income tax? No.

Types of investments available: Age-based portfolios (called enroll-ment-based option); static option where asset allocation stays fixed over the life of the investment with alloca-tion available to four different portfo-lios (Equity, Fixed Income, Balanced, and Preservation). T. Rowe Price manages all underlying funds.

FEES AND EXPENSES

Annual fee: $30, waived once assets reach $25,000 or if automatic deposits program is chosen.

Sales charges: None.

Program fee: 0.30% annually.

Expenses: Underlying expense ratio of funds ranges from 0.45% for cash reserves fund to 0.95% for equity growth fund.

Name of plan: University of Alaska College Savings Plan

Type of plan: 529 savings plan

Website: www.uacollegesavings.com

Phone: 800-478-0003

Manager: T. Rowe Price

Exclusively broker sold? No.

Are funds guaranteed by the state? No.

Who is eligible to open an account? Anyone.

CONTRIBUTION LIMITS

Minimum: $250 initial deposit; subsequent contributions at least $50.

Maximum: No further contributions once all accounts for same beneficiary reach $250,000.

Types of payment plans: Standard payments, automatic contributions available.

Are contributions deductible from income on state tax return? No. (Alaska has no income tax.)

Is the earnings portion of qualified withdrawals subject to state income tax? No.

Types of investments available: Age-based portfolios, (called enrollment-based option); static option where asset allocation stays fixed

over the life of the investment with allocation available to four different portfolios (Equity, Fixed Income, Balanced and Preservation). ACT option that is guaranteed by the program to keep pace with tuition increases at the University of Alaska. T. Rowe Price manages all underlying funds.

FEES AND EXPENSES

Annual fee: $30, is waived once assets reach $25,000 or if automatic deposits program is chosen. Also waived for ACT option.

Program fee: 0.30% annually.

Sales charges: None.

Expenses: Underlying expense ratio of funds ranges from 0.45% for cash reserves fund to 0.95% for equity growth fund.

STATE OF ARIZONA

Name of plan: Arizona Family College Savings Plan (SM&R)

Type of plan: 529 savings plan

Website: www.smrinvest.com/college

Phone: 888-66-READY

Manager: Securities Management & Research

Exclusively broker sold? No.

Are funds guaranteed by the state? No.

Who is eligible to open an account? Anyone.

CONTRIBUTION LIMITS

Minimum: $250 initial deposit; subsequent contributions of at least $25.

Maximum: No further contributions once all accounts for same beneficiary reach $187,000.

Types of payment plans: Standard payments; automatic contributions available.

Are contributions deductible from income on state tax return? No.

Is the earnings portion of qualified withdrawals subject to state income tax? No.

Types of investments available: 10 individual fund options including four equity funds managed by Fred Alger Management. There are no age-based or static allocations. The asset allocation is determined by the account owner by selecting from among the 10 fund options.

FEES AND EXPENSES

Enrollment fee: $10 per fund chosen.

Sales charges: None if funds are purchased directly from SM&R. Fees may apply if an advisor is used.

Expenses: Underlying expense ratio of funds ranges from 0.73% for bond fund to 2.10% for Alger Technology Fund. Expenses include 12b-1 fees.

Name of plan: Arizona Family College Savings Plan (CSB)

Type of plan: 529 savings plan

Web site: arizona.collegesavings.com

Phone: 888-66-READY

Manager: College Savings Bank

Exclusively broker sold? No.

Are funds guaranteed by the state? No. However, funds on deposit insured by FDIC up to $100,000.

Who is eligible to open an account? Anyone.

CONTRIBUTION LIMITS

Minimum: $250 initial deposit; subsequent contributions at least $25.

Maximum: No further contributions once all accounts for same beneficiary reach $187,000.

Types of payment plans: Standard payments; automatic contributions available.

Are contributions deductible from income on state tax return? No.

Is the earnings portion of qualified withdrawals subject to state income tax? No.

Types of investments available: Variable rate certificate of deposit with minimum 3% interest rate. Variable rate tied to an index of private college costs as compiled by The College Board. Variable rate equals index return less 1.00%.

Fees and expenses: None;, $10 state enrollment fee paid by College Savings Bank. There is a $50 fee for account owner or beneficiary change (fee waived for first change).

Name of plan: Waddell & Reed InvestEd Plan

Type of plan: 529 savings plan

Website: www2.waddell.com

Phone: 888-WADDELL

Manager: Waddell & Reed

Exclusively broker sold? Yes.

Are funds guaranteed by the state? No.

Who is eligible to open an account? Anyone.

CONTRIBUTION LIMITS

Minimum: $500 initial deposit; subsequent contributions at least $25.

Maximum: No further contributions once all accounts for same beneficiary reach $187,000.

Types of payment plans: Standard payments; automatic contributions available.

Are contributions deductible from income on state tax return? No.

Is the earnings portion of qualified withdrawals subject to state income tax? No.

Types of investments available: Three "fund of fund" portfolios: Growth, Balanced, and Conservative. These same portfolios are also used as age-based.

FEES AND EXPENSES

Enrollment fee: $10.

Sales charges: Choice between A shares (5.75% sales load plus up to 1.22% program expense); B shares (up to 5% deferred sales charge, waived after 6 years, plus up to 2.02% program expense); and C shares (1.00% deferred sales charge, waived after 1 year, plus up to 1.83% program expense).

Expenses: Underlying expense ratio of funds ranges from 0.40% for cash management fund to 0.85% for small cap fund.

STATE OF ARKANSAS

Name of plan: GIFT College Investing Plan

Type of plan: 529 savings plan

Website: www.thegiftplan.com

Phone: 877-615-4116

Manager: Mercury Funds

Exclusively broker sold? No, for Arkansas residents; Yes, for nonresidents.

Are funds guaranteed by the state? No.

Who is eligible to open an account? Anyone (nonresidents must use an advisor.)

CONTRIBUTION LIMITS

Minimum: $250 initial deposit (residents). nonresident accounts must have $1000 initial deposit. Subsequent contributions must be at least $50.

Maximum: No further contributions once all accounts for same beneficiary reach $245,000.

Types of payment plans: Standard payments; automatic contributions available.

Are contributions deductible from income on state tax return? No.

Is the earnings portion of qualified withdrawals subject to state income tax? No.

Types of investments available: Age-based portfolios; four static portfolios: Growth, Growth, and Income, Balanced, and Fixed Income.

FEES AND EXPENSES

Enrollment fee: None.

Annual fee: $25, waived for residents. Also waived for nonresidents with balances above $25,000.

Sales charges: Residents who open accounts directly with plan pay 0.60% program management fee. Accounts opened through an advisor choose between A shares (3.0% sales load plus 0.60% program expense); B shares (up to 2.5% deferred sales charge, waived after 6 years, plus up to 0.95% program expense for first six years, then reduced to 0.60%); and C shares (no sales charge, 0.95% program expense).

Expenses: Underlying expense ratio of funds ranges from 0.50% for total return fund to 1.74% for large-cap core fund.

STATE OF CALIFORNIA

Name of plan: Golden State ScholarShare College Savings Trust

Type of plan: 529 savings plan

Website: www.scholarshare.com

Phone: 877-SAV-4EDU (877-728-4338)

Manager: TIAA-CREF

Exclusively broker sold? No.

Are funds guaranteed by the state? No.

Who is eligible to open an account? Any adult or emancipated minor living in United States.

CONTRIBUTION LIMITS

Minimum: $25 per deposit; $15 for automatic deposits.

Maximum: No further contributions once all accounts for same beneficiary reach $124,799–$174,648 (depends on age of beneficiary, with those born in 2002–2003 eligible for lower amount and those born after 1986 eligible for higher amount).

Types of payment plans: Standard payments; automatic contributions available.

Are contributions deductible from income on state tax return? No.

Is the earnings portion of qualified withdrawals subject to state income tax? No.

Types of investments available: Age-based portfolios, "aggressive" age-based portfolios, three fixed portfolios: High equity, Social choice, and Guaranteed. The Guaranteed portfolio is not guaranteed by California, but is an obligation of TIAA-CREF Life with minimum 3% return.

FEES AND EXPENSES

Enrollment fee: None.

Annual fee: None.

Sales charges: None.

Expenses: Program management fee: 0.70%; Administrative Investment Board fees up to additional 0.10%. Underlying expense of funds is included in program management fee.

STATE OF COLORADO

Name of plan: CollegeInvest/ Prepaid Tuition Fund

Type of plan: 529 prepaid plan

Web site: www.collegeinvest.org

Phone: 800-478-5651 (In Colorado: 888-SAVE-NOW)

Manager: CO Student Obligation Bond Authority (CSOBA)

Exclusively broker sold? No.

Are funds guaranteed by the state? No.

Who is eligible to open an account? No new accounts can be currently opened. Program is to be revamped.

Name of plan: CollegeInvest / Scholars Choice College Savings Program

Type of plan: 529 savings plan

Web site: www.scholars-choice.com

Phone: 888-5-SCHOLAR (888-572-4652)

Manager: Citigroup Global Markets

Exclusively broker sold? No.

Are funds guaranteed by the state? No.

Who is eligible to open an account? Anyone.

CONTRIBUTION LIMITS

Minimum: $25 initial deposit; $15 subsequent deposit.

Maximum: No further contributions once all accounts for same beneficiary reach $235,000.

Types of payment plans: Standard payments; automatic contributions available.

Are contributions deductible from income on state tax return? Yes, residents may deduct all contributions without limitation.

Is the earnings portion of qualified withdrawals subject to state income tax? No.

Types of investments available: Age-based portfolios (same portfolios used as "years to enrollment" portfolios); three fixed portfolios: Equity, Balanced, and Fixed income.

FEES AND EXPENSES

Enrollment fee: None.

Annual fee: None for Colorado residents; nonresidents: $30.

Sales charges: Direct purchasers purchase shares without load but pay 0.99% program service fee. Purchasers who use advisor choose between A shares (3.50% sales charge plus 0.25% distribution fee); B shares (up to 2.50% deferred sales charge, waived after 6 years plus 0.95% distribution fee, reduced to 0.25% after 6 years); or C shares (no sales charge, 0.65% distribution fee).

Expenses: All holders pay 0.10% authority administration fee. Direct purchasers have underlying fund fees and expenses included in program service fee. Purchasers who use advisors pay underlying fees and expenses ranging from 0.38% for cash portfolio to 1.00% for MFS Government Securities.

STATE OF CONNECTICUT

Name of plan: Connecticut Higher Education Trust (CHET)

Type of plan: 529 savings plan

Web site: www.aboutchet.com

Phone: 888-799-CHET

Manager: TIAA-CREF

Exclusively broker sold? No.

Are funds guaranteed by the state? No.

Who is eligible to open an account? Any adult or emancipated minor living in the United States.

CONTRIBUTION LIMITS

Minimum: $25 per deposit; $15 for automatic deposits.

Maximum: No further contributions once all accounts for same beneficiary reach $235,000.

Types of payment plans: Standard payments; automatic contributions available.

Are contributions deductible from income on state tax return? No.

Is the earnings portion of qualified withdrawals subject to state income tax? No.

Types of investments available: Age-based portfolios, two fixed portfolios: High equity and Principal Plus. The Principal Plus option is an obligation of TIAA-CREF Life with minimum 3% return.

FEES AND EXPENSES

Enrollment fee: None.

Annual fee: None.

Sales charges: None.

Expenses: Program management fee: 0.57%. After underlying expense of funds, total expenses not to exceed 0.79%. Funds in Principal Plus option subject to additional 0.02% expense.

STATE OF DELAWARE

Name of plan: Delaware College Investment Plan

Type of plan: 529 savings plan

Web site: www.fidelity.com/delaware

Phone: 1-800-544-1655

Manager: Fidelity Investments

Exclusively broker sold? No.

Are funds guaranteed by the state? No.

Who is eligible to open an account? Any U.S. resident over 18.

CONTRIBUTION LIMITS

Minimum: $500 initial deposit; $50 subsequent deposits; $50 minimum initial deposit for automatic deposits.

Maximum: No further contributions once all accounts for same beneficiary reach $250,000.

Types of payment plans: Standard payments; automatic contributions available.

Are contributions deductible from income on state tax return? No.

Is the earnings portion of qualified withdrawals subject to state income tax? No.

Types of investments available: Age-based portfolios; three fixed portfolios: 100% equity, 70% equity, and Conservative.

FEES AND EXPENSES

Enrollment fee: None.

Annual fee: $30, waived if account balance over $25,000.

Sales charges: None.

Expenses: Program management fee: 0.30%. Underlying expense of funds (weighted average by portfolio) ranges from 0.85% to 1.13%.

DISTRICT OF COLUMBIA

Name of plan: DC 529 College Savings Plan

Type of plan: 529 savings plan

Website: www.dccollegesavings.com

Phone: 1-800-368-2745

Manager: Calvert Group

Exclusively broker sold? No.

Are funds guaranteed by the state? No.

Who is eligible to open an account? Any U.S. resident over 18.

CONTRIBUTION LIMITS

Minimum: $100 initial deposit; $25 subsequent deposits; $25 minimum initial deposit for automatic deposits.

Maximum: No further contributions once all accounts for same beneficiary reach $260,000.

Types of payment plans: Standard payments; automatic contributions available.

Are contributions deductible from income on state tax return? Yes, up to $3000 (single), $6000 (joint).

Is the earnings portion of qualified withdrawals subject to state income tax? No.

Types of investments available: Age-based portfolios; six fixed portfolios: Income, Balanced, Index, Large Cap, Mid Cap, and Small Cap. Three of the fixed portfolios are socially conscious. Stability of principal option with guaranteed minimum 3% return (obligation of Acasia Life).

FEES AND EXPENSES

Enrollment fee: None for residents; nonresidents: $25.

Annual fee: $15 for residents; $30 for nonresidents.

Sales charges: None.

Expenses: Program management fee: 0.25%. Underlying expense of funds (weighted average by portfolio, including single fund portfolios) ranges from 1.04% to 1.76%.

STATE OF FLORIDA

Name of plan: Florida Prepaid College Program

Type of plan: 529 prepaid plan

Web site: www.fsba.state.fl.us/prepaid

Phone: 800-552-GRAD (800-552-4723)

Manager: State of Florida

Are funds guaranteed by the state? Yes, contracts are a direct obligation of the state.

Who is eligible to open an account? Anyone over 18 can open an account.; Beneficiary must be in 11th grade or younger. Beneficiary must be a Florida resident. Beneficiary is also eligible if noncustodial parent is Florida resident.

Contributions: Contract prices are dependent on age of beneficiary and length of contract. Enrollment period is each November through January. Contract prices range from $11,413 to $15,629 for four years of tuition. These are lump-sum payments. Installment payments are also available for four-year contracts ranging from $105 to $417 per month.

What do contract payments cover? Various plans cover either tuition at two-year community college or four-year state university in Florida.

Optional plans for room and board also available.

Are contributions deductible from income on state tax return? No. Florida has no income tax. However, assets in the plan are not subject to the Florida Intangible Tax.

Is the earnings portion of qualified withdrawals subject to state income tax? No.

Can contract benefits be used at private schools or out-of-state schools? Yes, most accredited out-of-state colleges are eligible. Benefit will equal what the plan would normally pay a public college in Florida.

FEES AND EXPENSES

Enrollment fee: $50.

Name of plan: Florida College Investment Plan

Type of plan: 529 savings plan

Web site: www.florida529plans.com

Phone: 800-552-GRAD (800-552-4723)

Manager: State of Florida

Exclusively broker sold? No.

Are funds guaranteed by the state? No.

Who is eligible to open an account? Any U.S. resident over 18.

CONTRIBUTION LIMITS

Minimum: $25.

Maximum: No further contributions once all accounts for same beneficiary reach $283,000.

Types of payment plans: Standard payments; automatic contributions available.

Are contributions deductible from income on state tax return? No. Florida has no income tax. However, all plan assets are exempt from Florida Intangible Tax.

Is the earnings portion of qualified withdrawals subject to state income tax? No.

Types of investments available: Age-based portfolios, four fixed portfolios: Equity, Fixed Income, Balanced, and Money Market.

FEES AND EXPENSES

Enrollment fee: $50.

Annual fee: None.

Sales charges: None.

Expenses: Program management fee: 0.75%. Underlying expense of funds is included in program management fee.

STATE OF GEORGIA

Name of plan: Georgia Higher Education Savings Plan

Type of plan: 529 savings plan

Web site: www.gacollegesavings.com

Phone: 877-424-4377

Manager: TIAA-CREF

Exclusively broker sold? No.

Are funds guaranteed by the state? No.

Who is eligible to open an account? Any adult or emancipated minor living in the United States.

CONTRIBUTION LIMITS

Minimum: $25 per deposit; $15 for automatic deposits.

Maximum: No further contributions once all accounts for same beneficiary reach $235,000.

Types of payment plans: Standard payments; automatic contributions available.

Are contributions deductible from income on state tax return? Yes, up to $2000 deductible per beneficiary per year. This deduction is reduced by $400 per beneficiary for each $1000 of adjusted gross income above $100,000 for a joint return or $50,000 for an individual return.

Is the earnings portion of qualified withdrawals subject to state income tax? No.

Types of investments available: Age-based portfolios, "Aggressive" age-based portfolios. Three fixed portfolios: 100% Equity, Balanced, and Guaranteed. The Guaranteed option is an obligation of TIAA-CREF Life with minimum 3% return.

FEES AND EXPENSES

Enrollment fee: None.

Annual fee: None.

Sales charges: None.

Expenses: Program management fee: 0.85%. Underlying expense of funds included in program management fee.

STATE OF HAWAII

Name of plan: TuitionEDGE

Type of plan: 529 savings plan

Web site: www.tuitionedge.com

Phone: 866-529-EDGE (866-529-3343); Hawaii residents only: (808-643-4529)

Manager: Delaware Investments

Exclusively broker sold? No.

Are funds guaranteed by the state? No.

Who is eligible to open an account? Any adult living in the United States. Nonresidents of Hawaii have higher fee structure.

CONTRIBUTION LIMITS

Minimum: $15.

Maximum: No further contributions once all accounts for same beneficiary reach $253,000.

Types of payment plans: Standard payments; automatic contributions available.

Are contributions deductible from income on state tax return? No.

Is the earnings portion of qualified withdrawals subject to state income tax? No.

Types of investments available: Age-based portfolios, three fixed portfolios: Conservative, Balanced, and Aggressive. A bank savings account option is also available.

FEES AND EXPENSES

Enrollment fee: None.

Annual fee: $25, waived for residents of Hawaii and nonresident accounts over $10,000.

Sales charges: None for Hawaii residents (when account is established directly through plan). Nonresidents have choice between A shares (up to 5.75% load and 0.30% fee); B shares (up to 5% deferred load, waived after 7 years plus 1.00% fee); and C shares (1% deferred load, waived after 1 year plus 1.00% fee).

Expenses: Program management fee: 0.95%. Underlying expense of funds included in program management fee.

STATE OF IDAHO

Name of plan: Idaho College Savings Program (Ideal)

Type of plan: 529 savings plan

Web site: www.idsaves.org

Phone: 866-433-2533

Manager: TIAA-CREF

Exclusively broker sold? No.

Are funds guaranteed by the state? No.

Who is eligible to open an account? Any adult or emancipated minor living in the United States.

CONTRIBUTION LIMITS

Minimum: $25 per deposit; $15 for automatic deposits.

Maximum: No further contributions once all accounts for same beneficiary reach $235,000.

Types of payment plans: Standard payments; automatic contributions available.

Are contributions deductible from income on state tax return? Yes, up to $4000 deductible per individual return ($8000 for joint return).

Is the earnings portion of qualified withdrawals subject to state income tax? No.

Types of investments available: Age-based portfolios; two fixed portfolios: 100% Equity and Guaranteed. The Guaranteed option is an obligation of TIAA-CREF Life with minimum 3% return.

FEES AND EXPENSES

Enrollment fee: None.

Annual fee: None.

Sales charges: None.

Expenses: Program management fee: 0.70%. Underlying expense of funds: Guaranteed option 0%; Age-based options 0.16%–0.21%; 100% Equity option 0.23%.

STATE OF ILLINOIS

Name of plan: College Illinois!

Type of plan: 529 prepaid plan

Web site: www.collegeillinois.com

Phone: 877-877-3724

Manager: Illinois Student Assistance Commission

Are funds guaranteed by the state? Contracts are a legal obligation of a state commission, with a moral (but not legal) backing of the state.

Who is eligible to open an account? Anyone over 18 can open an account. Either owner or beneficiary must have been an Illinois resident for at least 12 months prior to contract purchase. There are no age limitations for beneficiary.

Contributions: Contract prices are dependent on age of beneficiary and length of contract. Enrollment period is each November through March (extended to August for newborns). Contract prices range from $23,699 to $27,020 (in 2002–2003) for eight semesters of tuition and fees at a state university. These are lump-sum payments. Installment payments are also available. Contracts for community college tuition are also available.

What do contract payments cover? Various plans cover either tuition at two-year community college or four-year state university in Illinois.

Are contributions deductible from income on state tax return? No.

Is the earnings portion of qualified withdrawals subject to state income tax? No.

Can contract benefits be used at private schools or out-of-state schools? Yes, most accredited out-of-state colleges are eligible. Benefit will equal the mean-weighted average of tuition and fees charged by Illinois public universities or community colleges at the time of the beneficiary's enrollment in college.

FEES AND EXPENSES

Enrollment fee: $75.

Name of plan: Bright Start College Savings Program

Type of plan: 529 savings plan

Web site: www.brightstartsavings.com

Phone: 1-877-43-BRIGHT (1-877-432-7444)

Manager: Citigroup Global Markets

Exclusively broker sold? No.

Are funds guaranteed by the state? No.

Who is eligible to open an account? Anyone.

CONTRIBUTION LIMITS

Minimum: $25 initial deposit; $15 subsequent deposit.

Maximum: No further contributions once all accounts for same beneficiary reach $235,000.

Types of payment plans: Standard payments; automatic contributions available.

Are contributions deductible from income on state tax return? Yes, residents may deduct all contributions without limitation.

Is the earnings portion of qualified withdrawals subject to state income tax? No.

Types of investments available: Age-based portfolios (can be supplemented with bank deposits). Three fixed portfolios: Equity, Fixed income, and Principal protection. Fixed income can be supplemented with bank deposits.

FEES AND EXPENSES

Enrollment fee: $30 (only if opened through a bank).

Annual fee: None.

Sales charges: None.

Expenses: 0.99% program service fee. Underlying fund fees and expenses included in program service fee.

STATE OF INDIANA

Name of plan: CollegeChoice 529 Plan

Type of plan: 529 savings plan

Web site: www.collegechoiceplan.com

Phone: 866-400-PLAN (866-400-7526)

Manager: One Group Mutual Funds/Banc One Investment Advisors

Exclusively broker sold? Yes. (Accounts can be opened directly but advisor sales load still applies.)

Are funds guaranteed by the state? No.

Who is eligible to open an account? Anyone over 18.

CONTRIBUTION LIMITS

Minimum: $50 initial deposit; $25 subsequent deposit.

Maximum: No further contributions once all accounts for same beneficiary reach $236,750.

Types of payment plans: Standard payments; automatic contributions available.

Are contributions deductible from income on state tax return? No.

Is the earnings portion of qualified withdrawals subject to state income tax? No.

Types of investments available: Age-based portfolios; seven fixed portfolios: Equity Index, Growth, Growth and Income, Balanced, Conservative, Bond, and Tuition (money market). Single stock portfolios: Fidelity

Advisor Inflation-Protected Bond Fund, Templeton Foreign Fund, Massachusetts Investors Growth Fund, Mutual Shares Fund, and the Royce Low-Priced Stock Fund.

FEES AND EXPENSES

Enrollment fee: None.

Annual fee: $10 (Indiana residents); $30 (nonresidents).

Sales charges: Choice of fee structure A (3.5% initial sales charge plus 0.40% annual administrative fee); fee structure B (2.50% deferred sales charge, waived after six years plus 0.95% administrative fee for first six years, 0.40% thereafter); or fee structure C (1% deferred sales charge, waived after 1 year plus 0.65% administrative fee).

Expenses: Underlying fund fees and expenses range from 0.52% for money fund to 1.05% for small-cap growth fund.

STATE OF IOWA

Name of plan: College Savings Iowa

Type of plan: 529 savings plan

Web site: www.collegesavingsiowa.com

Phone: 888-672-9116

Manager: Vanguard

Exclusively broker sold? No.

Are funds guaranteed by the state? No.

Who is eligible to open an account? Anyone over 18; beneficiary must be under 18 when account is opened.

CONTRIBUTION LIMITS

Minimum: $25, must contribute at least $50 per year to maintain account.

Maximum: No further contributions once all accounts for same beneficiary reach $146,000.

Types of payment plans: Standard payments; automatic contributions available.

Are contributions deductible from income on state tax return? Yes, Iowa residents can deduct up to $2150 of contributions for each beneficiary.

Is the earnings portion of qualified withdrawals subject to state income tax? No.

Types of investments available: Age-based portfolios; no fixed portfolios.

FEES AND EXPENSES

Enrollment fee: None.

Annual fee: None.

Sales charges: None.

Expenses: 0.65% management fee. Underlying fund fees and expenses are included in management fee.

STATE OF KANSAS

Name of plan: Learning Quest Education Savings Program

Type of plan: 529 savings plan

Web site: www.learningquestsavings.com

Phone: 800-579-2203

Manager: American Century

Exclusively broker sold? No.

Are funds guaranteed by the state? No.

Who is eligible to open an account? Any U.S. resident.

CONTRIBUTION LIMITS

Minimum: $500 initial contribution (Kansas resident); $2500 initial contri-

bution (non-nresident); subsequent minimum contribution: $50.

Maximum: No further contributions once all accounts for same beneficiary reach $235,000.

Types of payment plans: Standard payments; automatic contributions available.

Are contributions deductible from income on state tax return? Yes, Kansas residents can deduct up to $2000 of contributions for each beneficiary (joint returns can deduct up to $4000 for each beneficiary).

Is the earnings portion of qualified withdrawals subject to state income tax? No.

Types of investments available: Age-based portfolios (aggressive, moderate, or conservative); no fixed portfolios.

FEES AND EXPENSES

Enrollment fee: None.

Annual fee: $40, reduced to $10 after account reaches $100,000; fee waived for Kansas residents.

Sales charges: None (if account is opened directly with plan)

Expenses: 0.39% management fee. Underlying fund fees by portfolio range from 0.51% to 0.93%.

STATE OF KENTUCKY

Name of plan: Kentucky Education Savings Plan Trust

Type of plan: 529 savings plan

Web site: www.kentuckytrust.org

Phone: 877-598-7878

Manager: TIAA-CREF

Exclusively broker sold? No.

Are funds guaranteed by the state? No.

Who is eligible to open an account? Any adult or emancipated minor living or working in Kentucky. Former residents or those with family members in Kentucky are also eligible. A nonresident can also open an account if the beneficiary is a current or former resident of Kentucky.

CONTRIBUTION LIMITS

Minimum: $25 per deposit; $15 for automatic deposits.

Maximum: No further contributions once all accounts for same beneficiary reach $235,000.

Types of payment plans: Standard payments; automatic contributions available.

Are contributions deductible from income on state tax return? No.

Is the earnings portion of qualified withdrawals subject to state income tax? No.

Types of investments available: Age-based portfolios; 100% Equity fixed portfolio.

FEES AND EXPENSES

Enrollment fee: None.

Annual fee: None.

Sales charges: None.

Expenses: Program management fee: 0.80%. Underlying expense of funds are included in program management fee.

Name of plan: Kentucky's Affordable Prepaid Tuition (KAPT)

Type of plan: 529 prepaid plan

Web site: www.getkapt.com

Phone: 888-919-KAPT

Manager: State board chaired by Kentucky State Treasurer

Are funds guaranteed by the state? No, but 75% of state's unclaimed property fund is dedicated to covering any unfunded liability.

Who is eligible to open an account? Anyone over 18 can open an account; beneficiary must be Kentucky resident.

Contributions: Three types of contracts available: Value Plan, which guarantees tuition at a Kentucky community college; Standard Plan, which covers tuition at a Kentucky public university; and Premium Plan, which covers higher cost private schools but is guaranteed to grow at the rate of a Kentucky public university. Lump-sum prices in 2002– 2003 were $3850 for a two-year Value Plan contract, $16,388 for a four-year Standard Plan contract, and $55,110 for a four-year Premium Plan contract. Monthly payment plans are available.

What do contract payments cover? Depending on plan purchased, one to five years of tuition.

Are contributions deductible from income on state tax return? No.

Is the earnings portion of qualified withdrawals subject to state income tax? No.

Can contract benefits be used at private schools or out-of-state schools? Yes, most accredited out-of-state colleges are eligible for benefits.

FEES AND EXPENSES

Enrollment fee: $50.

Account Maintenance Fee: $10 per year for plans that were cancelled prior to qualified distribution.

STATE OF LOUISIANA

Name of plan: Student Tuition Assistance and Revenue Trust Program (START)

Type of plan: 529 savings plan

Web site: http://osfantweb.osfa.state.la.us/start5.nsf/

Phone: 800-259-5626 (x1012)

Manager: Louisiana Office of Student Financial Assistance

Exclusively broker sold? No.

Are funds guaranteed by the state? No.

Who is eligible to open an account? Anyone can open an account. However, either the account owner or the beneficiary must be a Louisiana resident at the time the account is opened.

CONTRIBUTION LIMITS

Minimum: $10.

Maximum: No further contributions once all accounts for same beneficiary reach an amount equal to five times the current one-year cost of attendance at the highest-cost Louisiana college (approximately $173,000).

Types of payment plans: Standard payments; automatic contributions available.

Are contributions deductible from income on state tax return? Yes, Louisiana residents may deduct up to $2400 per beneficiary per year. The state will also "enhance" earnings on the account by matching contributions by between 2% and 14% depending on income.

Is the earnings portion of qualified withdrawals subject to state income tax? No.

Types of investments available: Fixed Income portfolio only.

FEES AND EXPENSES

Enrollment fee: None.

Annual fee: None.

Sales charges: None.

Expenses: None: all costs are absorbed by the State of Louisiana.

STATE OF MAINE

Name of plan: NextGen College Investing Plan

Type of plan: 529 savings plan

Web site: www.nextgenplan.com

Phone: 877-463-9843

Manager: Merrill Lynch

Exclusively broker sold? No.

Are funds guaranteed by the state? No.

Who is eligible to open an account? Any U.S. resident.

CONTRIBUTION LIMITS

Minimum: $250 initial deposit. Subsequent deposits $50. Minimum initial and subsequent deposit is $25 per portfolio if investing in multiple portfolios.

Maximum: No further contributions once all accounts for same beneficiary reach $235,000.

Types of payment plans: Standard payments; automatic contributions available.

Are contributions deductible from income on state tax return? No; however, Maine will provide matching funds to resident account holders with financial need. Beneficiaries with household incomes below $50,000 are eligible for initial matching grants of up to $200 and subsequent grants of up to $100.

Is the earnings portion of qualified withdrawals subject to state income tax? No.

Types of investments available: Age-based portfolios, three fixed portfolios: 100% Equity, 75% Equity, and Fixed Income.

FEES AND EXPENSES

Enrollment fee: None.

Annual fee: $50, waived for Maine residents or account balances above $20,000. Also waived in a year contributions totaled at least $2000.

Sales charges: None (provided account opened directly; advisor accounts have additional fees).

Expenses: 0.55% program management fee. Underlying fund expenses range from 0.70% for Cash Allocation Account to 1.59% for Merrill Lynch Large Cap Core Fund.

STATE OF MARYLAND

Name of plan: College Savings Plans of Maryland—Prepaid College Trust

Type of plan: 529 prepaid plan

Web site: www.collegesavingsmd.org

Phone: 888-4MD-GRAD (888-463-4723)

Manager: State of Maryland

Are funds guaranteed by the state? Not a legal obligation of State, but legislature is required to consider appropriation to cover any unfunded liability.

Who is eligible to open an account? Either account owner or beneficiary must be Maryland resident.

Contributions: Contracts are available for either community colleges or universities. Prices vary based on type of plan and age of beneficiary. For example, a lump-sum contract for an infant covering community college tuition is priced (2002—2003 enrollment period) at $5435. The same contract for a 9th grade student is priced at $5896. For a five-year contract covering university tuition, prices range from $31,280 for an infant to $31,992 for a 9th grade student. Monthly payment plans are available.

What do contract payments cover? Depending on plan purchased, one to five years of tuition.

Are contributions deductible from income on state tax return? Yes, each account holder can deduct contributions up to $2500 per year, per beneficiary. Contributions in excess of $2500 can be carried over for a deduction in the following year.

Is the earnings portion of qualified withdrawals subject to state income tax? No.

Can contract benefits be used at private schools or out-of-state schools? Yes, most accredited out-of-state colleges are eligible.

FEES AND EXPENSES

Enrollment fee: $90 and $75 fee for contract cancellation.

Name of plan: College Savings Plans of Maryland—College Investment Plan

Type of plan: 529 savings plan

Web site: www.collegesavingsmd.org

Phone: 888-4MD-GRAD (888-463-4723)

Manager: T. Rowe Price

Exclusively broker sold? No.

Are funds guaranteed by the state? No.

Who is eligible to open an account? Anyone.

CONTRIBUTION LIMITS

Minimum: $250 initial or subsequent deposit; automatic contributions of at least $25.

Maximum: No further contributions once all accounts for same beneficiary reach $250,000.

Types of payment plans: Standard payments; automatic contributions available.

Are contributions deductible from income on state tax return? Yes, each account holder can deduct contributions up to $2500 per year, per beneficiary. Contributions in excess of $2500 can be carried over for a deduction in the following year.

Is the earnings portion of qualified withdrawals subject to state income tax? No.

Types of investments available: Age-based portfolios (called enrollment-based option); static option where asset allocation stays fixed over the life of the investment with allocation available to three different portfolios (Equity, Fixed Income, and Balanced). T. Rowe Price manages all underlying funds.

FEES AND EXPENSES

Enrollment Fee: $90.

Annual fee: $30, waived once assets reach $25,000 or if automatic deposit program is chosen.

Sales charges: None.

Program Fee: 0.38% annually.

Expenses: Underlying expense ratio of funds ranges from 0.35% for Equity Index 500 to cash reserves fund to 0.96% for Blue Chip Growth Fund.

STATE OF MASSACHUSETTS

Name of plan: Massachusetts U.Fund

Type of plan: 529 savings plan

Web site: www.mefa.org/savings

Phone: 1-800-544-2776

Manager: Fidelity Investments

Exclusively broker sold? No.

Are funds guaranteed by the state? No.

Who is eligible to open an account? Any U.S. resident over 18.

CONTRIBUTION LIMITS

Minimum: $1000 initial deposit; $50 subsequent deposits; $50 minimum initial deposit for automatic deposits.

Maximum: No further contributions once all accounts for same beneficiary reach $230,000.

Types of payment plans: Standard payments; automatic contributions available.

Are contributions deductible from income on state tax return? No.

Is the earnings portion of qualified withdrawals subject to state income tax? No.

Types of investments available: Age-based portfolios; three fixed portfolios: 100% equity, 70% equity and Conservative.

FEES AND EXPENSES

Enrollment fee: None.

Annual fee: $30, waived if account balance over $25,000.

Sales charges: None.

Expenses: Program management fee: 0.30% underlying expense of funds (weighted average by portfolio) approximately 0.73%

Name of plan: Massachusetts U. Plan

Type of plan: prepaid tuition plan (not qualified as a 529 plan)

Web site: www.mefa.org

Phone: 800-449-MEFA (800-449-6332)

Manager: Massachusetts Educational Financing Authority

Are funds guaranteed by the state? Represents a full-faith obligation of Massachusetts. Funds are invested in a Massachusetts general obligation bond.

Who is eligible to open an account? There is no residency requirement. Enrollment is open from May to June of each year.

Contributions: Tuition Certificates can be redeemed at maturity for a predetermined percentage of tuition and mandatory fees at any participating college or university. For example, a $1000 Tuition Certificate may represent 7% of a year's tuition at college X, 15% at college Y, and 25% at college Z.

What do contract payments cover? Tuition Certificates will cover a percentage of undergraduate tuition and mandatory fees as charged by the participating colleges and universities at the time of enrollment. Tuition Certificates will not cover the cost of room and board, books, supplies, or graduate education costs.

Are contributions deductible from income on state tax return? No.

Is the earnings portion of qualified withdrawals subject to state income tax? No.

Can contract benefits be used at private schools or out-of-state schools? Yes, most accredited out-of-state colleges are eligible.

Fees and expenses: None.

STATE OF MICHIGAN

Name of plan: Michigan Education Trust

Type of plan: 529 prepaid plan

Web site: www.michigan.gov/treasury

Phone: 800-MET4KID (800-638-4543)

Manager: Michigan Department of Treasury, Bureau of Investments

Are funds guaranteed by the state? No.

Who is eligible to open an account? Beneficiary must be a resident of Michigan.

Contributions: Contracts are available for either full benefits (any Michigan public college or university), limited benefits (institutions with tuition no more than 105% of the average Michigan public college or university), and community colleges (in-district costs at a community college for one or two years). Lump-sum prices for contracts (2002 prices) ranged from $1643 (one-year community college) to $22,048 (four-year full benefits). Monthly payment plans are available.

What do contract payments cover? Depending on plan purchased, one to four years of tuition.

Are contributions deductible from income on state tax return? Yes, each account holder can deduct all contract payments made.

Is the earnings portion of qualified withdrawals subject to state income tax? No.

Can contract benefits be used at private schools or out-of-state schools? Yes, most accredited out-of-state colleges are eligible.

Enrollment fee: $85, reduced to as low as $25 if contract is purchased early in the annual enrollment period.

Name of plan: Michigan Education Savings Program

Type of plan: 529 savings plan

Web site: www.misaves.com

Phone: 877-861-MESP

Manager: TIAA-CREF

Exclusively broker sold? No.

Are funds guaranteed by the state? No.

Who is eligible to open an account? Any adult or emancipated minor living in the United States.

CONTRIBUTION LIMITS

Minimum: $25 per deposit; $15 for automatic deposits.

Maximum: No further contributions once all accounts for same beneficiary reach $235,000.

Types of payment plans: Standard payments; automatic contributions available.

Are contributions deductible from income on state tax return? Yes, up to $5000 deductible per individual return ($10,000 for joint return). However, a contribution to an account that has already had a withdrawal is not eligible for tax deduction. Matching grants are also available up to $200 for resident accounts where the beneficiary is under 6 years old and household income is less than $80,000.

Is the earnings portion of qualified withdrawals subject to state income tax? No.

Types of investments available: Age-based portfolios; two fixed portfo-lios: 100% Equity and Guaranteed. The Guaranteed option is an obligation of TIAA-CREF Life with minimum 3% return.

FEES AND EXPENSES

Enrollment fee: None.

Annual fee: None.

Sales charges: None.

Expenses: Program management fee: 0.65%. Underlying expenses of funds are included in program management fee.

STATE OF MINNESOTA

Name of plan: Minnesota College Savings Plan

Type of plan: 529 savings plan

Web site: www.mnsaves.org

Phone: 877-338-4646

Manager: TIAA-CREF

Exclusively broker sold? No.

Are funds guaranteed by the state? No.

Who is eligible to open an account? Any adult or emancipated minor living in the United States.

CONTRIBUTION LIMITS

Minimum: $25 per deposit; $15 for automatic deposits.

Maximum: No further contributions once all accounts for same beneficiary reach $235,000.

Types of payment plans: Standard payments; automatic contributions available.

Are contributions deductible from income on state tax return? No. However, matching grants of 5% to 15% (up to $300) are available for resident accounts where household income is less than $80,000.

Is the earnings portion of qualified withdrawals subject to state income tax? No.

Types of investments available: Age-based portfolios; two fixed portfolios: 100% Equity and Guaranteed. The Guaranteed option is an obligation of TIAA-CREF Life with minimum 3% return.

FEES AND EXPENSES

Enrollment fee: None.

Annual fee: None.

Sales charges: None.

Expenses: Program management fee: 0.65%.; underlying expense of funds: included in program management fee.

STATE OF MISSISSIPPI

Name of plan: Mississippi Prepaid Affordable College Tuition Program (MPACT)

Type of plan: 529 prepaid plan

Web site: www.treasury.state.ms.us/mpact.htm

Phone: 800-987-4450

Manager: State of Mississippi Treasury Department

Are funds guaranteed by the state? Yes, funds are a direct obligation of the State of Mississippi.

Who is eligible to open an account? Account owner or beneficiary must be a resident of Mississippi. Beneficiary must be 18 or younger.

Contributions: Contracts are available for one through five years of tuition and fees at any public university or community college. For five-year senior college/university contract, lump-sum 2002 prices range from

$15,083 for a newborn to $17,487 for a high school student. One-year community college contracts range in price from $1229 to $1292. Monthly payment plans are available.

What do contract payments cover? Depending on plan purchased, one to five years of tuition.

Are contributions deductible from income on state tax return? Yes, each account holder can deduct all contract payments made.

Is the earnings portion of qualified withdrawals subject to state income tax? No.

Can contract benefits be used at private schools or out-of-state schools? Yes, most accredited out-of-state colleges are eligible.

FEES AND EXPENSES

Enrollment fee: $60.

Name of plan: Mississippi Affordable College Savings

Type of plan: 529 savings plan

Web site: www.collegesavingsms.com

Phone: 877-338-4646

Manager: TIAA-CREF

Exclusively broker sold? No.

Are funds guaranteed by the state? No.

Who is eligible to open an account? Any adult or emancipated minor living in the United States.

CONTRIBUTION LIMITS

Minimum: $25 per deposit; $15 for automatic deposits.

Maximum: No further contributions once all accounts for same beneficiary reach $235,000.

Types of payment plans: Standard payments; automatic contributions available.

Are contributions deductible from income on state tax return? Yes, up to $10,000 per year ($20,000 for joint returns) may be deducted from state income tax.

Is the earnings portion of qualified withdrawals subject to state income tax? No.

Types of investments available: Age-based portfolios; two fixed portfolios: 100% Equity and Money Market.

FEES AND EXPENSES

Enrollment fee: None.

Annual fee: None.

Sales charges: None.

Expenses: Program management fee: 0.70%; underlying expense of funds: age-based options 0.16% –0.21%, 100% equity option 0.23%.

STATE OF MISSOURI

Name of plan: Missouri Saving for Tuition Program (Mo$T)

Type of plan: 529 savings plan

Web site: www.missourimost.org

Phone: 888-414-MOST (888-414-6678)

Manager: TIAA-CREF

Exclusively broker sold? No.

Are funds guaranteed by the state? No.

Who is eligible to open an account? Any adult or emancipated minor currently living in the United States.

CONTRIBUTION LIMITS

Minimum: $25 per deposit; $15 for automatic deposits.

Maximum: No further contributions once all accounts for same beneficiary reach $235,000.

Types of payment plans: Standard payments; automatic contributions available.

Are contributions deductible from income on state tax return? Yes, up to $8000 per year may be deducted from state income tax.

Is the earnings portion of qualified withdrawals subject to state income tax? No.

Types of investments available: Age-based portfolios; two fixed portfolios: 100% Equity and Guaranteed. The Guaranteed option is an obligation of TIAA-CREF Life with minimum 3% return.

FEES AND EXPENSES

Enrollment fee: None.

Annual fee: None.

Sales charges: None.

Expenses: Program management fee: 0.65%. Underlying expense of funds are included in program management fee.

STATE OF MONTANA

Name of plan: Montana Family Education Savings Program

Type of plan: 529 savings plan

Website: http://montana.collegesavings.com

Phone: 800-888-2723

Manager: College Savings Bank

Exclusively broker sold? No.

Are funds guaranteed by the state? No. However funds on deposit are insured by the FDIC up to $100,000.

Who is eligible to open an account? Anyone.

CONTRIBUTION LIMITS

Minimum: $250 initial deposit; subsequent contributions at least $25.

Maximum: No further contributions once all accounts for same beneficiary reach $187,000.

Types of payment plans: Standard payments; automatic contributions available.

Are contributions deductible from income on state tax return? Yes, up to $3000 for an individual return and $6000 for a joint return.

Is the earnings portion of qualified withdrawals subject to state income tax? No.

Types of investments available: Variable rate certificate of deposit with minimum 3% interest rate. Variable rate tied to an index of private college costs as compiled by The College Board. Variable rate equals index return less 1.00%.

Fees and expenses: None.

Name of plan: Pacific Funds 529 College Savings Plan

Type of plan: 529 savings plan

Web site: www.pacificlife.com

Phone: 800-888-2723 (direct sales to Montana residents)

Manager: Pacific Funds

Exclusively broker sold? No, accounts can be opened directly by Montana residents, but this plan is exclusively broker sold to nonresidents.

Are funds guaranteed by the state? No.

Who is eligible to open an account? Anyone.

CONTRIBUTION LIMITS

Minimum: $250 initial or subsequent deposit. A; automatic contributions of at least $25.

Maximum: No further contributions once all accounts for same beneficiary reach $250,000.

Types of payment plans: Standard payments; automatic contributions available.

Are contributions deductible from income on state tax return? Yes, up to $3000 for an individual return and $6000 for a joint return.

Is the earnings portion of qualified withdrawals subject to state income tax? No.

Types of investments available: Five fixed "portfolio optimization" options. Also, 14 individual funds managed by a variety of managers including AIM, INVESCO, Janus, Lazard, MFS, PIMCO, Pacific Life, Putnam, and Salomon Brothers.

FEES AND EXPENSES

Enrollment Fee: $25 (waived for Montana residents or once assets reach $25,000).

Annual fee: None.

Sales charges: None for Montana residents; nonresidents choose between Class A shares with initial sales loads of 5.5% (4.75% for purchases over $50,000); Class B shares with 5% deferred sales charges (eliminated after 8 years); and Class C shares with 1% front end load and 1% deferred sales charge (deferred charge eliminated after 1 year). Sales charges do not apply to money market fund class A shares.

Expenses: Program fee: None. Underlying expense ratio of funds ranges from 0.95% for Class A Pacific Life Money Market to 2.55% for three of the equity funds (Class B or C).

STATE OF NEBRASKA

Name of plan: College Savings Plan of Nebraska

Type of plan: 529 savings plan

Web site: www.planforcollegenow.com

Phone: 888-993-3746

Manager: Union Bank and Trust

Exclusively broker sold? No.

Are funds guaranteed by the state? No.

Who is eligible to open an account? Any U.S. resident over 18.

CONTRIBUTION LIMITS

Minimum: None.

Maximum: No further contributions once all accounts for same beneficiary reach $250,000.

Types of payment plans: Standard payments; automatic contributions available.

Are contributions deductible from income on state tax return? Yes, up to $1000, or $500 for married filing separate status.

Is the earnings portion of qualified withdrawals subject to state income tax? No.

Types of investments available: Age-based portfolios with four different risk levels: Aggressive, growth, balanced or conservative. Six fixed portfolios and 22 different individual mutual funds are available. Managers include: Vanguard, PIMCO, American Century, Janus, T. Rowe Price, and Fidelity.

FEES AND EXPENSES

Enrollment Fee: None.

Annual fee: $20.

Sales charges: None for accounts directly opened. Sales loads apply if an advisor is used.

Expenses: Program fee: 0.60%. Underlying expense ratio of funds ranges from 0.05% for the Vanguard Institutional Index fund to 1.17% for the Fidelity Advisor Diversified International Fund.

Name of plan: AIM College Savings Plan

Type of plan: 529 savings plan

Website: www.aimfunds.com

Phone: 877-246-7526

Manager: AIM Funds (Investment Manager)/ Union Bank (Program Manager)

Exclusively broker sold? Yes.

Are funds guaranteed by the state? No.

Who is eligible to open an account? Any U.S. resident over 18.

CONTRIBUTION LIMITS

Minimum: $500 per portfolio; $50 with automatic contributions.

Maximum: No further contributions once all accounts for same beneficiary reach $250,000.

Types of payment plans: Standard payments; automatic contributions available.

Are contributions deductible from income on state tax return? Yes, up to $1000, or $500 for married filing separate status.

Is the earnings portion of qualified withdrawals subject to state income tax? No.

Types of investments available: Age-based portfolios; three fixed portfolios: Aggressive, Growth and Balanced. In addition, there are eight individual AIM funds that can be purchased.

FEES AND EXPENSES

Enrollment Fee: None.

Annual fee: $25, waived for accounts over $50,000 or accounts over $25,000 with automatic investment plan.

Sales charges: Choose between A shares with 5.5% initial sales charge (5.25% for purchases over $25,000) and 0.35% administrative service fee; B shares with 5.0% deferred sales charge that diminishes to zero after eight years and 1.1% administrative service fee that reduces to 0.35% after eight years; or C shares with 1% deferred sales charge (waived after 1 year) and 1.1% administrative service fee.

Expenses: Underlying expense ratio of funds ranges from 1.06% for AIM Cash Reserves to 1.70% for AIM International Core Equity.

Name of plan: The State Farm College Savings Plan

Type of plan: 529 savings plan

Website: www.statefarm.com/mutual.529.htm

Phone: 800-447-4930

Manager: AIM Funds (Investment Manager)/Union Bank (Program Manager)

Exclusively broker sold? Yes.

Are funds guaranteed by the state? No.

Who is eligible to open an account? Any U.S. resident over 18.

CONTRIBUTION LIMITS

Minimum: $500 per portfolio; $50 with automatic contributions.

Maximum: No further contributions once all accounts for same beneficiary reach $250,000.

Types of payment plans: Standard payments; automatic contributions available.

Are contributions deductible from income on state tax return? Yes, up to $1000 or $500 for married filing separate status.

Is the earnings portion of qualified withdrawals subject to state income tax? No.

Types of investments available: Age-based portfolios; three fixed portfolios: Aggressive Growth and Balanced. In addition, there are eight individual AIM funds that can be purchased.

FEES AND EXPENSES

Enrollment Fee: None.

Annual fee: $25, waived for accounts over $50,000 or accounts over $25,000 with automatic investment plan.

Sales charges: Choose between A shares with 5.5% initial sales charge (5.25% for purchases over $25,000) and 0.35% administrative service fee; B shares with 5.0% deferred sales charge that diminishes to zero in seventh year after purchase and 1.1% administrative service fee that reduces to 0.35% in eight years; or C shares with 1% deferred sales charge (waived after 1 year) and 1.1% administrative service fee.

Expenses: Underlying expense ratio of funds ranges from 1.06% for AIM Cash Reserves to 1.70% for AIM International Core Equity.

Name of plan: TD Waterhouse College Savings Plan

Type of plan: 529 savings plan

Web site: www.tdwaterhouse.com

Phone: 877-408-4644

Manager: Union Bank and Trust (program manager)/TD Waterhouse (distributor)

Exclusively broker sold? No.

Are funds guaranteed by the state? No.

Who is eligible to open an account? Any U.S. resident over 18.

CONTRIBUTION LIMITS

Minimum: None.

Maximum: No further contributions once all accounts for same beneficiary reach $250,000.

Types of payment plans: Standard payments; automatic contributions available.

Are contributions deductible from income on state tax return? Yes, up to $1000, or $500 for married filing separate status.

Is the earnings portion of qualified withdrawals subject to state income tax? No.

Types of investments available: Age-based portfolios with four different risk levels: Aggressive, growth, balanced, or conservative. Six fixed portfolios (100% equity, 80% equity, 60% equity, 40% equity, 20% equity, and Conservative). Managers include: Vanguard, PIMCO, American Century, Janus, T. Rowe Price, and Fidelity.

FEES AND EXPENSES

Enrollment Fee: None.

Annual fee: $30.

Sales charges: None.

Expenses: Program fee: 0.85%. Underlying expense ratio of funds ranges from 0.175% for the State Street 500 Index–S&P 500 Index Securities Lending Common Trust Fund to 1.12% for the Fidelity Diversified International Fund.

STATE OF NEVADA

Name of plan: Nevada Prepaid Tuition Program/America's College Savings Plan

Type of plan: 529 prepaid plan

Web site: www.nevadatreasurer.com/prepaid

Phone: 888-477-2667

Manager: State of Nevada Treasury Department

Are funds guaranteed by the state? No.

Who is eligible to open an account? Account owner or beneficiary must be a resident of Nevada. Beneficiary must be in 9th grade or younger.

Contributions: Contracts are available for either two or four years at a state university, two years at a community college, or a hybrid program that combines two years at a community college with two years at a state university. Enrollment currently open only for newborns. Program being revamped for older children with planned enrollment period scheduled for fall 2003. Lump-sum 2002 newborn pricing ranged from $2338 for two-year community college plan to $7460 for four-year university plan. Monthly payment plans are available.

What do contract payments cover? Depending on plan purchased, two to four years of tuition.

Are contributions deductible from income on state tax return? No, there is no Nevada income tax.

Is the earnings portion of qualified withdrawals subject to state income tax? No.

Can contract benefits be used at private schools or out-of-state schools? Yes, most accredited out-of-state colleges are eligible.

FEES AND EXPENSES
Enrollment fee: $60

Name of plan: American Skandia College Savings Program

Type of plan: 529 savings plan

Web site: www.americanskandia.com

Phone: 800-SKANDIA

Manager: Strong Capital Management (program manager)/ American Skandia (distributor)

Exclusively broker sold? Yes.

Are funds guaranteed by the state? No.

Who is eligible to open an account? Any U.S. resident over 18.

CONTRIBUTION LIMITS
Minimum: Initial contribution $250; subsequent contributions $50.

Maximum: No further contributions once all accounts for same beneficiary reach $250,000.

Types of payment plans: Standard payments; automatic contributions available.

Are contributions deductible from income on state tax return? No. Nevada has no income tax.

Is the earnings portion of qualified withdrawals subject to state income tax? No.

Types of investments available: Age-based portfolios with three different risk levels: Aggressive, moderate, or conservative. Three fixed portfolios (75% equity, 55% equity, and 25% equity).

FEES AND EXPENSES
Enrollment Fee: None.

Annual fee: $30.

Sales charges: Choice between A shares with 5.75% initial sales charge or C shares with 1.00% deferred charge (waived after 1 year) plus 0.95% annual program service fee.

Expenses: Underlying expense ratio of funds ranges from 0.94% for the Strong Government Securities Fund to 2.20% for ASAF Strong International Equity Fund.

Name of plan: Strong 529 Plan (formerly America's College Savings Plan)

Type of plan: 529 savings plan

Web sites: www.strong529plan.com and www.americas529plan.com

Phone: 877-529-5295

Manager: Strong Capital Management

Exclusively broker sold? No.

Are funds guaranteed by the state? No.

Who is eligible to open an account? Any U.S. resident over 18.

CONTRIBUTION LIMITS
Minimum: Initial contribution $250; subsequent contributions $50.

Maximum: No further contributions once all accounts for same beneficiary reach $250,000.

Types of payment plans: Standard payments; automatic contributions available.

Are contributions deductible from income on state tax return? No. Nevada has no income tax.

Is the earnings portion of qualified withdrawals subject to state income tax? No.

Types of investments available: Five age-based portfolios; five fixed portfolios. (The age-based portfolios gradually shift between the fixed portfolios): Aggressive, Moderate, Balanced, Conservative, and All Bond.

FEES AND EXPENSES

Enrollment Fee: $25

Annual fee: $25 (waived once account balance reaches $25,000).

Sales charges: None.

Expenses: Management fee 1.25% (0.85% for All Bond Portfolio). Underlying expense ratio of funds: included in management fee.

Name of plan: Upromise College Fund

Type of plan: 529 savings plan

Web site: www.upromisecollegefund.com

Phone: 800-587-7305

Manager: Upromise Investments Inc.

Exclusively broker sold? No.

Are funds guaranteed by the state? No.

Who is eligible to open an account? Any U.S. resident over 18.

CONTRIBUTION LIMITS

Minimum: Initial contribution $250; subsequent contributions $50.

Maximum: No further contributions once all accounts for same beneficiary reach $250,000.

Types of payment plans: Standard payments; automatic contributions available.

Are contributions deductible from income on state tax return? No. Nevada has no income tax.

Is the earnings portion of qualified withdrawals subject to state income tax? No.

Types of investments available: Age-based portfolios managed by Vanguard with three tracks: Conservative, Moderate and Aggressive. Eight fixed portfolios managed by Vanguard: Aggressive Growth, Growth, Moderate Growth, Conservative Growth, Income, 500 Index, Total Bond Market, and Prime Money Market. Age-based portfolio managed by Strong. Six fixed portfolios managed by Strong: Moderate, Balanced, Conservative, All Bond, Growth, and Government Securities.

FEES AND EXPENSES

Enrollment Fee: None.

Annual fee: $20.

Sales charges: None.

Expenses: Management fee: 0.65% for all Vanguard portfolios; 1.00% for Strong All Bond and Government Securities; 1.30% for Strong Conservative, Balanced, or Moderate; 1.59% for Strong Growth Portfolio. Underlying expense ratio of funds: included in management fee.

Name of plan: The Vanguard 529 College Savings Plan

Type of plan: 529 savings plan

Web site: www.vanguard.com

Phone: 866-734-4530

Manager: Upromise Investments Inc. (program manager)/Vanguard Group Inc (investment manager)

Exclusively broker sold? No.

Are funds guaranteed by the state? No.

Who is eligible to open an account? Any U.S. resident over 18.

CONTRIBUTION LIMITS

Minimum: Initial contribution $3000 ($50 for automatic contributions); subsequent contributions $50.

Maximum: No further contributions once all accounts for same beneficiary reach $250,000.

Types of payment plans: Standard payments; automatic contributions available.

Are contributions deductible from income on state tax return? No. Nevada has no income tax.

Is the earnings portion of qualified withdrawals subject to state income tax? No.

Types of investments available: Age-based portfolios managed by Vanguard with three tracks: Conservative, Moderate, and Aggressive. Three fixed multi-fund portfolios managed by Vanguard: Aggressive Growth Portfolio, Growth Portfolio, Moderate Growth Portfolio, Conservative Growth Portfolio, and Income Portfolio. In addition there are 13 Single Vanguard Fund portfolios: Total Stock Market, Total International, 500 Index, Growth Index, Value Index, Mid Cap Index, Small Cap Index, Balanced Index, Total Bond Market Index, Long-Term Bond Index, Inflation Protected Securities, High-Yield Bond, and Prime Money Market.

FEES AND EXPENSES

Enrollment Fee: None.

Annual fee: None, but $20 fee for accounts under $3000.

Sales charges: None.

Expenses: Management fee: ranges from 0.65% to 0.85% (for Total International Index Portfolio). Underlying expense ratio of funds are included in management fee.

Name of plan: USAA College Savings Plan

Type of plan: 529 savings plan

Web site: www.usaa.com

Phone: 800-645-6268

Manager: Strong Capital Management

Exclusively broker sold? No.

Are funds guaranteed by the state? No.

Who is eligible to open an account? Any U.S. resident over 18. Membership in USAA also required to access account opening information.

CONTRIBUTION LIMITS

Minimum: Initial contribution $2000; subsequent contributions $50.

Maximum: No further contributions once all accounts for same beneficiary reach $250,000.

Types of payment plans: Standard payments; automatic contributions available.

Are contributions deductible from income on state tax return? No. Nevada has no income tax.

Is the earnings portion of qualified withdrawals subject to state income tax? No.

Types of investments available: Age-based portfolios, six fixed portfolios with funds managed by Strong and USAA.

FEES AND EXPENSES

Enrollment Fee: None.

Annual fee: $15.

Sales charges: None.

Expenses: Management fee: 1.30%. Underlying expense ratio of funds: included in management fee.

STATE OF NEW HAMPSHIRE

Name of plan: Fidelity Advisor 529 Plan

Type of plan: 529 savings plan

Web site: www.advisorxpress.fidelity.com

Phone: 1-800-522-7297

Manager: Fidelity Investments

Exclusively broker sold? Yes.

Are funds guaranteed by the state? No.

Who is eligible to open an account? Any U.S. resident over 18.

CONTRIBUTION LIMITS

Minimum: $1000 initial deposit; $50 subsequent deposits; $50 minimum initial deposit for automatic deposits.

Maximum: No further contributions once all accounts for same beneficiary reach $233,240.

Types of payment plans: Standard payments; automatic contributions available.

Are contributions deductible from income on state tax return? No. There is no state income tax in New Hampshire.

Is the earnings portion of qualified withdrawals subject to state income tax? No.

Types of investments available: Eight age-based portfolios; two fixed portfolios: 100% equity and 70% equity.

FEES AND EXPENSES

Enrollment fee: None.

Annual fee: $30, waived if account balance over $25,000.

Sales charges: No information available. A shares have initial sales charge while B shares have deferred sales charge and higher asset-based management fee.

Expenses: No information available.

Name of plan: UNIQUE College Investing Plan

Type of plan: 529 savings plan

Web site: www.fidelity.com/unique

Phone: 1-800-544-1722

Manager: Fidelity Investments

Exclusively broker sold? No.

Are funds guaranteed by the state? No.

Who is eligible to open an account? Any U.S. resident over 18.

CONTRIBUTION LIMITS

Minimum: $1000 initial deposit; $50 subsequent deposits; $50 minimum initial deposit for automatic deposits.

Maximum: No further contributions once all accounts for same beneficiary reach $233,240.

Types of payment plans: Standard payments; automatic contributions available.

Are contributions deductible from income on state tax return? No. There is no state income tax in New Hampshire.

Is the earnings portion of qualified withdrawals subject to state income tax? No.

Types of investments available: Age-based portfolios; three fixed portfolios: 100% equity, 70% equity, and Conservative.

FEES AND EXPENSES

Enrollment fee: None.

Annual fee: $30, waived if account balance over $25,000.

Sales charges: None.

Expenses: Program management fee: 0.30%. Underlying expense of funds (weighted average by portfolio) ranges from 0.90% (college age-based portfolio) to 1.10% (100% equity portfolio).

STATE OF NEW JERSEY

Name of plan: New Jersey Better Educational Savings Trust (NJBEST)

Type of plan: 529 savings plan

Web site: www.hesaa.org/students/njbest

Phone: 877-4NJBEST

Manager: New Jersey Department of the Treasury, Division of Investment

Exclusively broker sold? No.

Are funds guaranteed by the state? Yes. The State of New Jersey has placed moral obligation behind account value. The program will request that the state legislature appropriate funds so that at least the full amount of contributions will be available for withdrawal.

Who is eligible to open an account? Any U.S. resident over 18. Either the account owner or beneficiary must be a New Jersey resident.

CONTRIBUTION LIMITS

Minimum: In order to keep account open, at least $25 per month or $300 per year must be contributed until account balance reaches $1200.

Maximum: No further contributions once all accounts for same beneficiary reach $185,000.

Types of payment plans: Standard payments; automatic contributions available.

Are contributions deductible from income on state tax return? No. However, NJBEST offers a scholarship program to beneficiaries who attend public or private schools in New Jersey. Minimum scholarship of $500 is available for accounts that had contributions of at least $1200 over four years. The maximum scholarship is $1500 for accounts that had contributions of at least $3600 over 12 years.

Is the earnings portion of qualified withdrawals subject to state income tax? No.

Types of investments available: Age-based portfolios ranging from 60%–80% equity for beneficiaries under age 4 to 0%—20% equity for beneficiaries 16 years of age or older.

FEES AND EXPENSES

Enrollment fee: None.

Annual fee: $5.

Sales charges: None.

Expenses: Program management fee: 0.50%. Underlying expense of funds included in program management fee.

STATE OF NEW MEXICO

Name of plan: The Education Plan of New Mexico—The Prepaid Tuition Program

Type of plan: 529 prepaid plan

Web site: www.tepnm.com

Phone: 800-499-7581

Manager: Schoolhouse Capital (administrator)/ Education Trust Board of New Mexico (sponsor)

Are funds guaranteed by the state? No.

Who is eligible to open an account? Account owner or beneficiary must be a resident of New Mexico. Contracts must be purchased at least five years prior to use.

Contributions: Contracts are available for one through five years at three different categories of New Mexico public colleges: Branch and Community Colleges, Comprehensive Universities, and Research Universities. Lump-sum 2002 pricing ranged from $899 for a one-year Community College contract to $18,361 for five years at a Research University. Monthly payment plans are available.

What do contract payments cover? Depending on plan purchased, one to five years of tuition.

Are contributions deductible from income on state tax return? Yes, all contributions are fully deductible.

Is the earnings portion of qualified withdrawals subject to state income tax? No.

Can contract benefits be used at private schools or out-of-state schools? Yes, most accredited out-of-state colleges are eligible.

FEES AND EXPENSES

Enrollment fee: None.

Name of plan: The Education Plan of New Mexico —The College Savings Program

Type of plan: 529 savings plan

Web site: www.theeducationplan.com

Phone: 800-499-7581 or 877-EDPLAN8

Manager: Schoolhouse Capital (administrator)/ Education Trust Board of New Mexico (sponsor)/State Street Global Markets (distributor)

Exclusively broker sold? No.

Are funds guaranteed by the state? No.

Who is eligible to open an account? Any U.S. resident over 18.

CONTRIBUTION LIMITS

Minimum: $250 initial contribution; $25 subsequent contribution.

Maximum: No further contributions once all accounts for same beneficiary reach $251,000.

Types of payment plans: Standard payments; automatic contributions available.

Are contributions deductible from income on state tax return? Yes, all contributions are deductible for New Mexico residents. However, residents who take tax deduction may not make withdrawals or take rollover distributions during the first year the account is open.

Is the earnings portion of qualified withdrawals subject to state income tax? No.

Types of investments available: Five age-based portfolios, three fixed portfolios (100% Equity, 100% Bonds, and 100% Short Term Yield). In addition, each of the five age-based portfolios can be selected as a fixed portfolio.

FEES AND EXPENSES

Enrollment fee: None.

Annual fee: $30

Sales charges: None.

Expenses: Program management fee: 0.30%. Underlying expense of funds range from 0.46% for SsgA Bond Market Fund to 1.52% for Janus Advisor Growth and Income.

Name of plan: Scholar's Edge

Type of plan: 529 savings plan

Web site: www.scholarsedge529.com

Phone: 866-529-7283

Manager: Schoolhouse Capital and Oppenheimer Funds.

Exclusively broker sold? Yes.

Are funds guaranteed by the state? No.

Who is eligible to open an account? Any U.S. resident over 18.

CONTRIBUTION LIMITS

Minimum: $250 initial contribution; $100 subsequent contribution.

Maximum: No further contributions once all accounts for same beneficiary reach $251,000.

Types of payment plans: Standard payments; automatic contributions available.

Are contributions deductible from income on state tax return? Yes, all contributions are deductible for New Mexico residents. However, residents who take tax deduction may not make withdrawals or take rollover distributions during the first year the account is open.

Is the earnings portion of qualified withdrawals subject to state income tax? No.

Types of investments available: Five age-based portfolios, three fixed portfolios (100% Equity, 100% Bonds, and 100% Short Term Yield). In addition, each of the five age-based portfolios can be selected as a fixed portfolio.

FEES AND EXPENSES

Enrollment fee: None.

Annual fee: $25 (Waived for New Mexico Residents and accounts over $25,000).

Sales charges: A shares have 4.75% load plus 0.35% annual program management fee. C shares have 1.00% deferred sales charge (waived after 18 months) plus 1.20% Program management fee.

Expenses: Underlying expense of funds range from 0.68% for Oppenheimer Money Market Fund to 1.67% for Oppenheimer Quest Capital Value A fund.

Name of plan: College Sense 529 Higher Education Savings Plan

Type of plan: 529 savings plan

Web site: www.collegesense.com

Phone: 866-529-SENSE (866-529-7367)

Manager: Schoolhouse Capital and New York Life

Exclusively broker sold? Yes.

Are funds guaranteed by the state? No.

Who is eligible to open an account? Any U.S. resident over 18.

CONTRIBUTION LIMITS

Minimum: $250 initial contribution; $100 subsequent contribution.

Maximum: No further contributions once all accounts for same beneficiary reach $251,000.

Types of payment plans: Standard payments; automatic contributions available.

Are contributions deductible from income on state tax return? Yes, all contributions are deductible for New

Mexico residents. However, residents who take tax deduction may not make withdrawals or take rollover distributions during the first year the account is open.

Is the earnings portion of qualified withdrawals subject to state income tax? No.

Types of investments available: Five age-based portfolios, three fixed portfolios (100% Equity, 100% Bonds, and 100% Short Term Yield). In addition, each of the five age-based portfolios can be selected as a fixed portfolio.

FEES AND EXPENSES

Enrollment fee: None.

Annual fee: $25 (Waived for New Mexico Residents and accounts over $25,000).

Sales charges: A shares have 3.5% load plus 0.25% annual program management fee. C shares have 1.00% deferred sales charge (waived after 12 months) plus 0.75% Program management fee.

Expenses: Underlying expense of funds range from 0.46% for SsgA Bond Market Fund to 2.17% for MainStay International Equity Fund A.

Name of plan: Arrive Education Savings Plan

Type of plan: 529 savings plan

Web site: www.arrive529.com

Phone: 877-277-4838

Manager: Schoolhouse Capital

Exclusively broker sold? Yes.

Are funds guaranteed by the state? No.

Who is eligible to open an account? Any U.S. resident over 18.

CONTRIBUTION LIMITS

Minimum: $250 initial contribution; $100 subsequent contribution.

Maximum: No further contributions once all accounts for same beneficiary reach $251,000.

Types of payment plans: Standard payments; automatic contributions available.

Are contributions deductible from income on state tax return? Yes, all contributions are deductible for New Mexico residents. However, residents who take tax deduction may not make withdrawals or take rollover distributions during the first year the account is open.

Is the earnings portion of qualified withdrawals subject to state income tax? No.

Types of investments available: Five age-based portfolios, three fixed portfolios (100% Equity, 100% Bonds, and 100% Short Term Yield). In addition, each of the five age-based portfolios can be selected as a fixed portfolio. There are also 14 individual funds that can be allocated separately. Managers include Jennison Associates, Marsico Capital Management, Harris Associates/ Oakmark Funds, Janus, Thornburg Investment Management, Pilgrim Baxter, and Bank of Ireland.

FEES AND EXPENSES

Enrollment fee: None.

Annual fee: $25 (Waived for New Mexico Residents and accounts over $25,000).

Sales charges: A shares have 5.75% load plus 0.25% annual program management fee. B shares have 5% deferred sales charge (decreasing to zero by year 7) plus 1% annual program fee (reverting to 0.25% after 7 years). C shares have 1.00% deferred sales charge (waived after 18 months) plus 1.00% program management fee.

Expenses: Administration fee: 0.40%. Underlying expense of funds range from 0.68% to 1.60%.

STATE OF NEW YORK

Name of plan: New York's College Savings Program

Type of plan: 529 savings plan

Web site: www.nysaves.com

Phone: 877-NYSAVES (877-697-2837)

Manager: TIAA-CREF (Upromise Investments, with Vanguard Group and Columbia Management Group, will serve as program manager after November 14, 2003.)

Exclusively broker sold? No.

Are funds guaranteed by the state? No.

Who is eligible to open an account? Any adult or emancipated minor living in the United. States.

CONTRIBUTION LIMITS

Minimum: $25 per deposit; $15 for automatic deposits.

Maximum: No further contributions once all accounts for same beneficiary reach $235,000.

Types of payment plans: Standard payments; automatic contributions available.

Are contributions deductible from income on state tax return? Yes, up to $5000 per year ($10,000 for joint returns) may be deducted from income on state income tax return. (Tax deduction is recaptured on both nonqualified withdrawals and qualified rollovers to other plans.)

Is the earnings portion of qualified withdrawals subject to state income tax? No; however, the earnings portion of qualified rollovers is subject to state tax.

Types of investments available: Age-based portfolios (also aggressive age-based); two fixed portfolios: 100% Equity and Guaranteed. The Guaranteed option is an obligation of TIAA-CREF Life with minimum 3% return.

FEES AND EXPENSES

Enrollment fee: None.

Annual fee: None.

Sales charges: None.

Expenses: Program management fee: 0.60%. Underlying expense of funds is included in program management fee.

STATE OF NORTH CAROLINA

Name of plan: North Carolina's National College Savings Program

Type of plan: 529 savings plan

Website: www.cfnc.org/savings

Phone: 800-600-3453

Manager: College Foundation

Exclusively broker sold? No.

Are funds guaranteed by the state? No.

Who is eligible to open an account? Account owner must live or work in North Carolina, or beneficiary must be North Carolina resident. Nonresidents can open an account if they are being assisted by a fee-based financial advisor whose principal place of business is in North Carolina.

CONTRIBUTION LIMITS

Minimum: $5.

Maximum: No further contributions once all accounts for same beneficiary reach $268,804.

Types of payment plans: Standard payments; automatic contributions available.

Are contributions deductible from income on state tax return? No.

Is the earnings portion of qualified withdrawals subject to state income tax? No.

Types of investments available: A series of age-based portfolios managed by J. & W. Seligman & Co. Four fixed options: Dependable Income, managed by North Carolina State Treasurer; Protected Stock fund (Minimum 3% return guaranteed by Met Life with 70% of the return of the S&P 500 if above the minimum return; investment must be held 5 years.); Balanced Fund managed by Wachovia Bank/ Evergreen; Aggressive Stock Fund split between NCM Focused Equity and Legg Mason Value Trust. Age-based portfolios can also be chosen as fixed portfolio.

FEES AND EXPENSES

Enrollment fee: None.

Annual fee: $25 for accounts under $1000.

Sales charges: None.

Expenses: Program administration fee: 0.25% (0.10% for amounts invested in Seligman funds). Underlying expense of Seligman age-based portfolios range from 0.62% to 1.05%.

Name of plan: North Carolina's National College Savings Program/ Seligman CollegeHorizon Funds (Advisor-Sold Program)

Type of plan: 529 savings plan

Web site: www.seligman529.com

Phone: 800-600-3453

Manager: College Foundation/ Seligman

Exclusively broker sold? Yes.

Are funds guaranteed by the state? No.

Who is eligible to open an account? Any U.S. resident.

CONTRIBUTION LIMITS

Minimum: $250 initial; $100 subsequent.

Maximum: No further contributions once all accounts for same beneficiary reach $268,804.

Types of payment plans: Standard payments; automatic contributions available.

Are contributions deductible from income on state tax return? No.

Is the earnings portion of qualified withdrawals subject to state income tax? No.

Types of investments available: A series of age-based portfolios managed by J. & W. Seligman & Co. Age-based portfolios can also be chosen as fixed portfolio.

FEES AND EXPENSES

Enrollment fee: None.

Annual fee: $25 (waived for accounts over 25,000); additional $25 fee for accounts under $1000.

Sales charges: A shares: 4.75% initial charge plus 0.50% annually; B shares: 5% deferred sales charge reduced to zero after 6 years plus 1.25 % annually (0.50% after 8 years); C shares 1.00% initial charge plus 1.00% deferred charge (waived after 18 months), plus 1.25% annually.

Expenses: Underlying expense of Seligman age-based portfolios range from 0.62% to 1.05%.

STATE OF NORTH DAKOTA

Name of plan: College SAVE

Type of plan: 529 savings plan

Web site: www.collegesave4u.com

Phone: 866-728-3529

Manager: Morgan Stanley

Exclusively broker sold? No.

Are funds guaranteed by the state? No.

Who is eligible to open an account? Any U.S. resident.

CONTRIBUTION LIMITS

Minimum: $25 ($300 minimum balance by end of first year).

Maximum: No further contributions once all accounts for same beneficiary reach $269,000.

Types of payment plans: Standard payments; automatic contributions available.

Are contributions deductible from income on state tax return? No.

Is the earnings portion of qualified withdrawals subject to state income tax? No.

Types of investments available: Three tracks of age-based portfolios (aggressive, moderate, and conservative). Four fixed portfolios are also available: Aggressive/active management, Aggressive/passive management, Balanced/active management, and Balanced/passive management.

FEES AND EXPENSES

Enrollment fee: None.

Annual fee: $30 (waived for North Dakota residents).

Sales charges: None.

Expenses: 0.50% Program management fee (waived for North Dakota residents). Underlying expense of portfolios range from 0.67% to 1.21%.

STATE OF OHIO

Name of plan: CollegeAdvantage 529 Savings Plan (Ohio resident plan)

Type of plan: 529 savings plan

Web site: www.collegeadvantage.com

Phone: 800-AFFORD-IT (1-800-233-6734)

Manager: Putnam Investments

Exclusively broker sold? No.

Are funds guaranteed by the state? Yes, there is one investment option (Guaranteed Savings Fund) that is backed by the State of Ohio.

Who is eligible to open an account? Any U.S. resident, but either account owner or beneficiary must be a resident of Ohio.

CONTRIBUTION LIMITS

Minimum: $15.

Maximum: No further contributions once all accounts for same beneficiary reach $232,000.

Types of payment plans: Standard payments; automatic contributions available.

Are contributions deductible from income on state tax return? Yes. Up to $2000 per contributor (or married couple) can be deducted (by Ohio taxpayers) per beneficiary, with unlimited carryforward in future years.

Is the earnings portion of qualified withdrawals subject to state income tax? No.

Types of investments available: Four fixed asset allocations and 10 individual funds are available. In addition a guaranteed savings option is available that is designed to keep pace with tuition increases at public colleges in Ohio.

FEES AND EXPENSES

Enrollment fee: None.

Annual fee: $25 (waived for guaranteed option or for accounts over $25,000).

Sales charges: None.

Expenses: 0.99% (including underlying fund expenses). Putnam International Voyager Fund has additional expenses.

Name of plan: Putnam College-Advantage 529 Savings Plan

Type of plan: 529 savings plan

Web site: www.putnaminvestments.com

Phone: 800-225-1581

Manager: Putnam Investments

Exclusively broker sold? Yes.

Are funds guaranteed by the state? No.

Who is eligible to open an account? Any U.S. resident. This plan however, is not designed for residents of Ohio. See Ohio resident plan.

CONTRIBUTION LIMITS

Minimum: $25.

Maximum: No further contributions once all accounts for same beneficiary reach $232,000.

Types of payment plans: Standard payments; automatic contributions available.

Are contributions deductible from income on state tax return? Yes. Up to $2000 per contributor (or married couple) can be deducted (by Ohio residents) per beneficiary, with unlimited carryforward in future years.

However, this plan is designed for nonresidents.

Is the earnings portion of qualified withdrawals subject to state income tax? No.

Types of investments available: Four fixed asset allocations and 10 individual funds are available.

FEES AND EXPENSES

Enrollment fee: None.

Annual fee: $25 (waived for accounts over $25,000).

Sales charges: A shares have 3.5%–5.75% initial sales charge (depending on asset class selected) plus 0.40% annual administration fee. B shares have 2.5%–5.0% deferred sales charge (declining to zero after 7 years) plus 0.95%–1.15% annual administration fee for the first six years and 0.40% thereafter. C shares have 1.00% deferred sales fee (waived after first year) plus 0.65%–1.15% annual administration fee.

Expenses: Underlying fund expenses range from 0.49% for Putnam Money Market Fund to 1.23% for Putnam International Voyager Fund.

STATE OF OKLAHOMA

Name of plan: Oklahoma College Savings Plan

Type of plan: 529 savings plan

Web site: www.ok4saving.org

Phone: 877-654-7284

Manager: TIAA-CREF

Exclusively broker sold? No.

Are funds guaranteed by the state? No.

Who is eligible to open an account? Any adult or emancipated minor living in the United States.

CONTRIBUTION LIMITS

Minimum: $25 per deposit; $15 for automatic deposits.

Maximum: No further contributions once all accounts for same beneficiary reach $235,000.

Types of payment plans: Standard payments; automatic contributions available.

Are contributions deductible from income on state tax return? Yes, up to $2500 deductible per account.

Is the earnings portion of qualified withdrawals subject to state income tax? No.

Types of investments available: Age-based portfolios; two fixed port-folios: 100% Equity and Principal plus interest.

FEES AND EXPENSES

Enrollment fee: None.

Annual fee: None.

Sales charges: None.

Expenses: Program management fee: 0.55%; underlying expense of funds: age-based options 0.16%–0.21%, 100% equity option 0.23%.

STATE OF OREGON

Name of plan: Oregon College Savings Plan

Type of plan: 529 savings plan

Web site: www.oregoncollegesavings.com

Phone: 866-772-8464

Manager: Strong Capital Management

Exclusively broker sold? No.

Are funds guaranteed by the state? No.

Who is eligible to open an account? Anyone of legal age.

Both owner and beneficiary must have Social Security numbers.

CONTRIBUTION LIMITS

Minimum: $250 initial deposit; $25 for automatic deposits.

Maximum: No further contributions once all accounts for same beneficiary reach $250,000.

Types of payment plans: Standard payments; automatic contributions available.

Are contributions deductible from income on state tax return? Yes, up to $2000 ($1000 for married taxpayers filing separately).

Is the earnings portion of qualified withdrawals subject to state income tax? No.

Types of investments available: Age-based portfolios; six fixed "lifestyle" portfolios.

FEES AND EXPENSES

Enrollment fee: None.

Annual fee: $30 (waived for Oregon residents, accounts greater than $25,000 or accounts with automatic investment plan).

Sales charges: None for accounts directly opened; sales charges may apply if account is opened through an advisor.

Expenses: 1.00% for Broad Equity Market Portfolio; 1.25% for other port-folios. Underlying expense of funds included in total expenses.

Name of plan: MFS 529 Savings Plan

Type of plan: 529 savings plan

Web site: www.mfs.com

Phone: 866-529-1637

Manager: MFS Investment Management

Exclusively broker sold? Yes.

Are funds guaranteed by the state? No.

Who is eligible to open an account? Any adult or emancipated minor living in the United States.

CONTRIBUTION LIMITS

Minimum: $250 initial deposit; $50 subsequent deposits.

Maximum: No further contributions once all accounts for same beneficiary reach $250,000.

Types of payment plans: Standard payments; automatic contributions available.

Are contributions deductible from income on state tax return? Yes, up to $2000 ($1000 for married taxpayers filing separately).

Is the earnings portion of qualified withdrawals subject to state income tax? No.

Types of investments available: Age-based portfolios; four fixed allocations; 20 individual fund selections.

FEES AND EXPENSES

Enrollment fee: None.

Annual fee: $25 (waived for Oregon residents, accounts greater than $25,000 or accounts with automatic investment plan).

Sales charges: A shares have 5.75% initial sales charge (4.75% for bond funds, no initial sales charge for cash reserve fund); B shares have 4% deferred sales charge (waived after 6 years or for qualified withdrawal for educational expenses); C shares have 1% deferred sales charge in first year.

Expenses: Allocation portfolios: 0.70% for A shares, 1.35% for B or C shares (includes 0.62% fee waiver). Other individual funds range from 1.05% for class A Cash Reserve fund (2.05% for class B or Class C) to 2.01% for Class A Research International Fund (2.66% for B or C Class).

Name of plan: USA CollegeConnect

Type of plan: 529 savings plan

Web site: www.usacollegeconnect.com

Phone: 800-457-9001

Manager: Schoolhouse Capital (Federated Investors is marketing agent)

Exclusively broker sold? Yes.

Are funds guaranteed by the state? No.

Who is eligible to open an account? Any adult or emancipated minor living in the United States.

CONTRIBUTION LIMITS

Minimum: $500 initial deposit; $100 subsequent deposits for age-based portfolio option ; $5000 initial deposit for individual mutual fund portfolio option with minimum $1000 in each portfolio; $100 subsequent deposit in each portfolio.

Maximum: No further contributions once all accounts for same beneficiary reach $250,000.

Types of payment plans: Standard payments; automatic contributions available.

Are contributions deductible from income on state tax return? Yes, up to $2000 ($1000 for married taxpayers filing separately).

Is the earnings portion of qualified withdrawals subject to state income tax? No.

Types of investments available: Age-based portfolios; 10 individual fund selections.

FEES AND EXPENSES

Enrollment fee: None.

Annual fee: $30 (waived for Oregon residents, accounts greater than $25,000 or accounts with automatic investment plan).

Sales charges: A shares have 5.5% initial sales charge (4.5% for fixed income funds or conservative age-based portfolio; B shares have 5.5% deferred sales charge (waived after 6 years); C shares have 1% deferred sales charge during first year.

Expenses: 0.45% Administration fee; Asset-based fee: 0% for Class A shares, 0.75% for first eight years for Class B shares, 0.75% for Class C shares. Underlying mutual fund expenses are additional and range from 0.85% for Total Return Bond Fund to 2.00% for International Capital Appreciation (both after partial fee waivers).

STATE OF PENNSYLVANIA

Name of plan: TAP 529 Guaranteed Savings Plan

Type of plan: 529 guaranteed savings plan

Web site: www.tap529.com

Phone: 800-440-4000

Manager: Pennsylvania Treasury Department/Delaware Investments

Are funds guaranteed by the state? No; however, funds are guaranteed by the TAP Guaranteed Savings Program.

Who is eligible to open an account? Account owner or beneficiary must be a resident of Pennsylvania.

Contributions: Participants purchase "TAP Credits" which then grow at a rate equivalent to one of five average tuition levels: State-Related School Average, State System School Average, Community College Average, Ivy League School Average, or Private Four-year College Average.

CONTRIBUTION LIMITS

Minimum: $25.

Maximum: No further contributions once all accounts for same beneficiary reach $290,000.

What do contract payments cover? Although credits are designed to keep up with tuition, excess funds in account can be used for room and board in addition to tuition.

Are contributions deductible from income on state tax return? No.

Is the earnings portion of qualified withdrawals subject to state income tax? No; however, if a Pennsylvania resident invests in an out-of-state plan, earnings from that plan would be subject to Pennsylvania state tax.

Can contract benefits be used at private schools or out-of-state schools? Yes, most accredited out-of-state colleges are eligible.

FEES AND EXPENSES

Enrollment fee: $50.

Annual fee: $25.

Name of plan: TAP 529 Investment Plan

Type of plan: 529 savings plan

Web site: www.tap529.com

Phone: 800-440-4000

Manager: Delaware Investments

Exclusively broker sold? No, state residents can open accounts directly. However, nonresidents must purchase through an advisor.

Are funds guaranteed by the state? No.

Who is eligible to open an account? Any adult or emancipated minor living in the United States.

CONTRIBUTION LIMITS

Minimum: $1000 initial deposit ($50 for automatic contributions); $50 subsequent deposits.

Maximum: No further contributions once all accounts for same beneficiary reach $290,000.

Types of payment plans: Standard payments; automatic contributions available.

Are contributions deductible from income on state tax return? No.

Is the earnings portion of qualified withdrawals subject to state income tax? No; however, if a Pennsylvania resident invests in an out-of-state plan, earnings from that plan would be subject to Pennsylvania state tax.

Types of investments available: Age-based portfolios (aggressive and conservative); seven fixed allocations.

FEES AND EXPENSES

Enrollment fee: None.

Annual fee: $25 (waived for accounts greater than $20,000 or accounts with automatic investment plan).

Sales charges: A shares have 5.75% initial sales charge (2.75% for most conservative allocation) plus 0.30% annual sales fee. B shares have 5% deferred sales charge (reduced to zero after 7 years) plus 1% annual sales fee (reverting to 0.30% in 7th year). C shares have 1% deferred sales charge during first year plus 1% annual sales fee.

Expenses: Underlying fund expenses range from 0.55% for Delaware Corporate Bond Fund to 1.69% for Delaware International Value Equity Fund.

STATE OF RHODE ISLAND

Name of plan: College Bound fund

Type of plan: 529 savings plan

Web site: www.collegeboundfund.com

Phone: 888-324-5057

Manager: Alliance Capital Management

Exclusively broker sold? No, state residents can open accounts directly. However, nonresidents must purchase through an advisor.

Are funds guaranteed by the state? No.

Who is eligible to open an account? Any adult living in the United States.

CONTRIBUTION LIMITS

Minimum: $1000 initial deposit; $50 subsequent deposits.

Maximum: No further contributions once all accounts for same beneficiary reach $287,070.

Types of payment plans: Standard payments; automatic contributions available.

Are contributions deductible from income on state tax return? Yes, up to $500 per individual return ($1000 for a joint return). Contributions in excess of those amounts can be carried over to future tax years.

Is the earnings portion of qualified withdrawals subject to state income tax? No.

Types of investments available: Age-based portfolios (aggressive growth and growth); four fixed allocations (Aggressive Growth, Growth, Balanced, and Principal Protection). In addition nine of Alliance's funds are available as options.

FEES AND EXPENSES

Enrollment fee: None.

Annual fee: $25 (waived for Rhode Island residents or for accounts greater than $25,000 or accounts with automatic investment plan).

Sales charges: A shares have 4.25% initial sales charge plus 0.25% annual sales fee. B shares have 4% deferred sales charge (reduced to zero after 4 years) plus 1% annual sales fee (reverting to 0.25% in 9th year). C shares have 1% deferred sales charge during first year plus 1% annual sales fee.

Expenses: Underlying fund expenses range from 0.61% for Alliance Bond Fund–Quality Bond Portfolio to 1.63% for Alliance Quasar Fund.

Name of plan: JPMorgan Higher Education Plan

Type of plan: 529 savings plan

Web site: www.jpmorganfleming.com

Phone: 877-JMF-529

Manager: Alliance Capital Management and J.P. Morgan Fleming Asset Management

Exclusively broker sold? Yes.

Are funds guaranteed by the state? No.

Who is eligible to open an account? Any adult living in the United States.

CONTRIBUTION LIMITS

Minimum: $1000 initial deposit.; $50 subsequent deposits.

Maximum: No further contributions once all accounts for same beneficiary reach $287,070.

Types of payment plans: Standard payments; automatic contributions available.

Are contributions deductible from income on state tax return? Yes, up to $500 per individual return ($1000 for a joint return). Contributions in excess of those amounts can be carried over to future tax years.

Is the earnings portion of qualified withdrawals subject to state income tax? No.

Types of investments available: Age-based portfolios; three fixed allocations (Equity Growth, Balanced, and Conservative).

FEES AND EXPENSES

Enrollment fee: None.

Annual fee: $25 (waived for Rhode Island residents or for accounts greater than $25,000 or accounts with automatic investment plan).

Sales charges: A shares have 4.25% initial sales charge plus 0.25% annual sales fee. B shares have 4% deferred sales charge (reduced to zero after 4 years) plus 1% annual sales fee (reverting to 0.25% in 9th year).

Expenses: Underlying fund expenses range from 0.45% for AFD Exchange Reserves to 1.54% for JP Morgan Select International Equity Fund.

STATE OF SOUTH CAROLINA

Name of plan: Future Scholar 529 College Savings Plan.

Type of plan: 529 savings plan

Web site: www.futurescholar.com

Phone: 800-765-2668

Manager: Banc of America Advisors LLC

Exclusively broker sold? nonresidents must open an account through an advisor. However, South Carolina Residents may directly open an account (with slightly different investment options).

Are funds guaranteed by the state? No.

Who is eligible to open an account? Any U.S. resident (no age restrictions).

CONTRIBUTION LIMITS

Minimum: $250 initial deposit; $50 subsequent deposits.

Maximum: No further contributions once all accounts for same beneficiary reach $250,000.

Types of payment plans: Standard payments; automatic contributions available.

Are contributions deductible from income on state tax return? Yes, unlimited deductions on South Carolina return.

Is the earnings portion of qualified withdrawals subject to state income tax? No.

Types of investments available: Age-based portfolios; six fixed allocations (Aggressive Growth, Growth, Balanced Growth, Balanced, Income, and Growth and Income); 10 individual fund portfolios are also available. For directly opened resident accounts, instead of the 10 individual fund choices, three single-fund portfolios (LargeCap Index, MidCap Index, and Stable Capital) are available.

FEES AND EXPENSES

Enrollment fee: $25 (waived for South Carolina residents and for accounts over $10,000).

Annual fee: $25 (waived for South Carolina residents and for accounts over $10,000)

Sales charges: None for South Carolina residents. For nonresidents, A shares have 5.75% initial sales charge (4.75% for High Yield Bond Fund, 3.25% for Bond Portfolios or Allocation Portfolios) plus 0.25% annual sales fee. B shares have 5% deferred sales charge, which is reduced to zero after 6 years (except for Bond Portfolio where deferred charge is 3%, reduced to zero in 5th year and for Allocation Portfolios where deferred charge is 2.5%, reduced to zero in 6th year). B shares have 1% (0.70% for Allocation Portfolio) annual sales fee for first seven years and reverting to 0.25% in 8th year. C shares have 1% deferred sales charge during first year plus 1% (0.50% for Allocation Portfolios) annual sales fee.

Expenses: Underlying fund expenses range from 0.20% for Nations Cash Reserves to 1.23% for Nations International Value Fund.

Name of plan: South Carolina Tuition Prepayment Program

Type of plan: 529 prepaid plan

Web site: www.scgrad.org

Phone: 888-7SC-GRAD

Manager: State of South Carolina.

Are funds guaranteed by the state? The plan does not have a full faith and credit guarantee by the state. However, if the plan is cancelled, the state has a "moral obligation" to pay a minimum 4% return on contributions.

Who is eligible to open an account? Any adult can contribute, but beneficiary must be a resident of South Carolina for 12 months prior to account opening and not yet completed 10th grade.

Contributions: Contracts are available for either two or four years of tuition at a South Carolina public college or university. Lump-sum 2002 pricing ranged from $10,061 for a two-year contracts for a newborn to $11,076 for a two-year contract for a 10th grade student. Four-year lump-sum contracts ranged from $19,267 for a newborn to $21,828 for a student in 10th grade. Monthly payment plans are available.

What do contract payments cover? Depending on plan purchased, two or four years of tuition.

Are contributions deductible from income on state tax return? Yes, all contributions are fully deductible.

Is the earnings portion of qualified withdrawals subject to state income tax? No.

Can contract benefits be used at private schools or out-of-state schools? Yes, most accredited out-of-state colleges are eligible.

FEES AND EXPENSES

Enrollment fee: $75.

Enrollment period: Generally each October through January.

STATE OF SOUTH DAKOTA

Name of plan: College Access 529

Type of plan: 529 savings plan

Web site: www.collegeaccess529.com

Phone: 866-529-7462

Manager: PIMCO Funds Distributors

Exclusively broker sold? Non-residents must open an account through an advisor. However, South Dakota residents may directly open an account

Are funds guaranteed by the state? No.

Who is eligible to open an account? Any U.S. resident over 18. This plan also allows two individuals as joint owners to open an account.

CONTRIBUTION LIMITS

Minimum: $1000 initial deposit; $250 minimum initial deposit per portfolio; $50 subsequent deposits.

Maximum: No further contributions once all accounts for same beneficiary reach $305,000.

Types of payment plans: Standard payments; automatic contributions available.

Are contributions deductible from income on state tax return? No, South Dakota does not have a state income tax.

Is the earnings portion of qualified withdrawals subject to state income tax? No.

Types of investments available: Age-based portfolios; five fixed allocations (Capital Appreciation, Core Equity, Total Return Plus, Real Return Plus, and Money Market Plus). In addition, 16 individual fund portfolios are available.

FEES AND EXPENSES

Enrollment fee: None.

Annual fee: $25 per portfolio (waived for direct accounts opened by South Dakota residents and for accounts over $10,000).

Sales charges: South Dakota residents who open direct accounts pay an annual 0.65% distribution fee for class CII units. For nonresidents, A shares have 5.50% initial sales charge plus 0.70% annual servicing and management fee. B shares have 5% deferred sales charge, which is reduced to zero after 7 years. B shares have 0.70% annual servicing and management fees plus 0.75% annual distribution fee. Advisor-sold C shares have 1% deferred sales charge during first year plus 0.70% annual servicing and management fees plus 0.75% annual distribution fee.

Expenses: Underlying fund expenses range from 0.35% for UBS S&P 500 Index Fund to 1.41% for MFS Institutional International Research Equity Fund. Individual portfolios have weighted average expense ratios ranging from 0.50% to 0.79%.

STATE OF TENNESSEE

Name of plan: Tennessee BEST Prepaid Tuition Plan

Type of plan: 529 prepaid plan

Web site: www.treasury.state.tn.us/best/index.htm

Phone: 888-486-BEST

Manager: State of Tennessee.

Are funds guaranteed by the state? No.

Who is eligible to open an account? Either account owner or beneficiary must be a resident of Tennessee.

Contributions: The plan sells contracts by "Units." The plan is designed so that the average tuition at a Tennessee State University is 100 credits per year. 2002 prices awere $37 per unit. The value of each unit is to grow at the same rate as tuition at Tennessee State Universities. Monthly payment plans are available. Contribution maximum is $235,000.

What do contract payments cover? Units can be used for tuition, room and board, and fees.

Are contributions deductible from income on state tax return? No, Tennessee does not have an income tax.

Is the earnings portion of qualified withdrawals subject to state income tax? No.

Can contract benefits be used at private schools or out-of-state schools? Yes, most accredited out-of-state colleges are eligible.

FEES AND EXPENSES

Enrollment fee: None.

Enrollment period: Repricing of contracts usually takes place in August.

Name of plan: Tennessee's BEST Savings Plan

Type of plan: 529 savings plan

Web site: www.tnbest.com

Phone: 888-486 BEST

Manager: TIAA-CREF

Exclusively broker sold? No.

Are funds guaranteed by the state? No.

Who is eligible to open an account? Any adult or emancipated minor living in the United States.

CONTRIBUTION LIMITS

Minimum: $25 per deposit; $15 for automatic deposits.

Maximum: No further contributions once all accounts for same beneficiary reach $235,000.

Types of payment plans: Standard payments; automatic contributions available.

Are contributions deductible from income on state tax return? No, there is no income tax in Tennessee.

Is the earnings portion of qualified withdrawals subject to state income tax? No.

Types of investments available: Age-based portfolios; one fixed portfolio: 100% Equity.

FEES AND EXPENSES

Enrollment fee: None.

Annual fee: None.

Sales charges: None.

Expenses: Program management fee: 0.95%. Underlying expense of funds are included in management fee.

STATE OF TEXAS

Name of plan: Texas Guaranteed Tuition Plan

Type of plan: 529 prepaid plan

Web site: www.tgtp.org

Phone: 800-445-GRAD

Manager: State of Texas.

Are funds guaranteed by the state? Yes, funds in the plan are a full faith and credit obligation of the State of Texas.

Who is eligible to open an account? An account can be opened for a beneficiary who has been a Texas resident for last 12 months. A parent can also be an account owner for a nonresident child beneficiary provided the parent is a Texas resident. Beneficiary must not have completed high school. As of June 2003, the plan limited new enrollments to beneficiaries under one year old.

Contributions: Contracts range from one year at a community college to a five-year plan covering private schools. Lump-sum payments (in 2002) ranged from $1766 for a one-year community college plan for a newborn beneficiary to $65,391 for a five-year private college plan (any age beneficiary).

What do contract payments cover? Public college contracts cover full tuition at a Texas public college. Private college contracts provide average tuition amounts.

Are contributions deductible from income on state tax return? No, Texas does not have an income tax.

Is the earnings portion of qualified withdrawals subject to state income tax? No.

Can contract benefits be used at private schools or out-of-state schools? Yes, most accredited out-of-state colleges are eligible.

FEES AND EXPENSES

Enrollment fee: $50.

Name of plan: Tomorrow's College Investment Plan

Type of plan: 529 savings plan

Web site: www.enterprise529.com

Phone: 800-445-GRAD

Manager: Enterprise Capital Management

Exclusively broker sold? Nonresidents must open an account through an advisor. However, Texas residents may directly open an account.

Are funds guaranteed by the state? No.

Who is eligible to open an account? Any U.S. resident.

CONTRIBUTION LIMITS

Minimum: $25

Maximum: No further contributions once all accounts for same beneficiary reach $257,460.

Types of payment plans: Standard payments; automatic contributions available.

Are contributions deductible from income on state tax return? No, Texas does not have a state income tax.

Is the earnings portion of qualified withdrawals subject to state income tax? No.

Types of investments available: Age-based portfolios; two fixed allocations (100% stock and Balanced). In addition, 13 individual fund portfolios are available.

FEES AND EXPENSES

Enrollment fee: None.

Annual fee: $30 (waived for direct accounts opened by Texas residents and for accounts over $25,000).

Sales charges: Texas residents who open direct accounts pay an annual 1.00% fee which includes underlying fund expense. For accounts opened with an advisor, A shares have 4.0% initial sales charge plus 0.25% annual marketing fee and 0.20% administrative fee. B shares have 2.5% deferred sales charge, which is reduced to zero after 6 years. B shares have 0.55% annual marketing fee plus 0.20% administrative fee. B shares revert to A share pricing after eight years. C shares have 1% deferred sales charge during first two years plus 0.75% marketing fee and 0.20% administrative fee.

Expenses: Underlying fund expenses range from 0.17% for SSgA S&P 500 Index Fund to 1.75% for Enterprise Global Socially Responsive Fund. Individual portfolios have weighted average expense ratios ranging from 0.94% to 1.26%.

STATE OF UTAH

Name of plan: UESP (Utah Educational Savings Plan Trust)

Type of plan: 529 savings plan

Web site: www.uesp.org

Phone: 800-418-2551

Manager: State of Utah

Exclusively broker sold? No.

Are funds guaranteed by the state? No.

Who is eligible to open an account? Any U.S. resident with a Social Security number.

CONTRIBUTION LIMITS

Minimum: $25 (at least $300 per year must be contributed).

Maximum: No further contributions once all accounts for same beneficiary reach $260,000.

Types of payment plans: Standard payments; automatic contributions available.

Are contributions deductible from income on state tax return? Yes, each Utah taxpayer that who contributes to an account can deduct the contribution (up to $1410 in 2002, indexed in future years). Each member of a married couple can take the deduction, provided each contributes to an account separately.

Is the earnings portion of qualified withdrawals subject to state income tax? No.

Types of investments available: Five age-based portfolios (two of which mix S&P 500 index fund from Vanguard with Vanguard Total Bond Market Index fund; three other portfolios are diversified options with allocations between large-cap, mid-cap, small-cap, and international funds). Four fixed options (Public Treasurer's Investment Fund, Vanguard Institutional Index Fund, Vanguard Institutional Total Bond Market Index Fund, and a diversified option) are also available. All investments are on a "pooled basis" and short-term returns may not match those of underlying funds. Withdrawals from the plan must begin when the beneficiary reaches the age of 22.

FEES AND EXPENSES

Enrollment fee: None.

Annual fee: None for Option 1 (Public Treasurer's Investment Fund). For other options, $5 per $1000 of account balances up to a maximum fee of $25.

Sales charges: None.

Expenses: Management fee of 0.28% for stock investments and 0.30% for bond investments. Underlying fund expenses are included in this fee.

STATE OF VERMONT

Name of plan: Vermont Higher Education Investment Plan

Type of plan: 529 savings plan

Web site: ww.vsac.org/investment_plan/main.htm

Phone: 800-637-5860

Manager: TIAA-CREF

Exclusively broker sold? No.

Are funds guaranteed by the state? No.

Who is eligible to open an account? Any adult or emancipated minor living in the United States.

CONTRIBUTION LIMITS

Minimum: $25 per deposit; $15 for automatic deposits.

Maximum: No further contributions once all accounts for same beneficiary reach $240,100.

Types of payment plans: Standard payments; automatic contributions available.

Are contributions deductible from income on state tax return? No. However, starting in 2004, contributions up to $2000 will be eligible for a 5% tax credit.

Is the earnings portion of qualified withdrawals subject to state income tax? No.

Types of investments available: Age-based portfolios; two fixed portfolios: 100% Equity and Interest Income.

FEES AND EXPENSES

Enrollment fee: None.

Annual fee: None.

Sales charges: None.

Expenses: Program management fee: 0.80% (no fee for Interest Income portfolio). Underlying expenses of funds are included in program management fee.

STATE OF VIRGINIA

Name of plan: CollegeAmerica

Type of plan: 529 savings plan

Web site: www.americanfunds.com

Phone: 800-421-0180

Manager: Virginia College Savings Plan and American Funds

Exclusively broker sold? Yes.

Are funds guaranteed by the state? No.

Who is eligible to open an account? Any U.S. resident.

CONTRIBUTION LIMITS

Minimum: $250 per fund.

Maximum: No further contributions once all accounts for same beneficiary (across all plans administered by the Virginia College Savings Plan) reach $250,000.

Types of payment plans: Standard payments; automatic contributions available.

Are contributions deductible from income on state tax return? Yes, up to $2000 per year (with unlimited carryover to future years). Taxpayers over age 70 can deduct unlimited contributions.

Is the earnings portion of qualified withdrawals subject to state income tax? No.

Types of investments available: 21 different mutual funds are available: seven growth funds, five growth-and-income funds, two equity income funds, one balanced fund, five bond funds, and one money market fund.

FEES AND EXPENSES

Enrollment fee: $10.

Annual fee: $10.

Sales charges: Class A shares have initial sales charge of up to 5.75% (no upfront sales charge for Cash Management Trust). B shares have a contingent deferred sales charge of up to 5% (reduced to zero after six years). B shares have expenses about 0.80% higher than Class A shares. B shares convert to A shares after eight years. Class C shares have a 1.00% contingent deferred sales charge (reduced to zero after one year). C share expenses are about 0.80% higher than Class A shares.

Expenses: Underlying fund expenses range from 0.59% for Cash Management Trust of America to 1.47% for New World Fund.

Name of plan: Virginia Prepaid Education Program

Type of plan: 529 prepaid plan

Website: www.virginia529.com

Phone: 888-567-0540

Manager: State of Virginia (Virginia College Savings Plan).

Are funds guaranteed by the state? Yes, State legislation passed in 1998 provides a financial guarantee in each year's state budget to cover contractual obligations in the event of a funding shortfall.

Who is eligible to open an account? Either the account owner or the account beneficiary must be a Virginia resident at the time the contract application is signed. The beneficiary must be in ninth grade or younger.

Contributions: Contracts range from one year at a community college to a five-year plan covering state university. Lump-sum payments (in 2002) range from $1204 for a one-year community college plan for a newborn beneficiary to $23,520 for a five-year university plan (ninth grade beneficiary).

What do contract payments cover? Contracts cover full tuition at a public college.

Are contributions deductible from income on state tax return? Yes, up to $2000 per year (with unlimited carryover). Account owners age 70 or older get an unlimited deduction from income on their Virginia income tax return.

Is the earnings portion of qualified withdrawals subject to state income tax? No.

Can contract benefits be used at private schools or out-of-state schools? Yes, most accredited out-of-state colleges are eligible. However, contract earnings for out-of-state schools are at a lower level.

FEES AND EXPENSES

Enrollment fee: $85 ($25 if already enrolled in another Virginia 529 plan).

Name of plan: Virginia Education Savings Trust (VEST)

Type of plan: 529 savings plan

Web site: www.virginia529.com

Phone: 888-567-0540

Manager: Virginia College Savings Plan

Exclusively broker sold? No

Are funds guaranteed by the state? No.

Who is eligible to open an account? Any U.S. resident.

CONTRIBUTION LIMITS

Minimum: $25 initial investment; account balance must reach $250 within one year of account opening.

Maximum: No further contributions once all accounts for same beneficiary (across all plans administered by the Virginia College Savings Plan) reach $250,000.

Types of payment plans: Standard payments; automatic contributions available.

Are contributions deductible from income on state tax return? Yes, up to $2000 per year (with unlimited carryover to future years). Taxpayers over age 70 can deduct unlimited contributions.

Is the earnings portion of qualified withdrawals subject to state income tax? No.

Types of investments available: Age-based portfolios that use combinations of Vanguard 500 Index fund, Rothschild Small/Mid-Cap Domestic Equity Fund, Vanguard Small Cap Index Fund, American Funds' EuroPacific Growth Fund, Templeton Foreign Equity Series, Western Asset Fixed-Income Fund, and PIMCO Stable Value Fund. Four fixed portfolios (Aggressive, Moderate, Conservative and Money Market) are also available. Each of the four fixed portfolios uses Vanguard funds. All contributions are invested by the program twice a month (either on the 15th or last business day of the month) with a minimum two-week delay. Any interest earned on funds during this interim period is retained by Virginia College Savings Plan to defray administrative and operating expenses.

FEES AND EXPENSES

Enrollment fee: $85 ($25 if already enrolled in another Virginia 529 plan).

Annual fee: None.

Sales charges: None.

Expenses: Expenses of age-based portfolios range from 0.85% to 1.00%. Fixed portfolio expenses range from 0.93% to 0.98%. Underlying fund expenses are included in total.

STATE OF WASHINGTON

Name of plan: Guaranteed Education Tuition (GET)

Type of plan: 529 prepaid plan

Web site: www.get.wa.gov

Phone: 877-GET-TUIT

Manager: State of Washington Investment Board.

Are funds guaranteed by the state? Yes, accounts are a direct obligation of the State of Washington.

Who is eligible to open an account? Anyone can open an account. However, the beneficiary must be a Washington resident at the time of enrollment. Units cannot be used for two years after purchase.

Contributions: Units can be purchased from the plan. 100 units are guaranteed to cover one academic year of resident tuition at the Washington public university with the highest cost. Up to 500 units can be purchased per beneficiary and up to 125 units can be used per year. In 2002, each unit was priced at $52.

What do contract payments cover? Contracts cover full tuition at a public college. Excess units can be used for room and board and fees.

Are contributions deductible from income on state tax return? No.

Is the earnings portion of qualified withdrawals subject to state income tax? No.

Can contract benefits be used at private schools or out-of-state schools? Yes, most accredited out-of-state colleges are eligible.

FEES AND EXPENSES

Enrollment fee: $50; $100 maximum per family in the same household.

STATE OF WEST VIRGINIA

Name of plan: Smart529 Prepaid Tuition Plan

Type of plan: 529 prepaid plan

Web site: www.smart529.com

Phone: 866-574-2542

Manager: West Virginia State Treasurer and Hartford Life Insurance Co.

Are funds guaranteed by the state? No.

Who is eligible to open an account? Either the account owner or beneficiary must be a resident of West Virginia. Beneficiary must be in ninth grade or younger.

Contributions: Units can be purchased from the plan. Each unit covers one semester of tuition and fees at a West Virginia public college. Lump-sum 2002 prices ranged from $1778 for a single unit purchased for a newborn to $18,320 for 10 units purchased for a ninth-grade student.

What do contract payments cover? Contracts cover full tuition at a public college.

Are contributions deductible from income on state tax return? Yes, all contributions to the plan are deductible from income by West Virginia taxpayers.

Is the earnings portion of qualified withdrawals subject to state income tax? No.

Can contract benefits be used at private schools or out-of-state schools? Yes, most accredited out-of-state colleges are eligible.

FEES AND EXPENSES

Enrollment fee: None; however, a $50 fee is assessed if funds are rolled over into another 529 plan.

Name of plan: Smart529 College Savings Option

Type of plan: 529 savings plan

Web site:
www.smart529.com (residents) and www.hartfordinvestor.com/products/collegesp.htm (nonresidents)

Phone: 866-574-3542

Manager: Hartford Life Insurance Co.

Exclusively broker sold? No, West Virginia residents may directly open an account. Nnonresidents must use an advisor.

Are funds guaranteed by the state? No.

Who is eligible to open an account? Any U.S. resident.

CONTRIBUTION LIMITS

Minimum: $100 initial investment, $15 subsequent (direct accounts); $500 initial investment, $50 subsequent (advisor sold accounts).

Maximum: No further contributions once all accounts for same beneficiary reach $265,620.

Types of payment plans: Standard payments; automatic contributions available.

Are contributions deductible from income on state tax return? Yes, unlimited deduction for West Virginia taxpayers.

Is the earnings portion of qualified withdrawals subject to state income tax? No.

Types of investments available: Age-based portfolios; three static portfolios (Aggressive Growth, Growth, and Balanced), eight individual fund portfolios (Capital Appreciation, Midcap, Global Leaders, Stock, Dividend and Growth, Advisors, Bond Income Strategy, and Stable Value).

FEES AND EXPENSES

Enrollment fee: None.

Annual fee: $25 (waived for accounts over $25,000 or for accounts in automatic investment program; also waived for direct accounts opened by West Virginia residents).

Sales charges: None for direct West Virginia resident accounts. For nonresident accounts, Class A shares have initial sales charge of up to 5.50% plus 0.30% annual distribution fee. B shares have a contingent deferred sales charge of up to 5% (reduced to zero after six years) plus annual distribution fee of 0.80%. B shares convert to A shares after eight years. Class C shares have a 1.00% contingent deferred sales charge (reduced to zero after one year). C shares have an annual distribution fee of 0.99%.

Expenses: In addition to individual distribution fees, annual charges for all classes are 1.16%. Underlying fund expenses are included in this charge.

STATE OF WISCONSIN

Name of plan: EdVest College Savings Program

Type of plan: 529 savings plan

Web site: www.edvest.com

Phone: 888-338-3789

Manager: Strong Capital Management

Exclusively broker sold? No.

Are funds guaranteed by the state? No.

Who is eligible to open an account? Any U.S. resident.

CONTRIBUTION LIMITS

Minimum: $250 initial investment; $25 subsequent.

Maximum: No further contributions once all accounts for same beneficiary reach $246,000.

Types of payment plans: Standard payments; automatic contributions available.

Are contributions deductible from income on state tax return? Yes, up to $3000 per beneficiary (provided beneficiary is either a dependent or grandchild).

Is the earnings portion of qualified withdrawals subject to state income tax? No.

Types of investments available: Age-based portfolios, five fixed portfolios (Aggressive, Moderate, Balanced, Index, and Bond)

FEES AND EXPENSES

Enrollment fee: $10.

Annual fee: $10 (waived for accounts over $25,000).

Sales charges: None for direct accounts. For accounts opened through an advisor, Class A shares have initial sales charge of up to 5.75% (4.50% for purchases above $50,000) plus 0.40% annual distribution and service fee. B shares have a contingent deferred sales charge of up to 2.5% (reduced to zero after six years) plus annual distribution fee of 0.95%. B shares convert to A shares after eight years. Class C shares have a 1.00% contingent deferred sales charge (reduced to zero after one year). C shares have an annual distribution fee of 1.15%.

Expenses: In addition to individual distribution fees, expenses are 1.15% (0.90% for Stable Value Portfolio). Underlying fund expenses are included in this charge.

Name of plan: Tomorrow's Scholar

Type of plan: 529 savings plan

Web site: www.tomorrowsscholar.com

Phone: 866-677-6933

Manager: Strong Capital Management

Exclusively broker sold? Yes, primarily through American Express Financial Advisors.

Are funds guaranteed by the state? No.

Who is eligible to open an account? Any U.S. resident.

CONTRIBUTION LIMITS

Minimum: $250 initial investment; $25 subsequent .

Maximum: No further contributions once all accounts for same beneficiary reach $246,000.

Types of payment plans: Standard payments; automatic contributions available.

Are contributions deductible from income on state tax return? Yes, up to $3000 per beneficiary (provided beneficiary is either a dependent or grandchild).

Is the earnings portion of qualified withdrawals subject to state income tax? No.

Types of investments available: Age-based portfolios; three fixed portfolios (Aggressive, Balanced, and Conservative).

FEES AND EXPENSES

Enrollment fee: $20.

Annual fee: $10 (waived for accounts over $25,000).

Sales charges: Class A shares have initial sales charge of 3.5% plus 0.40% annual distribution and service fee. B shares have a contingent deferred sales charge of up to 2.5% (reduced to zero after six years) plus annual distribution fee of 0.95%. B shares convert to A shares after eight years. Class C shares have a 1.00% contingent deferred sales charge (reduced to zero after one year). C shares have an annual distribution fee of 1.00%.

Expenses: In addition to individual distribution fees, expenses are 1.27%. Underlying fund expenses are included in this charge.

STATE OF WYOMING

Name of plan: College Achievement Plan

Type of plan: 529 savings plan

Web site: www.collegeachievementplan.com

Phone: 877-529-2655

Manager: Mercury Advisors

Exclusively broker sold? No.

Are funds guaranteed by the state? No.

Who is eligible to open an account? Any U.S. resident.

CONTRIBUTION LIMITS

Minimum: $1000 initial investment ($250 for Wyoming residents); $50 subsequent.

Maximum: No further contributions once all accounts for same beneficiary reach $245,000.

Types of payment plans: Standard payments; automatic contributions available.

Are contributions deductible from income on state tax return? No.

Is the earnings portion of qualified withdrawals subject to state income tax? No.

Types of investments available: Age-based (Active Allocation) portfolios; four fixed portfolios (100% equity, 75% equity, Balanced, and Fixed Income).

FEES AND EXPENSES

Enrollment fee: None.

Annual fee: $25 (waived for accounts over $25,000 or for Wyoming residents).

Sales charges: None.

Expenses: Management fee 0.25%, distribution fee 0.35%, Wyoming administration fee 0.15%. In addition, underlying fund expenses range from 0.67% for Summit Cash Reserves to 1.77% for MFS Research International Fund.

INDEX

South Dakota, College Access 529, 227–228
S&P 500, as stock benchmark, 47, 59
Stafford Loans, 76, 122
Standard & Poor's Corporation:
  Business Week, 62
  Fund Services, 59
  The Outlook, 61–62
  Stock Appreciation Ranking System (STARS), 61
State colleges and universities. *See* Public colleges and universities
State Farm College Savings Plan (Nebraska), 208
State University of New York:
  National Merit scholarships, 116
  presidential scholarships, 114
Stock Appreciation Ranking System (STARS), 61
Stocks:
  as contributions to UTMA/UGMA accounts, 37
  corporate bonds versus, 47–49
  deductibility of losses in 529 plans, 29
  equity funds, 52–55, 56–59
  investing in individual, 59–62
  investment options for 529 plans, 17, 29, 53–59
  nonallowability of contributions to 529 plans, 27
  small-capitalization versus large-capitalization, 48–49, 56–58
  S&P 500 as benchmark for, 47, 59
Strong 529 Plan (Nevada), 211
Strong Capital Management, 210, 212, 222, 236–237
Student Tuition Assistance and Revenue Trust Program (START; Louisiana), 199
Summer employment, 106, 121

T. Rowe Price, 184–186, 200
T. Rowe Price College Savings Plan (Alaska), 185–186
TAP 529 Guaranteed Savings Plan (Pennsylvania), 224
TAP 529 Investment Plan (Pennsylvania), 224–225
Taxes, 63–72
  Coverdell Education Savings Accounts (ESAs) and

advantages of paying taxes and penalties on plan distributions, 36
excise tax on excess contributions, 32, 36–37
income taxes and penalties on nonqualified distributions, 35
tax-free status of distributions and earnings, 32, 35
filers using form 1040-A or 1040-EZ, 75, 80, 81, 83
529 plans and, 69–70
  advantages of paying taxes and penalties on plan distributions, 21–22
  estate tax reduction, 4–5, 23–24, 27, 129–130
  gift tax exclusion for plan contributions, 23–24, 129–130
  nonqualified plan distributions, 20–22, 28, 29, 64, 69–70
state tax deduction recapture for nonqualified distributions, 20–21, 29, 69–70
state tax deductions for plan contributions, 17–22
state taxes on withdrawals for rollovers to other state 529 plans, 29, 156
tax-free withdrawal status for qualified expenses, 16, 17–19, 20, 32
withdrawals/distributions reported on form 1099Q, 20, 69
impact of savings in parent's name on taxable basis, 42–43
on retirement plan withdrawals
  401(k) accounts, 43–44
  IRAs, 41–44
savings strategy to maximize tax benefits, 70–72
tax credits, 63–68. *See also* Hope Credit; Lifetime Learning Credit
Tuition Tax Deduction, 36, 37–38, 68–69
on U.S. Savings Bonds, 39–40
UTMA/UGMA accounts and, 37
TD Waterhouse College Savings Plan (Nebraska), 208
Tennessee:
  Tennessee BEST Prepaid Tuition Plan, 228–229
  Tennessee's BEST Savings Plan, 228–229